The Creative Cosmos

To the free minds of my generation
— who will understand it;
and the generation of my children
— who will live it.

A contribution of the General Evolution Research Group

The Creative Cosmos

A Unified Science of Matter, Life and Mind

Ervin Laszlo

Floris Books

First published in 1993 by Floris Books, Edinburgh
© Ervin Laszlo 1993

British Library CIP Data available

ISBN 0-86315-172-8

Printed in Great Britain
by Cromwell Press, Melksham, Wilts

Contents

Acknowledgments

Researching and writing this book has been a singular adventure, with periods of euphoria alternating with nights of desperation. Yet only the implications and explications of the basic insight I sought to communicate have ever been in question, not the core of that insight itself. This gave me the strength to go on with the months and years of rethinking and rewriting, and from time to time to seek out the advice of friends and colleagues whom I knew to be similarly oriented and deeply motivated.

I take, then, this opportunity to acknowledge the many constructive criticisms and assessments that it was my good fortune to receive. They came first of all from the members of the General Evolution Research Group, an international and interdisciplinary research network I founded in 1987 with the help of Jonas Salk. My evolutionary colleagues were always sympathetic — they shared the quest of searching for general laws of the evolutionary process — yet they were frank in their assessments and criticisms. The comments of Robert Artigiani, Vilmos Csányi, David Loye, Jonathan Schull and Ignazio Masulli were especially detailed and constructive. The late David Bohm was encouraging from the very first: he has placed many valuable materials in my hands. Karl Pribram has read and reread parts of the manuscript and gave insightful comments and precise suggestions. I am grateful to John Wheeler and to Henry Stapp for detailed in-depth discussions. Ib Ravn, Mark Braham, David Dunn, Pál Greguss, Stanley Krippner, Henry Margenau, Roberto Peccei, Rupert Sheldrake, Mauro Ceruti, Ignazio Licata, Dario Schena Sterza and Roberto Fondi have all read various sections of the manuscript and provided constructive suggestions. David Peat has helped with the presentation of the more esoteric concepts of the new physics, and Jean Staune, in whose series at Editions Fayard (Paris) the French translation of this work first appeared, produced a score of valuable comments and an unending stream of enthusiastic encouragement. Last but not least, I note the deep gratitude I owe to Christopher Moore, my editor at Floris, whose sustained and penetrating interest led to a collaboration that was punctuated by periods of intense work and discussion in the sunny hills of Tuscany. The text now in the hands of the reader owes its final shape to this collaborative effort.

Montescudaio, Tuscany
June 1993

Foreword

by Karl Pribram

The Creative Cosmos is a superb example of postmodern deconstruction at its very best. Its first two parts demonstrate the anomalies and lacunae in the current narrative we call science. The next sections boldly develop a new narrative that aims to carry our comprehension beyond these limitations. For these parts, I would caution the reader to adhere to a maxim once issued by Warren McCulloch: 'Do not bite my finger; look where I am pointing.'

The term 'narrate' is closely linked to the Latin *gnarus* which in turn is kin to *gnoscere*, to know. Thus narration is a form of knowing, just as is 'science,' *scire*, kin to *scindere*, to cut. However, the accepted language of science is mathematics, a sharply honed tool for cutting, analysing, observations into packets that allow observations to be shared (replicated). Paradoxically, mathematics also allows predictions to be made, predictions which lead to new observations.

Twentieth-century science has been eminently successful in its pursuit of *scire*. Cognitively, however, mathematical formulations are, by themselves, incomplete. The narrative aspects of science, the concepts and meanings to which the computations point, have been neglected, often deliberately as in the ever popular Copenhagen interpretation of quantum physics. This neglect has produced considerable malaise in some of us; and more important, it has led to a coverup of the anomalies and lacunae addressed in *The Creative Cosmos*.

The Creative Cosmos ably summarizes what is missing in today's account of science-as-narrative. Of course, Laszlo is not alone in his lament. Einstein, Dirac, Bohm and Bell have all attempted to *understand* their formulations in physics; Koestler, in biology and psychology. But the received wisdom in the classroom has, for the most part, emphasized the elegance of what has been achieved often with the advice that any attempt at further understanding would simply confuse.

Laszlo is to be commended in that he provides us with a plausible alternative. All of the scientists noted above have groped in the direction now taken by Laszlo. He points out, that as the twentieth century comes to a close, scientists are again becoming more comfortable with the concept of 'field' which has been eclipsed for most of the century by an almost exclusive emphasis on the particulate.

Fields are invoked to account for (inter-) actions at a distance. Newton conceptualized such actions and interactions in terms of force. Today we have become so accustomed to this innovation that we think of the force of gravity as a thing. Actually, of course, all we have are the observations of actions at a distance. As Laszlo indicates, this means that we are inferring gravity from our observations: gravity is not an observable; as in the case of field concepts, gravity is inferred.

The reason why we have become so accustomed to the inference that gravitational fields exist, is that there properties have been clearly stated and shared observations have made them common cognizance. Of course, these commonalities hold only for two interacting bodies; the three body problem is only now beginning to yield to nonlinear computations.

Gravitational, electromagnetic, the strong and weak nuclear forces have all become relatively familiar, at least to scientists, because their inferred properties do not invoke any radical departure from the measurements that have served scientists so well. These four fields are inferred from interactions among entities. These interactions take place in space and over time. Probabilities of occurrence must be invoked for the nuclear forces; the inverse square law is replaced by the Pauli exclusion principle etc., but on the whole the inferences are manageable, albeit barely.

The postulated fifth field is different. It is not inferred from an interaction among spatially and temporally separated entities. As Bohm has described it, space and time become implicate, enfolded. Mathematically, the fifth field is spectrally, holographically organized. The organization is composed of interference patterns, that is, of the amplitudes (amounts) of energy present at intersections among waveforms. The equations that describe the transformations from spacetime to spectrum are called spread functions because the changes in form spread entities into a distributed manifold of such amplitudes. The relations among amplitudes can be conceived to compose a holoscape which can be represented by a contour map, similar to the familiar weather map of temperature gradients.

The fifth field is thus not a simple inference from observations. Rather the fifth field is a transformation of fields which are inferred from observations. It is this second order aspect of the fifth field which makes it so difficult to grasp. In fact, until the engineering instantiation of the holographic mathematical formulation, only mathematicians were able to imagine this type of organization. Leibniz was the first in describing what he called monads; Gabor was responsible for holography in the immediate past.

Scientists do not feel as comfortable with transformation as do mathematicians. Transformations imply action paths. Until recently, scientists have conceived of action paths mostly in terms of conservation laws, optimizations in favour of least action principles. Prigogine broke ground in pointing out the difference between stabilities that occur far from equilibrium and those that reflect least action, i.e. equilibrium. The paths described by the transformations between spacetime and spectrum and back again may lead to stabilities far from equilibrium as well as to least action. When least action is involved, the path (integral) has the form of quantum mechanics. Gabor showed that this form is not limited to the quantum physics realm but is universal to communication. He therefore defined a quantum of information, a channel which can carry a unit of communication with the least amount of uncertainty.

The path to least uncertainty leads, of course, towards communication with maximum amount of information. By using the measure of the amount of information as a measure of diversity within some domain, (that is, a measure of complexity), we come directly to Prigogine's description of the path to order from chaos.

There are thus at least two classes of path that describe the transformations that occur between the spectral and the spacetime domains. Both begin by describing a phase space that combines the spectral and spacetime domains. One class emphasizes the spectral aspect as it describes the spatial composition of matter; the other emphasizes the spacetime aspect as it describes the time evolution of complexity.

There is only one aspect of this book to which I cannot wholeheartedly subscribe. As a physiologist, I know that the same or similar descriptions (even mathematical formulations) hold at various levels of organization. Some aggregates of molecules behave much as do some aggregates of cells — and even some aggregates of individuals. Thus laws of economics may be applicable to the operations of neural systems; and the feedback loops involved in homeostasis and homeo- rhesis are as applicable to control procedures in engineering as they are to the regulations of an organism's internal environment. Tele- phone communication systems used as information transmission net- works and the programming of computers make elegant metaphors for understanding how the brain operates to generate and control beha- viour and experience. But the nitty-gritty of the use of these metaphors is the construction of precise models that detail the similarities and differences in transformations, the transfer functions that describe *how* different levels influence one another. *The Creative Cosmos* fails in this regard when it relates the psi-field to brain function. Although I have formulated the hypothesis, based on evidence quoted by Laszlo, that hyperstimulation of the frontolimbic forebrain allows primates including humans to operate in a holistic, holographic-like mode, I have trouble imagining how the psi-field would influence the organism in any detailed and specific extrasensory fashion. In the same vein, I have difficulty attributing to the psi-field, the permanent human-type memory storage capability envisioned by Laszlo. As I conceive it, the psi-field enters the transformation process — that is, describes paths of transformation at *several* levels or scales — thus obviating the need to overarch from cosmos to quark.

But these may be my own limitations. When I was a child, I had trouble believing that heavier-than-air craft would be capable of mass transportation, dirigibles made much more sense to me. I am still awed by portable radios and their current walkman size. Television leaves me gaping in colour shock and the proximity of faces. Thus, my read of *The Creative Cosmos* reminded me of treasured adventure stories, such as *The Microbe Hunters* and Admiral Byrd's exploration of Antarctica. Laszlo has, indeed, filled the need for a twenty-first century renewal of the narrative of science which has been so neglec- ted during the twentieth century.

14

Introduction

This study tackles what in my view is *the* fundamental question of scientific inquiry into the nature of reality. The question is not, as theologians and philosophers from Thomas Aquinas to Gottfried Wilhelm Leibniz speculated: 'Why is there something in the world rather than nothing?' To such a query there is no answer this side of religion. For science, the fundamental question is more modest. That question is how the things that are, have *become* what they are. What is the dynamic at the heart of nature that generates what we see and what we are? Because what we see and what we are, even if not rigorously predetermined, cannot be the product of mere chance. After all, what there is in the world became on the whole ordered and consistent, rather than disordered and chaotic. If so, there must have been either a Creator that has ceaselessly willed it so, or a process dynamic that has constantly made it so. To discover the nature of that dynamic is a challenge to empirical science.

It is this challenge that the book before the reader takes up. The issue, of course, is mind-boggling — it encapsulates both the fundamental question for science regarding the nature of reality, and the further issue, whether the question has a single, consistent answer, or several disjointed ones. Scientific inquiry has not produced a consistent single answer regarding the process dynamics of the natural orders, though natural philosophers, natural theologians and process metaphysicians have been consistently probing for it. This state of affairs, however, may have more to do with the compartmentalized nature of scientific inquiry than with the nature of the reality that such inquiry seeks to understand.

In the three decades that I have been confronting the above question — my first book on the subject, *Essential Society: An Ontological Reconstruction*, appeared in 1963 — I have come to recognize not only the enormity of the challenge it poses, but also that scientific

15

inquiry is making remarkable headway towards tackling it. Now, in the 1990s, with the emergence of sophisticated cross-disciplinary concepts, methods and theories, and the determined shift in focus from what things *are* to how they are *becoming,* there is a reasonable expectation that science could grasp the essentials of the dynamics by which complexity and order is built in nature from indeterminism and turbulence — as the Greeks would say, how cosmos arises in the womb of chaos. For my part, I have looked for evidence of a funda-mental dynamics in the principal branches of the natural sciences, and sought the organizing insights first in Whitehead's process meta-physics, in Wiener's cybernetics and von Bertalanffy's general system theory, and then in Prigogine's dissipative systems theory and Bohm's theory of the implicate order. I was not satisfied, however: while each theory contributed something fundamental that was missing in its predecessors, none has revealed the basic concept upon which a unified process dynamics could be reliably constructed. Then, how-ever, my search took an unexpected turn.

As it happened, the insight on which this book is based came to me one quiet evening in the summer of 1986 as I was sitting in the company of a few close friends and colleagues under a sky of infinite depth and clarity on the shores of the Mediterranean. We were in a reflective mood, just recovering from the shock of the news of the passing away of a mutual friend whom we had all admired for his insight and creativity as well as for his deep humanism. As each of us recounted episodes from his rich and adventurous life, someone remarked how tragic it was that all his accumulated experience and wisdom should now have vanished without a trace. I replied, with a conviction that surprised me as much as the others, that the experience and wisdom of our friend had not vanished from this world: its trace still existed the same as the trace of all things that ever took place in the universe.

We fell silent. The truth of this assertion, bold as it was, had hit us all. After a few moments someone asked me how I could be so certain. I responded by drawing on a store of ideas and concepts that I had not known I possessed. I spoke of the parsimony of nature, of the rise and fall of all that has ever come to be in the universe and here on Earth. I said that a human life, the most remarkable adventure of matter in the universe, is not and could not be an exception to the law of preservation of all things and events in the cosmos. The wealth of impressions and insights of a person's life do not disappear without a trace but remain embedded and registered in the heart of reality. It was like the ray of light that came to our eyes from one of the myriad stars in the domed sky far above the quiet beach. At that very moment light from all parts of the universe was entering our eyes, bringing to us signals that stretched out across the whole history of the cosmos. Nothing in this world has been lost without a trace, neither a single photon from a star in gamma Centauri nor a cell in the network of neurons in the brain of our departed friend.

After a while we said good night and agreed to meet for a swim next morning. On the following day, as we dried ourselves in the bright morning sun, my friends asked if I was still convinced of last night's concept of a self-preserving cosmos. My first impulse was to dismiss the entire thought as the fruit of a poetical interlude without further significance. But I could not. The idea held me in its thrall; it felt intuitively right. This was not, I realized, something I just happened to think of the night before but something I had always known. I resolved to return to the concept and explore it at leisure.

It was months later, when I had completed my book on the general laws of evolution, that I realized that the insight of that summer evening furnished a possible avenue for comprehending the puzzle of the evolution of order in the universe. To understand how that insight — one that has been present in human consciousness for thousands of years — could furnish a meaningful solution to the greatest puzzle one could reasonably conceive, I should say something more about the nature of that puzzle.

If the world around us is what it is, and if it was not created ready-made but evolved in the course of time, then something more than mere chance must have governed its development. A random process could not have produced the kind of order that we meet with in our experience; it could not even have produced the kind of chaos that surrounds us at times. The fact is that pure, unadulterated chance could not have existed in the universe even if it coexisted with strands of order. If a series of chance events had punctuated the developmental process, the things that would have emerged out of that process would have randomly diverged among themselves. Higher levels of order could not have grown out of such a set of randomly diverging lower-level orders — unless, of course, all of reality, though made up of windowless monads, was governed by Leibniz's 'preestablished harmony.' Given a process that is subject to pure chance, even previously ordered things would each grow their own way.

The diversification of evolving systems in the absence of factors that would impose some form of coordination on their development is well illustrated, in nature as well as in the human world. For example, experiments show that the release of the linkages that bind cells within organisms makes for a rapid increase in their heterogeneity: living cells diversify far more in a culture than within the morphological structure of the whole animal. The tendency towards divergence rather than convergence in the absence of common ties is apparent in a more intuitive vein within our everyday experience: if two people — no matter how perfectly attuned they were to each other when they met — had no common bonds, their own, necessarily somewhat different, experiences would sooner or later make them grow apart. Such a couple, much as cells in a culture, is unlikely to remain united and part of one and the same social group or cultural community. Such examples tell us that in an uncoordinated, chance-riddled universe, the enormously complex orders that underlie the phenomena of life, mind, and culture are extremely unlikely to have come about. Yet life, mind, and the many layers of complexity in the cosmos and in the human world, did come about. Evidently, mere chance did not dominate the evolutionary process: there must also have been a significant degree of binding and coordination.

But how could the many things of the real world be bound and coordinated with each other? How could things — cells and people, as well as atoms and molecules, species, and whole ecologies — not only diverge but also converge with and towards one another, even if separated in space and time? Did a cosmic intelligence create ties of coordination between them — or did nature?

If the orders that we meet with in nature were the result of an evolutionary process, something must have been given in the universe to constrain the random play of events that would have otherwise split apart the evolutionary trajectories. This something could be an individual tie between the evolving entities themselves — such as love and sympathy between two human beings — or their integration within a larger system, such as a shared social group or cultural community (or, in the case of cells, a living organism). Such ties and integrations must be given throughout nature, since matter did build into complex structures in the course of time, into veritable cathedrals of quanta within atoms, atoms within molecules, molecules within crystals ... within cells within organisms within societies within ecologies. This calls for an explanation.

The surprising recollection of that late summer may furnish it. If indeed all that occurs in the material universe remains in some way encoded in the womb of spacetime, nature may obtain that minute bias that would make randomly diverging developmental pathways into significantly converging ones. Because when a process acquires some element of self-referentiality, it is no longer entirely random: it is biased towards internal consistency. If the self-referentiality is not deterministic and monolithic, it will not lead to the mere repetition of already achieved orders; rather, it will create possibilities for attaining genuine novelty within the range of internal consistency. If the universe preserved and fed back the traces of its own evolution, 'in-forming' its parts consistently with the whole and the whole consistently with its parts, it could evolve towards order creatively and self-consistently, without either the mechanistic constraint of self-repetition, or the chaotic anarchy of unfettered randomness.

On first sight, the possibility that the trace of the whole state of the universe — physicists would say, the trace of the universe's wavefunction — would remain encoded in physical reality seems mind-boggling. On a closer look, however, it turns out to be considerably less mind-boggling than any other explanation of order in the cosmos that we could think of. That order in nature should follow a path that was laid down when the universe was set into motion has been surrendered with the downfall of the clockwork determinism of classical mechanics; while the partially random quantum universe that replaced

Newton's deterministic universe remains silent regarding the evolution of the higher (transphysical) forms and levels of order. The assumption that blueprints or archetypes actively mould processes in nature towards their realization suggests a teleology that stretches the permissible scope of scientific theory; and the thesis that the order we meet with in our experience has been created *ex nihilo* is a religious tenet entirely beyond the ken of science. Consequently the recurrent insight, that the physical universe 'in-forms' itself and thus evolves creatively as well as consistently without outside agency, may well be the most economical as well as the most reasonable of the available explanations.

Of course, if we are to demonstrate the cogency of a self-referential dynamics that could generate all that there is in the world, we must show how this world could 'in-form' itself in the course of its evolution. To search for, and identify, the interactive self-referential dynamics that could produce the kind of orders we meet with in experience is the basic objective to which this book is dedicated. Its theories and hypotheses are offered without dogmatism, in full recognition of the enormity of the question they tackle and the boldness of the answer they provide.

Boldness, if disciplined by method, is not misplaced, however. Science, though highly accomplished in a plethora of ways, is far from having penetrated all the walls of mystery; indeed, it is only at the first stretch of the long road that leads from mythical and intuitive notions towards a systematically elaborated and methodically tested knowledge of the fundamental nature of the world in which we, and all that we behold, have come to be. Yet science is well beyond the first steps. It may already have reached the portals of real insight into the unitary interactive process that generates the diverse and consistent orders of the distinct yet not categorically discrete realms we customarily identify as 'matter,' 'life,' and 'mind.'

We should not hesitate to press ahead.

PART ONE

The Search

– 1 –

The Cosmological Revolution

*There is one common flow, one common breathing, all things
are in sympathy.*

Hippocrates

The perennial dream

To understand the world around us, and to see ourselves as part of
that world, has always been a grand dream. It has been dreamt in all
cultures and in all civilizations — it has been the inspiration of
prehistoric myths and of early magic, the intuition of mystics, and the
vision of prophets. For the past two and a half thousand years, since
the thinkers of ancient Greece replaced mythical views and magical
formulas with rational explanations, the dream to know the stars above
and the mind within has also been a mainspring of philosophy. And
in the sixteenth and seventeenth centuries, when pioneering spirits
began to probe the nature of reality through observation and experiment, the dream of understanding ourselves and the world around us
infused the enterprise of science as well.

In the modern age the dream has been all but lost. The pursuit of
material progress often dominated the desire to find meaning in life
and wholeness in existence, and deprecated the integral belief systems
of earlier civilizations. The modern mind would not accept that the
many levels of the cosmos — the terrestrial sphere below and the
celestial sphere above — are bound together by encompassing sym-
pathies; that the microcosmos would reflect the macrocosmos and a

grain of sand could mirror the universe. For classical civilizations the intuition of Hippocrates and the principle of Hermes Trismegistos held undisputed validity: there is one common flow, and as it is above, so it is below. The modern mind, shaped by the eighteenth-century alliance between modern science and traditional handicrafts, looked at such sweeping notions as mere superstition. The industrial age opened fresh vistas for the satisfaction of material needs and demands and emphasised the mastery of the forces of nature at the expense of the perennial quest for their integral understanding. Instead of orientation by encompassing meaning, modern people were left with the idea of progress: linear and, as it seemed, indefinitely assured. Life became longer and more comfortable, but emptier and less meaningful.

Yet the dream of finding the unifying pattern that would underlie and connect the things and events we observe and experience has never been entirely surrendered. By the second half of the twentieth century, the spiritual vacuum left by fragmented systems of knowledge and belief resurrected it and fired a new search. Today, the search is intensifying. As we head towards the twenty-first century, the human and social world around us is becoming increasingly complex and threatens to escape control. The prospect of crisis is darkened by the spectre of disaster. To safeguard our planetary home, new ways of grasping the interconnection between people in societies, between societies, and between humankind and nature, are being explored. As the Apollo pictures from space reveal, our planet is a world within a larger world — the solar system, the galaxy, and the universe as a whole. The renewed striving towards integral vision embraces these wider realities as well, seeking to grasp our origins, our place, and our role in nature as well as in the cosmos.

The striving for a comprehensive vision permeates wide areas of contemporary culture and society. Its signs and manifestations are a renewed interest in holistic thinking, in oriental philosophy, in religion and in mysticism, and in natural ways of living. People are no longer content to see the world through the narrow slits of technical specialities: increasingly they want to see it all, and they want to see it whole. The striving for a unified view of the world is a sign of health and vitality in an age of chaos and uncertainty. It is proof that the basic

24

drive to know and to understand — a drive as basic as that for food or sex — has not been lost in the shuffle of a changing world. Degenerate cultures may be content with fragmentary concepts that lack deeper meaning, but vibrant cultures seek the contours of the whole of the reality they experience.

In the revitalization of the ancient dream, the role of science should not be underestimated. While theoretical science cannot replace art and religion or preempt intuitive insights into the nature of reality, it is more fundamental than is generally assumed. Science is not, like popular imagination depicts, merely a search for things and processes to observe and to describe. While there is observation and description, there is also explanation and interpretation. A simplistic cataloguing of all we could observe would yield a bewildering array of objects and events, with little evident connection among them. The search for meaning is an essential element in the scientific enterprise, even if the enterprise is disciplined by considered criteria and rigorous method. As science's analysis is complemented by synthesis, the diversity of the observed world is brought increasingly within the compass of a larger and more coherent unity.

In a number of scientific disciplines the search for integral understanding is about to reach a new phase. It is expressed in the quest for unified theories in the new physics and the new cosmology, in the elaboration of a science of dynamical systems in mathematics, chaos theory, and the emerging 'sciences of complexity,' and in the application of general theories of evolution and change in a variety of biological, social, and human fields. The horizons that open for a scientific knowledge of cosmos and consciousness are vast and breathtaking.

Science is on the threshold of another 'revolution.' This revolution promises to be even vaster — and certainly faster — than the Copernican revolution that replaced the model of a geocentric universe with that of a heliocentric one. The revolution now in the offing promises to replace the still prevalent materialistic-reductionist concept of matter and mind with an emerging whole-field concept.

The coming revolution, bringing to us tested knowledge that is unified in regard to the understanding of the essential features of

25

reality, responds to the ancient dream of comprehending the nature of matter, life and mind. This revolution cannot — and obviously will not — occur within the time-honoured confines of the disciplines; it can only unfold across the disciplines. The next great paradigm shift in science will be by nature transdisciplinary — it will be a *cosmological* revolution in the classical sense in which cosmology has always been the science of the whole of reality *(kosmos,* after all, means 'ordered whole' in classical Greek).

The concept of a fundamental revolution in science may come as a surprise to the non-scientist. The public image of science is one of a solid edifice, built little by little, in careful incremental steps. This image is false. Science does not add bits and pieces of new knowledge to secure storehouses of 'facts' established once and for all. All knowledge in science is open to disconfirmation — to 'falsification' in the term used by Karl Popper. Thus when new knowledge is added to the old, even the most established theories become exposed to disproof. Obviously, scientists do not readily dismiss established theories: there is usually an extended period during which researchers attempt to fit anomalous data into the established framework. But if and when new data refuse to fit, and further attempts to make them fit would only force nature into the Procrustean bed of outdated theory, established knowledge undergoes a mutation.

We have reached a point today where puzzles and anomalies accumulate in regard to several basic frameworks of established natural-scientific knowledge. Not just one theory is challenged, within one circumscribed field of investigation, but some of the most basic elements of our knowledge of the world are called into question: the nature of matter, the evolution of living species, the relationship between consciousness and cosmos, and the origins and destiny of the universe itself.

The time is ripe to look at the puzzles and anomalies in a fresh perspective. A rethinking of the received conceptual frameworks may lead to the formulation of a new scientific paradigm, one that transcends reductionism and materialism in favour of a unified concept — a concept of reality organically shaped by interacting universal fields.

The classical beginnings

To shed light on the dynamics by which universal fields interactively create the evolving cosmos, producing the diverse yet consistent orders that meet our eye, is the objective of the present study. This ambitious enterprise must be placed in a proper historical context. Thus, before embarking on it we shall briefly review the nature of sustained attempts to comprehend the fundamental properties of the known universe, tracing the evolution of systematic thinking about the experienced world from its classical beginnings to the latest of the great scientific revolutions.

Attempts to understand the nature of the experienced world go back to the civilizations of antiquity. The Sumerian, the Babylonian, the Egyptian, as well as the Indian and the Chinese cultures produced detailed accounts of what they believed to be the ultimate nature of man and cosmos. Mythic cosmologies were also developed in the pre-Colombian civilizations of the Mayas, the Incas, and the Aztecs, as well as by tribal cultures in Africa. But the foundations of rational thinking about the nature of the experienced world and therewith the conceptual foundations of modern science were laid by the philosophers of classical Greece.

In the sixth century BC the Ionian nature philosophers divested themselves of the mythological world views that until then had dominated the main strands of human civilization and attempted to comprehend the nature of the world essentially in relation to our experience of it. The first attempts focused on the origins of the universe. The question posed by the Greeks was the very same question posed in this book: how could the diversity and order that meets the eye today have arisen in the universe? The classical thinkers began the long chain of reasoning that led to modern natural science with the idea that order must have arisen from disorder, or at least from the potential for order: *kosmos* must have come from *khaos*.

The Hellenic philosophers maintained the view that beneath the diversity of the sights and sounds that reach the eye and the ear there is a deeper reality that is the ground of the order that we observe, and that this deeper reality is coherent and unitary. This echoed an ancient insight of Eastern philosophies: that all there is in the world emerged stepwise from an original Source that was indivisible and spaceless and timeless in its own primordial essence. But, unlike the sages of the East, the Hellenic philosophers insisted that this original Source and its gradual diversification into the world we now observe can be grasped by reason without recourse to mysticism, enlightenment, and intuition.

The rational attempts of the nature philosophers of Greece centred on understanding the variegated world of sense experience in terms of an underlying unity called 'the One.' The One was to be found in a grain of sand as well as in the totality of the universe. The microcosm reflects, they said, the macrocosm; the macrocosm shines forth in the microcosm. The Greeks were also aware of 'the many': they saw the great variety of things in the world, the plants, the animals, the people, as well as the sea and the clouds. They explained this diversity as emerging from a basic original 'stuff' or 'substance.' Unity, they said, is always present in the womb of diversity.

According to Thales, the original unitary substance was water, while his disciple Anaximander suggested that fire, earth and air played an equally important role: the primeval substance was undefined, limit-less, and all-encompassing. Anaximenes, in turn, maintained that the original substance was a mixture of water and earth that, warmed by the sun, generated plants, animals, and human beings by spontaneous creation.

The rational minds of the Greeks developed the kind of natural philosophy initiated by Thales to a high degree of sophistication. The atomist theory of Leucippus and Democritus was a shining example. Atoms, said the theory, are the only things that exist: all things are composed of them. Atoms are indivisible and indestructible. Atoms and the things composed of atoms constitute the domain of Being, but Being is not all there is in the world, for there is also non-being: the Void. Change can occur precisely because atoms play out their lives in the Void, adopting different positions and forming different things.

In the atomist theory the Democriteans grasped what they believed to be the ultimate nature of the world. This was a world made up of elementary and indestructible elements creating in combination all there is, and ever will be. Their theory endured for almost two thousand years; it fell apart only with the rise of modern experimental science.

With the golden age of Hellenic civilization on the decline, the attention of Greek philosophers shifted from cosmological speculation to human affairs. The great turnaround in Greek thought was introduced by Socrates, in whose wide-ranging discussions the morality of human actions came to dominate the earlier strands of natural philosophy. Yet, for Socrates' great disciple Plato, the wish to know the whole reappeared as the quest for grasping reality's ultimate principles. Plato called these principles Forms or Ideas. The highest among them, he said, are Truth, Goodness, and Beauty. Every object has its proper Form or Idea — indeed, the ultimate furnishings of reality are not solids, but the Forms described in geometry. The geometrical shape of the Forms was to account for the properties of material objects. The four-squareness of the cube, for example, explained the stability of matter, the sharp points of the tetrahedron the sting of fire, and the icosahedron, the closest among the regular solids to the sphere, the fluidity of water. The Forms themselves were not three-dimensional shapes but abstract and ideal entities, like numbers and other mathematical symbols.

Plato's philosophy gave rise to a long-lasting and influential school of thought founded by Plotinus. These 'neo-Platonists' revered the Forms, viewing them as sacred and mystical entities. They held that the experienced world is a lower region which only imperfectly expresses the Forms; the latter subsist in all their perfection in a higher sphere of reality.

The idealism of the Platonic tradition was counterbalanced by the naturalism of the school of Aristotle. In Aristotle's view the whole of the world consists of the interplay of four basic natural elements: earth, water, air, and fire. Each element seeks its natural place — earth the centre, water the next level, and fire and air the higher spheres. This gives order to the 'great chain of being' which extends from inanimate objects through plants and animals, all the way to humans. The inorganic becomes the organic by metamorphosis; nature proceeds gradually but constantly from the least to the most perfect and sensible. The process is not accidental — all things have their cause. But causes do not exist separately from their effects. The ultimate ground of reality, which for Plato was on a higher plane, Aristotle folded back into the natural world accessible to observation and reason.

Aristotelian philosophy became an integral part of the great medieval synthesis that culminated in the thirteenth century with the *Summa Theologica* of Thomas Aquinas. For a century thereafter it appeared that a satisfactory grasp had been achieved of the humanly knowable world. Whatever walls of mystery still remained could be ascribed to the inscrutable will of God.

However, the fourteenth century brought upheavals that shattered unquestioning faith in the Christian synthesis. This was a century of wars and conflicts, including the Hundred Years' War between England and France. Above all, it was the time when the plague known as the Black Death reached Europe. It appeared in 1349, and within twelve years killed perhaps a third of that continent's population. The effect on the public mind was soon apparent. The previous unity of thought and belief split into two; one of the new directions sought redemption by intensifying moral discipline and appealing to the divine powers; the other endeavoured to gain greater control over the physical world to escape unreasonable suffering and mitigate needless pain. The former direction reinforced the traditional doctrine and spirituality of the Catholic Church, while the latter planted the seed that would later grow into modern science and its applications in technology.

Then in the fifteenth and sixteenth centuries, the Renaissance weakened the hold of the redemption-oriented religious system on the European mind. Independent inquiry arose outside the monastic walls; humanism and religious reform became the subject of intense debate. There were attempts to reestablish pristine forms of Christianity as well as movements to revitalize civic humanism in the classical mould. The Catholic Church was challenged by the Reformation, its monopoly on knowledge contested. Independent minds, spearheaded by geniuses such as Galileo, Bruno, Copernicus, Kepler and Newton, evolved the fledgling sciences and created a cultural mutation that in the centuries that followed crystallized as the dominant worldview of the modern age.

The rise and fall of the mechanistic paradigm

Perhaps more than anyone else, Galileo can be regarded as the initiator of the new vision of the world. Instrumentally observed and mathematically described, this vision was that of a world as a grand mechanism, beyond human control. This was in line with what Galileo intended: his purpose was to find rules for understanding that were so inexorable and immutable that they could not be assailed. Inspired by the confirmation of the Copernican heliocentric universe through his observations with the newly invented telescope, Galileo claimed that nature observed through instruments would produce quantitative descriptions that are purged of the passions that divide men.

The mechanistic vision of the world pioneered by Galileo culminated in the mathematical principles of Newtonian physics — principles that remained unchallenged for over three centuries. Their strength derived from the demonstration that simple mathematical statements could lead to accurate predictions in a variety of fields of observation, including the positions of the planets, the paths of projectiles, and the motions of the individual mass points which were said to be the ultimate constituents of physical reality.

In Newton's classical mechanics the universe came to be viewed as a machine that implements the instructions laid down at the beginning of time. Once the machine has been set in motion, the instructions — the laws of motion — take charge: all motion is predetermined, nothing is left to chance. Little wonder that, when queried by Napoleon as to the place of God in this system, the mathematician Laplace is said to have responded that he had 'no need of that hypothesis.'

Physicists — and mathematicians who took their cue as to the nature of reality from physics — had indeed no need of 'God-hypotheses,' but biologists were in a more difficult position. There did not seem to be any simple way of understanding the relationship

31

between the living world and the physical universe. Newtonian physics did not know of any irreversible processes (time is reversible in the classical laws of motion), yet the biological world seemed to evolve in a manner that appeared on the whole irreversible. Moreover this evolution had an 'arrow of time' which was precisely opposed to that which nineteenth-century physics found in the universe at large. The second law of the classical thermodynamics founded by Clausius and Thompson and elaborated by Boltzmann said that, in any system closed to flows of energy across the system boundaries, the factor called entropy could only grow. This meant that closed systems that perform 'work' must inevitably run down. They use up whatever free energy is available within their structure and move towards a state of maximum randomness and disorganization — towards maximum entropy. Hence if the universe did not receive fresh energies from some source outside of itself, it, too, must ultimately run down.

Many classical thermodynamicists became convinced of the ultimate heat-death of the cosmos. Some, however, together with evolutionary philosophers such as Henri Bergson, were puzzled. How is it that one domain within the universe — the domain of living things — can move against the stream, building up, instead of breaking down? Boltzmann invoked the laws of probability, while Bergson suggested that life is driven by a specific force he called *élan vital.* Yet no explanation was entirely satisfactory.

Within the physical sciences the Newtonian paradigm was reinforced at the beginning of the nineteenth century with the revival of the atomist theory of Democritus by English chemist John Dalton. Dalton's theory, that all gases are made up of small and indivisible units called atoms, brought chemistry into the ambit of classical mechanics. But Dalton's interpretation was soon challenged. Within fifty years of the publication of his theory, experimenters discovered that atoms are not indivisible but are made up of still smaller particles. And even these particles could not be the ultimate 'atoms' of the physical world because, if they have finite extension in space, it is always possible that they could be further divided. Indeed, when sufficiently powerful experimental devices became available, even the nucleus of the atom proved fissionable.

With the splitting of the atom in the late nineteenth century, and of the atomic nucleus in the early twentieth, more had been fragmented than a physical entity. The entire edifice of atomistic natural philosophy was shaken. Experimental physics had demolished the theory that all of reality is built of indivisible atoms, but it could not put any comparably coherent and meaningful concept in its place. By the middle of the twentieth century the idea of an ultimate particle that is itself indivisible had entirely collapsed. Matter proved divisible again and again, but this would not yield a smallest particle: out of the divided entities pairs of smaller particles and antiparticles would emerge: 'pair-creation,' it seemed, could go on forever.

The universe of physics turned strange beyond all expectations: to quantum and particle physicists, matter itself seemed to have dematerialized. The physical basis of reality became, in Popper's words, more like a cloud than a rock.

Already in the late 1920s, quantum physicists, led by Niels Bohr, were forced to suspend speculation concerning the independent nature of what they were observing: they considered the subatomic entities they were investigating (entities that do not exceed the Planck-mass of 10^{-5} grams) simply as 'phenomena.' But when the only things one knows are 'phenomena,' objective reality evaporates. Phenomena, as Werner Heisenberg said, are not the 'works of nature' but merely the 'texts of science.' 'The atomic physicist has to resign himself to the fact that his science is but a link in the infinite chain of man's argument with nature, and that it cannot simply speak of nature "in itself".'[1] 'We are suspended in language,' Bohr concurred, 'physics concerns what we can say about nature.'[2] The works of nature — the objects of classical physics — seemed to have escaped the quantum physicists' grasp. The external world of physics, according to Eddington, had become a world of shadows. 'Nothing is real,' he wrote, 'not even one's wife. Quantum physics leads the scientist to the belief that his wife is a rather elaborate differential equation.' (But, Eddington added, he is probably tactful enough not to obtrude this opinion in domestic life.)[3]

Though forbidden to think about the nature of reality beyond observations, some physicists nevertheless went further. They speculated that the world to which language and the 'text of science' refers is mental rather than material. 'To put the conclusion crudely,' said Eddington, 'the stuff of the world is mind-stuff.'[4] Jeans agreed: '... the cumulative evidence of various pieces of probable reasoning makes it seem more and more likely that reality is better described as mental than as material ... the universe seems to be nearer to a great thought than a great machine.'[5] Heisenberg, perhaps the most philosophically oriented of all the great quantum physicists, took recourse to Platonic idealism. Just as Plato had dissolved the materialism of the pre-Socratic philosophers in the abstract world of ideal forms and ideas, so today the deterministic world of classical mechanics is dissolved in mathematical formulas. If atoms are not material bodies, he asserted, then they show 'a distinct formal similarity to the $\sqrt{-1}$ in mathematics.'[6] He spoke with conviction of the error of the 'philosophical doctrine of Democritus.' Ultimately every particle, Heisenberg said, consists of every other particle, and the concept of a fundamental particle must be replaced with the concept of a fundamental symmetry.[7] This is the basic idea of the so-called 'bootstrap' theories — theories that contest that the physical world is built of identifiable building blocks. There are no basic particles; everything is built of everything else. Particles are made of other particles by binding forces that are themselves created by the exchange of particles among particles — the observed world lifts itself into existence by its own bootstraps. In Heisenberg's view this bootstrapping world is built as a mathematical structure; thus there is no use asking to what, beyond themselves, the formulas of physics would refer.

By the second half of this century the ontological basic of science turned highly opaque. Not only could scientists not identify the basic entities that would underlie the diversity of manifest phenomena; they even contested that such entities existed in nature. Clearly, neither the Democritean atom nor the Newtonian mass-point was the ultimate ground of physical reality.

The rise of the cosmological revolution

With the Einsteinian revolution at the turn of the century physicists had moved irrevocably beyond the mechanistic paradigm. Then, some two decades later, with the advent of quantum theory, they abandoned the last vestiges of classical mechanistic thinking. Yet many scientists, especially in the human, social, and engineering fields, remained fascinated by the simplicity and power of the Newtonian formulas. When it came to being precise and pragmatic, there seemed to be no substitute for classical mechanics. The systems of immediate interest to humans were thought to be decomposable to their elements — ultimately to their atomic or molecular building blocks. These were believed to be related by simple and direct chains of cause and effect, so that interrelations, no matter how complex, could always be simplified for purposes of computation.

The instrument for computing interrelations was in place: it was the calculus, invented simultaneously by Newton and by Leibniz. It functioned best when causal relations among the observed phenomena could be reduced to simple cause-effect chains, and the entire set of relations changed smoothly and continuously. The calculus was held to be almost universally applicable: real world phenomena were believed to be generally computable ('integrable'), being subject only to smooth and continuous change and reducible to basic causal chains. Complex, 'non-integrable' systems were thought to be the exception and not the rule.

But the assumption of mechanistic reducibility could not be maintained when the modern computer appeared on the scene. Complex systems became available for investigation with non-conventional methods, and when they were investigated in detail even systems that were previously thought to be fully integrable turned out to be complex beyond the pale of the classical tools.

The computer enabled scientists to deal with *simultaneous* interactions among *nonlinear* processes. If a number of nonlinear processes interact, complex loops and feedbacks are produced, exhibiting features such as recursion and self-referentiality. While at one extreme, the behaviour that results may be so simple as to be almost linear, at the other it may be so complex as to appear chaotic. The classical tools dealt only with the former, and this gave rise to the belief that, as a rule, the phenomena themselves are simple and linear. Contemporary methods have corrected this assumption and succeeded in discovering order at higher levels of complexity, penetrating all the way to dimensions of order that were previously thought to be chaos-bound. The latter, mapped by so-called chaotic or strange attractors, turned out to have irreducible characteristics of their own. These include a high level of input- and initial-condition dependence, fractal dimensions, and basically indeterminate — and thus intrinsically unpredictable — evolutionary trajectories.

With the computer revolution, sciences such as cybernetics, general system theory, nonequilibrium thermodynamics, nonlinear dynamics, general evolution theory, and theories of self-organization and chaos experienced rapid development. Leading-edge scientists from von Bertalanffy to Prigogine, and from Wiener to Ashby and Abraham, learned to decode the dynamics intrinsic to complex systems, renouncing attempts to decompose them to their basic elements.

Within physics the properties of single components came to be analysed in terms of systems of interrelations, rather than attempting to reconstruct the interrelated systems on the basis of the properties of the single components. Theories making use of this method included Heisenberg's S-matrix theory and Chew's bootstrap theory. In quantum field theories the decisive systems came to be conceptualized in terms of field interactions. These interactions were taken to constitute the individual particles, instead of the particles constituting the fields.

On first sight, the difference between deriving the properties of the parts from the properties of the whole, and reconstructing the properties of the whole from the properties of the parts, may seem picayune. On a closer look, however, the distinction turns out to be decisive. A continuous field is not reducible to the particles that dot its continua, the same as a dynamical system that follows its own evolutionary trajectory is not reducible to the differential equations that define relations among its individual parameters. Taking the whole as constituting the parts is a non-trivial alternative to taking the parts as constituting the whole.

The approach from whole to part is not necessarily speculative. Already over a century ago, mathematicians William Hamilton and Karl Gustav Jacobi could show that it is possible to treat local events as a function of a total field without loss of rigour. Every particular motion can be viewed as a function of all prior motion, rather than as the result of the action of separate mechanical forces.

Things in a Hamilton-Jacobi universe are not separate entities but the products of an interconnected whole. There are no simple causes and isolated effects; all things cause and determine each other. Everything that occurs, no matter how minute and local, is the outcome of all that has occurred before and is the ground for all that will occur thereafter. Reality is like a system of interacting waves. Rather than discrete things and independent events, there are but ripples upon ripples upon waves upon waves in this universe, propagating and interpenetrating in a seamless sea.

Though it has been known to mathematicians for over a century, the concept of an ensemble that determines the behaviour of its parts has been seldom applied to the analysis of real world phenomena. For one thing, many fields of science remained dominated by the Newtonian concept of a mechanical world where motion can be computed in terms of independent forces acting on the trajectory of discrete particles. For another, calculating events and motions in the Hamilton-Jacobi framework proved only possible if the events and the interactions are few in number: it turned out that a large number of highly connected elements soon exceeds the possibilities of computation. In consequence the occasional empirical applications of the Hamilton-Jacobi theory tended to turn the basic concept on its head: scientists used the mathematics to calculate small ensembles of events as if they were separate and independent from the wide ensemble that is 'the rest of the universe.'

Today, however, the primacy of 'the rest of the universe' is rediscovered. In microphysics the state of a particle is seen as the product of the ensemble in which that particle is embedded, and that ensemble is made up of all other particles. Physics, as Ilya Prigogine has observed, is on the way to becoming a global science.[8] The primacy of the ensemble has also surfaced in physical cosmology, where the state of the cosmos at any one time, as well as the evolution of its states over time, are explained in reference to universal parameters. And the primacy of wholes *vis-à-vis* their parts is surfacing in macro-biology and in ecology, as well as in anthropology and in some fields of social science.

A more holistic, systemic approach is emerging in field after field. While there is still a long way to go, current trends augur that there is a new scientific revolution in the offing. Philosopher of science Errol Harris summed up its thrust. He said that the emerging new 'cosmology of wholeness' hopes to:

— account for the wholeness of the universe, a single, indivisible wholeness of distinguishable but inseparably related parts;
— furnish the principle of organization universal to the system, a principle immanent within all the parts of the universe each of which expresses and exemplifies it;
— provide the hierarchical scale of differentiation that stratifies all the parts in a progression of levels of emergent complexity, so that each successive part expresses and manifests the principle more fully and adequately than its precedecessors; and
— exhibit a complex network of interdependence where all elements are reciprocally adjusted in structure and function one to another.[9]

The present study is situated in the context of this 'cosmological revolution.' It seeks to identify the principle underlying order and organization in the cosmos — a venture, as Harris said, of those who seek a grand unified theory of reality.

In the chapters that follow we shall unfold this venture, looking first for the grounds of a new cosmology in current attempts to unify the scientific world picture, and then building the indicated concepts into a basic framework that could respond to the challenge to which this book is dedicated: to understand, in terms of an integrated dynamics, how the things that *are* in this world, have *come to be* the way they are.

– 2 –
Unification in Physics

In unfolding our venture to understand the orders that have emerged in the universe, we now review the thrust of the latest theories promulgated in the pertinent scientific fields. These are theories within the mainstream of the cosmological revolution: theories on the one hand in the new physics, and on the other in an emerging transdisciplinary domain that cuts across a number of classical boundaries. The new physics comes up with what physicists fondly if whimsically refer to as 'GUTs' (grand unified theories), while the new transdisciplinary theories either enlarge the application of physics to cover phenomena of life and mind, or focus on the processes of cosmic and biological evolution. We begin with the grand unified theories of the physicists.

The quest for grand unification

The objective of grand unification is not new to physics; in its time each major conceptual breakthrough unified the facts revealed to physical science up to that time. This was the case in the mechanics outlined by Galileo and the universal formulation of that mechanics at the hands of Newton; it was then the case in the electrodynamics of Maxwell and the thermodynamics of Boltzmann. In the beginning of this century, Einstein contributed the crucial breakthrough that unified the suddenly anomalous world picture of physics. This was not primarily the merit of Special Relativity, where the puzzles raised by nineteenth century physics found consistent and elegant resolution, but of General Relativity, where geometry and mechanics became fully and unexpectedly integrated. Space and matter, with the geometry of the one and the mechanics of the other, achieved a new and integral unity. The formerly mechanical force of gravity became an element of geometry; it was viewed as the effect of the curvature of space. The geometry of the latter, in turn, was traced to the distribution of matter. While it continued to be useful at times to think of space and matter as distinct entities, one had henceforth to keep in mind that they formed an integrated whole.

Not contented with the unification of geometry and mechanics, Einstein sought the further step that would integrate all known particles of matter with all known forces of spacetime within the in-itself timeless matrix of unified field theory. But Einstein's attempt embraced but two of the four universal forces of interaction — gravitation and electromagnetism — and left the weak and strong nuclear forces out of account. That it ultimately failed was due to this mistaken assumption about the universal forces of nature and not to the intrinsic unfeasibility of the enterprise. Today physicists encompass all four universal forces in attempts to create grand unified theories, together with the particles that have since come to light.

The unification of particles

Ever since the beginning of this century, each year has exhibited greater and greater detail in the inner structure of the atom and brought greater and greater complexity to atomic and subatomic theory. The atom itself was split at the end of the nineteenth century, and electrons were known to occupy its energy shells. But nobody suspected how many different particles would emerge later. The relevant discoveries came with the development of particle accelerators. With the commissioning of each new accelerator, more powerful than its predecessors, a whole new range of particle collisions became possible, and in the collisions entire arrays of new particles were spewed forth.

In the 1920s only three subatomic particles were known: the photon, the electron, and the proton. Ernest Rutherford then suggested that a further particle must be present in the nucleus: the neutron. When the existence of this particle was confirmed by experiment, the repertory of elementary particles had begun to expand. In 1930, in an attempt to explain the puzzling results of experiments on the decay of radioactive nuclei, the existence of the neutrino was suggested by Wolfgang Pauli. Twenty-five years later, also the neutrino was experimentally confirmed.

At that time quantum theory had already offered a good understanding of the outer shell of atoms, but the stability of the atomic nucleus remained puzzling. Hideki Yukawa suggested that a new elementary particle was involved. Since its mass was predicted to lie between that of the proton and the electron, he named it meson. According to Yukawa's theory, the stability of the atomic nucleus is due to the constant exchange of mesons between protons and neutrons.

When experiments were designed to trace the meson, physicists discovered not one particle but a whole family that included muons and pions. And, as more powerful particle accelerators came on line and nuclear collisions were investigated in cosmic rays high above the atmosphere, several further elementary particles came to light. Some were discovered as experimentalists followed up predictions by theoreticians; others emerged unforeseen in the experiments.

The first elementary particles — the electron, the proton, the neutron, and the early mesons — appeared as expected and fitted into the then-current theories of the structure of the atom. But as physicists moved the experiments to higher energy levels, observations refused to match theory. One mismatch involved the life-expectancy of exchange particles. Theory dictated that such particles should endure for only 10^{-23} second — a period during which a ray of light would have barely enough time to travel the width of an elementary particle — but experiment showed that the particles exist for 10^{-10} second: long enough for light to flash across the entire length of a room. Since the particles endure ten trillion times longer than expected, and are always produced in pairs, they came to be known as strange particles.

In order to create order among the many denizens of the emerging 'particle zoo,' Murray Gell-Mann suggested grouping particles in a particular 'eightfold' way (a term referring to the eightfold path of the Buddha). This ordering was based on the theory that particles are made up of a more fundamental entity called the 'quark.'[1] Originally, there were thought to be three varieties of quark: the up, the down, and the strange. The proton, for example, consists of two up and one

41

down quarks, the neutron of two down and one up quark, and the exchange particles have a strange quark in addition. Later, however, as more particles came to light, three quarks no longer sufficed and the family of quarks grew from three to six members.

Gell-Mann's theory of quarks resolved a persistent problem in the grouping of the particles: while leptons (low-mass particles such as the electron) had a coherent symmetry group, hadrons (heavy particles such as protons and neutrons) did not. If, however, each hadron is composed of three quarks, also the hadron family can be integrated in symmetry groups in reference to combinations of quarks.

The unification of forces

Ordering the vast array of particles into coherent symmetry groups was a major achievement, but genuine unification required that also the forces represented by the particles be unified. This endeavour was pioneered by Einstein in the unified field theory. His theory, though it considered only the gravitational and the electromagnetic forces and was hence condemned to fail, became the inspiration of an entire string of grand unified theories. Current GUTs and super-GUTs draw on quantum as well as on relativity theory and include four (rather than Einstein's two) universal fields of interaction: the strong and the weak nuclear forces, in addition to electromagnetism and gravitation. The physical universe is now thought to obey the laws of relativity, as well as of quantum mechanics.

Grand unification takes elementary particles as elements within the four universal fields. Field intensity at a specific point gives the statistical probability of finding a particle at that location: in a sense, particles are generated by variations in field intensity. Photons, electrons, nucleons, and the entire particle zoo are consequences of the quantum dynamics of these interacting fields.

The above concept has produced a profound shift in emphasis in physics, from particulate entities to the ensemble of the dynamical events that embed them. Steven Weinberg did not hesitate to assert that the real furnishings of the universe are fields; particles must be reduced to the status of epiphenomena.[2]

The foundations of quantum field theory were created in the 1920s and '30s by Jordan, Wigner, Dirac, Born, Pauli, Fermi, and Heisenberg among others. The mature form of the theory, known as quantum electrodynamics (QED) appeared during the 1940s. Its predictions found spectacular verification in the high-energy experiments that came on line in mid-century. As physicists succeeded in explaining disparate processes with field concepts, other quantum field theories followed, marking various stages in the unification of the physical forces of nature.

The first breakthrough came with the unification of the weak nuclear force with electromagnetism. Up to that point, the weak force appeared to behave in a very different way from that of electromagnetism. Sidney Sheldon, Steven Weinberg and Abdus Salam could show that these different forces emerge as two aspects of a single 'electroweak' force. It is now believed that in the early moments of the universe there was no distinction between electromagnetism and the weak nuclear force. But as structure began to emerge in the universe, this perfect symmetry became broken and the integrated force differentiated into the long-range force of electromagnetism and the short-range weak nuclear force.

Further unification could be effected with a deeper understanding of the strong nuclear force. Before the advent of quarks it was assumed that the exchange of intermediate force particles (mesons) produced the effect of the strong nuclear force. However, with the quark theory of hadrons it was necessary to postulate a force between the quarks themselves. It turned out that this force could be mathematically treated in a totally analogous way to the force of electromagnetism. Although the force acting between quarks had yet to be unified with the electroweak force, its formal appearance was very similar. By analogy with quantum electrodynamics (QED), the theory that achieved this unification came to be called quantum chromodynamics (QCD).

Super grand unification

With QED and QCD an entire array of grand unified theories appeared on the scene. The first stage in the program of grand unification had been the development of an integrated theory of the

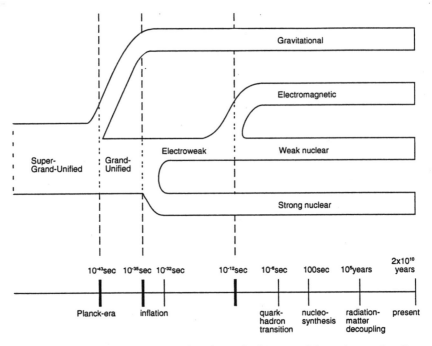

Figure 1. Spontaneous symmetry breaks in the history of the universe, leading to a successive separation of the four universal forces from the primal super-grand-unified force.

strong nuclear and the electroweak forces, together with the leptons and hadrons that constitute matter in the universe. The next stage was to extend this theory to include the force of gravitation (see Figure 1). This called for quantizing the gravitational field. The strong nuclear force had been quantized in terms of the gluon; and the electroweak force had been expressed in terms of the W and Z particles. The gravitational force could be quantized, in principle, in reference to a particle called the graviton.

Quantizing the gravitational field raised complex problems. Since Einstein's theory of gravitation was a geometrical theory of spacetime, quantizing that theory meant quantizing a geometry. Beyond this conceptual problem there were other difficulties: for one thing, there was no evidence that gravitons would exist in nature; for another, the mathematics that was needed to describe gravitons led to infinities. As a result a quantum theory of gravitation required a new approach, departing radically from earlier attempts at quantum field theory. So-called gauge symmetries had to be invoked, making use of super-symmetries and superspaces. In consequence a whole generation of 'super' theories was born.

The first breakthrough was the development of 'Susy,' the mathematics of supersymmetry. The quantum field theory incorporating Susy became 'quantum supergravity': it enabled physicists to unify fermions and bosons. This was a major achievement: the half-integral spin fermions were known to be the main 'matter'-particles, while the integral spin bosons were the 'force'-particles. (Fermions and bosons are distinguished by the values of their spin: bosons have integer values of spin [1, 2, 3, ...] while fermions have half-integral values [$\frac{1}{2}$, $\frac{3}{2}$, etc.]) Previously, the fermions could be grouped together in families and so could the bosons, but there was a clear-cut separation between the internally related family of fermions and the likewise internally related family of bosons. Now, thanks to supersymmetry, fermions and bosons — matter and force — could be related one to the other. In the higher dimensions of superspace, each can be 'reflected into' the other.

In order to unify fermions and bosons in superspace, a whole new set of particles had to be introduced: for every fermion and boson there had to be a supersymmetric partner. Just as photons acquired mirror-image particles called photinos and quarks acquired squarks, the 'graviton' had to be coupled with the 'gravitino.' This resolved the principal obstacle to the unification of gravitation with the electroweak force. Theoreticians could now postulate a grand unified force called 'supergravity.'

Nevertheless, super-grand-unified theories encountered further difficulties. First of all, quantum supergravity demanded that the supersymmetric partners should have masses higher than the particles of which they are mirror images. This introduced an element of unverifiability into the theory: the energy level of the supersymmetric particles turned out to be high enough to preclude creating them in particle accelerators. The new particles would remain entirely unobservable — unless, as some physicists believed, photinos could be detected in high-energy collisions between electrons and positrons, or protons and antiprotons.

Not only did the super-GUTs predict a host of new and experimentally unobservable particles, they also held another surprise: in most formulations they required eleven dimensions to work. Einstein's revolutionary innovation of adding the fourth time-dimension to the three spatial dimensions paled in comparison with theories that added as many as seven dimensions to the four of spacetime.

Physicists went to work, using complex mathematics to 'compactify' the seven extra dimensions of superspace in order to render Susy consistent with the four dimensions of relativity theory. It was assumed that the extra dimensions would exist but were 'rolled up' so that their effect would not be manifest even at the scale of elementary particles. But it soon appeared that the effort was doomed: there was no way to reduce seven of the eleven dimensions without compactifying the remaining four as well. This, however, would reduce the empirical entailments of the theory to zero dimensions.

For a time it appeared that the enterprise of super grand unification had to be abandoned. But then a younger generation of physicists came up with another, even more daring idea. Joel Scherk proposed that particles are not particulate at all but strings that spin and vibrate in space. All known phenomena of physical nature would be built from different combinations of these vibrations, much as the music of a string quartet is built from the vibrations of the strings of the four musical instruments.

The idea that rotating and vibrating strings would be fundamental to our understanding of nature dates back to the 1960s. At that time Gabriel Veneziano suggested that when elementary particles are arranged in order of their masses, they form a pattern similar to that of notes or resonances. Other physicists were later struck by the idea that the resonances could be produced by minuscule bodies vibrating strings the size of particles.

Scherk's string theory proved compatible with Gell-Mann's quark theory. The new theory explained why quarks are unobservable in nature: it is for the same reason that a string can never have a single end. When the ends of a string are separated, new ends are created.

The same way when hadrons are broken open, instead of single quarks, freshly paired quarks come into being.

In 1976, Scherk, Ferdinando Gliozzi and David Olive showed that supergravity can be introduced into string theory, making it into 'superstring theory.' Here the particle-strings vibrate in a higher-dimensional superspace. Yet the real triumph of the theory came in the mid-80s, just when supersymmetry theories seemed defeated by the problem of compactification. John Schwartz and Michael Green were able to show that a ten-dimensional superstring theory was perfectly compatible with four-dimensional spacetime; it did not encounter the problems of compactification. The new superstrings turned out to be smaller than the strings of the original theory: they are no larger than the Planck-length of 10^{-35} metre — far smaller than any known elementary particle.

Superstring theory is not free of problems and not even its basic concept is universally accepted by the physics community. Yet confidence that grand unification is achievable has grown, and few particle physicists would contest that, in time, all the forces and particles of the universe may be unified within a single theory.[3]

The factor of incompleteness

GUTs and super-GUTs are remarkable achievements of the new physics, but they are not the last word. In the present state of the art, unified theories are incomplete; they cannot account for the progressive, transphysical structuration of matter in the universe. Human experience indicates that matter coheres not only into particles, atoms and molecules, but also into cells, organisms and ecosystems on at least one planet. Although current GUTs describe the properties and interactions of particles, atoms and molecules, they do not show how particles, atoms and molecules generate the varied phenomena of the world we experience. In a truly unified theory of the universe, the progressive build-up of ever more complex and integrated configurations of matter with ever more differentiated characteristics must be an intrinsic feature.

That GUTs do not explain the build-up of the higher levels of complexity in space and time is a considerable lacunae. Hopes for a complete bootstrap theory — one that would explain progressive self-organization in nature not only in the physical but also in the biological and the human realm — have been surrendered; current schemes of self-organization do not penetrate much beyond the level of the physical universe.[4] It is with good reason that Stephen Hawking noted that, although the goal of physics is a complete understanding of everything around us, including our own existence, physics has not succeeded in reducing chemistry and biology to the status of solved problems, while the possibility of creating a set of equations through which it could account for human behaviour remains entirely remote.[5]

Complexity in the universe is an objective element, not a subjective chimera. A bacterium is objectively more complex than an atom, just as a mouse is more complex than a bacterium. It is reasonable, then, to require of scientific theory that it should give an account of the build-up of complexity in nature in rigorous and testable ways (see Appendix for note on *Complexity*).

A theory that can show how complexity is generated in the empirical world is by no means beyond the scope of science. Although laws that account for the progressive build-up of matter from particles to organisms are not easy to come by, the difficulties do not suggest that such laws do not exist. It is altogether too facile to shift the problem into the domain of metaphysics, or to dismiss it by claiming that complex phenomena arise haphazardly out of their simple constituents. To claim that the molecules, cells and tissues that make up a complex living organism would be the product of fortuitous accidents is just as unfounded as ascribing the complexity of the living to the action of mystical or metaphysical principles.

The challenge must be faced: it is to create an empirically consistent and internally coherent theory that would rise towards the pinnacles of complexity and order in nature with better logic than either chance or speculative metaphysics can provide.

– 3 –
Transdisciplinary Unification

Physicists deal with the physical foundations of the observable world; they do not ordinarily deal with phenomena of life and mind. Thus if we are to understand the dynamics of the process by which the orders intrinsic to life and mind came to be constituted, we need to go beyond the scope of contemporary physics. The unification of bosons and fermions, gravitation, strong and weak nuclear interactions and electromagnetism is important but it is not enough: we must also account for the higher-level orders that emerge within the womb of the unitary physical universe.

The physical foundations of the universe may or may not give us sufficient grounds for understanding how the transphysical domains of reality came to be generated. If the physical foundations turn out to suffice for grasping the nature of higher-order phenomena, unified theories could proceed on the basis of an enlarged concept of physics. But if such a knowledge does not suffice, the cosmological revolution would have to take another route: it would have to give the *laws* — the integrated dynamics — by which higher forms and dimensions of order emerge in nature.

We shall sample here two theories that fall into the first category of 'enlarged physics'; and two that belong to the second category we shall call 'general evolution theory.'

A sampling of leading-edge theories

Bohm's implicate order

Throughout his long career, and until his passing away just as this book was nearing completion, David Bohm fought dogmatism and complacency in physics and challenged the phenomenalism and idealism of quantum theory. In the 1950s he put forward the theory of hidden variables in an effort to transform the probabilistic understanding of the behaviour of subatomic particles into the deterministic behaviour demanded by Einstein. In recent years Bohm has developed a new concept, according to which all things, including the emergence of order and the interplay of chance and necessity, derive from a basic level that underlies the manifest world of experience.[1]

Bohm proceeds on the assumption that, over the past forty years, the basic theoretical notions in physics have been in a state of serious and sustained confusion. A profound change is overdue. Bohm's reform is radical — there are two levels of reality: one that reveals itself in phenomena, and another, lying below. A basic description of the universe must ultimately be based on this underlying level that Bohm calls 'implicate.' (The Latin sense of 'implicate' is to fold inward.) The essential feature of the implicate order is that everything that takes place in space and time is enfolded in it. An example is a vortex. It has a relatively constant, recurrent and stable form, yet it does not have an existence independent of the movement of the fluid in which it appears. The vortex may appear as an independent body, yet its order is derived from the dynamics of the flowing water.

Bohm illustrates the relationship between the underlying implicate order and the surface explicate order with a device consisting of two concentric glass cylinders with a viscous fluid such as glycerine between them. A droplet of insoluble ink is placed in the fluid and the outer cylinder is slowly rotated. The droplet is then drawn into a thread-like form. If a sufficiently large number of rotations are made, the original droplet seems to be lost within the glycerine. Yet when the cylinder is rotated in the opposite direction, the thread-like form draws back into the shape of a droplet.

The droplet is an aggregate of separate carbon particles carried along at the same speed as the glycerine in which it is inserted. When the particles are drawn out, they become visible as a thread-like form. If two droplets are inserted in the fluid, each constitutes an independent thread-like form, and if the threads intersect the particles in each droplet intermingle. Yet when the motion of the underlying fluid is reversed, the particles in each of the threads retrack back into separate droplets. Here Bohm emphasised the primacy of the total solution in which the droplets of ink are suspended relative to the particles of carbon. The particles are part of the ensemble in which they are enfolded, or 'implicated.'

According to Bohm, the totality of the manifest world derives from the implicate order as an explicate sub-totality of stable recurrent forms. Because all things are given together in the implicate order, there are no longer any chance events in nature; everything that happens in the explicate order is the expression of order in the order of the implicate realm. Nothing new or random can emerge on the level of manifest phenomena; evolution must be but appearance. Quarks as well as galaxies, the same as organisms and atoms, are once and for all part of the order that subtends the observed phenomena.

The implicate order acts on the explicate order by determining the motion of quanta. The pertinent factor is Q, the quantum potential. Much as the gravitational constant G, the quantum potential Q pervades spacetime. However, Q, originates in the implicate order, a sub-quantum domain beyond space and time. Out of this enfolded holographic order the quantum potential emerges as a 'pilot wave' that guides the motion of quanta. The effect in question depends uniquely on the form, and not on the energy of the holographic waveforms; hence, unlike the forces of gravitation and electromagnetism, Q does not diminish in space or attenuate in time.

Bohm's pilot-wave model of reality conforms to traditional ideas of physics, inasmuch as the evolution of the universe is governed by deterministic laws applying to particles and to fields. Bohm assumed that in addition to the wave function of quantum theory, reality contains factors that pertain to the physical world as classically conceived. By this assumption he could explain probabilistic quantum events by invoking deterministic laws. Every particle, he said, is accompanied by a wave that satisfies the Schrödinger wave function. This 'pilot wave' determines the quantum potential, which in turn determines the particle state. Hence particles do not possess both particle-like and wave-like properties: the observed wave-like properties follow from the general effect of the quantum wave-field on their structure.

Bohm's assumption is that a particle's behaviour resembles that of a ship guided by radar. The structure of particles — possibly between 10^{-16}m and the Planck-length of 10^{-35}m — is complex and subtle enough to respond to information from a pilot wave. However, as Bohm noted, there is no theory as yet as to the origin of this information.[2]

Bohm's two-layer universe does not evolve: it subsists. Everything that comes to be in the explicit order is already given in the implicate order. Yet the origins of this order are not explained: the implicate order of the holofield is merely postulated. Given that Q, the quantum potential, originates in the implicate order, it appears that the vital classical component in the quantum universe is to be accepted on faith alone. Its origins are explained neither in theory, nor by any possible empirical means — observation and experiment, after all, can only refer to the explicate order.

Stapp's Heisenberg quantum universe

Another theory that seeks to explain transphysical phenomena with an enlarged concept of physics is the legacy of Heisenberg, revived and expanded recently by Henry Stapp.[3]

Heisenberg himself was ambiguous about the reality interpretation of quantum theory: at times he implied a mentalistic, at other times a physicalist, interpretation. He wrote, for example, that 'we are finally led to believe that the laws of nature that we formulate mathematically in quantum theory deal no longer with the particles themselves but with our knowledge of the elementary particles. ... The conception of the objective reality of the particles has thus evaporated ... into the transparent clarity of a mathematics that represents no longer the behaviour of the elementary particles but rather our knowledge of this behaviour.'[4] However, elsewhere he maintained that 'If we want to describe what happens in an atomic event we have to realize that the word "happens" ... applies to the physical not the psychical act of observation, and we may say that the transition from the "possible" to the "actual" takes place as soon as the interaction between the object and the measuring device, and thereby with the rest of the world, has come into play; it is not connected with the act of registration of the result in the mind of the observer.'[5]

Now, if the above noted transition from the 'possible' to the 'actual' — that is, quantum theory's 'collapse of the wave-function' — is due to the interaction between the measuring device and the particle, the world to which our observations refer is ontologically real. If, however, the wave-function collapses with the registration of the result in the mind of the observer, the world beyond our observations of it remains essentially unreal — 'veiled' or 'smoky.' The former alternative represents an ontological interpretation of quantum mechanics, in contrast with the mentalistic interpretation of the Copenhagen school and the mainstream quantum establishment.

Stapp chooses the ontological interpretation. If we follow him we may inquire, as he does, about the limits of its applicability. Is probabilistic quantum reality limited to the subatomic domain where real world phenomena do not exceed the Planck mass of 10^{-5} grams, or does it apply to macroscopic phenomena as well?

According to Stapp, the model of physical reality that is the most widely accepted among contemporary physicists is the Heisenberg quantum universe complete with large-scale nonclassical effects.[6] He notes that this universe dispenses with Bohm's classical variables while retaining the idea that the probability distribution that occurs in quantum theory exists in nature, not only in the mind of the observer. The quantum probability distribution, together with its abrupt changes, makes for a complete representation of reality. This representation discloses that the evolution of the physical world proceeds by an alternation between two phases: a gradual evolution via deterministic laws that are analogous to the laws of classical physics; and the periodic occurrence of sudden, uncontrolled quantum jumps. The latter actualize one or the other of the various macroscopic possibilities generated by the deterministic laws of motion. The 'detection event' occurs once deterministic laws have decomposed the quantum probability distribution into well separated branches. This event actualizes one of the alternatives and eliminates the others. The actualized alternative may be a macroscopic event, distinguishable at the level of direct observation.

Stapp's interpretation of the Heisenberg quantum universe seeks not only to respond to some of the quantum anomalies we shall review in

Chapter 4, but to give a coherent quantum mechanical explanation of biological, even of mental phenomena. The evolving quantum state, although it is controlled in part by mathematical laws that are analogous to the laws of classical physics, no longer refers to anything substantive in the real world. The quantum state only represents the potentialities and probabilities associated with actual events. Consequently any 'stuff' or 'substance' that would be represented by the evolving quantum state would be more idea-like than matter-like in character. The matter-like aspects of phenomena are exhausted in certain mathematical properties, but these mathematical features can be understood just as well — and in fact better — as characteristics of an evolving idea-like world. There is, Stapp asserts, no natural place for matter in the quantum universe. This is the exact reverse of the situation created by classical physics, where there was no natural place for mind.

The idea-like character of the Heisenberg quantum universe does not reduce to the phenomenalism of the Copenhagen school: the universe, though idea-like, is ontologically real. This opens the possibility of integrating human consciousness into the physical sciences. The classical concept of matter was local-reductionist in nature — the physical world was decomposable into elementary local quantities that interact only with their immediately adjacent neighbours. On the other hand conscious thought appears to constitute complex wholes, both at the functional level and as directly experienced. It is not possible, Stapp claims, to conceptualize a thought as a part of the physical world when the latter is classically conceived. To bring human conscious thought into the physicist's conception of the world something is needed within that conception that has the required integrity and complexity.

The world of classical physics, being essentially reductionist, knows no irreducibly complex wholes. Not so the expanded physics of the quantum universe. Here the actual quantum event can be the actualization, as a unit, of an entire high-level pattern of neural firings. Such a pattern could have the complexity of conscious thought and be at the same time a single actualized structure. The analysis of the basic features of high-level brain functions and of conscious mental processes could reveal an isomorphism between the intrinsic structure of conscious mental events and the intrinsic structure of a certain class of brain events, described in the language of quantum theory.

Stapp concludes that, if the nonclassical mathematical regularities identified by quantum theory are accepted as characteristics of an essentially idea-like world, then we 'appear to have found in quantum theory the foundation for a science that may be able to deal successfully in a mathematically and logically coherent way with the full range of scientific thought, from atomic physics, to biology, to cosmology, including also the area that had been so mysterious within the framework of classical physics, namely the connection between processes in human brains and the stream of human conscious experience.'[7]

The Heisenberg quantum universe appears here as the major candidate for transdisciplinary unified theory. This theory, based on an expanded concept of physics, is at present essentially incomplete. Even aside from the difficult question, whether an idea-like objective reality is satisfactory in view of the intrinsic realism of natural science, there is a problem highlighted by the query: 'whence the quantum jump?' As Stapp admits, these jumps are not strictly controlled by any known law of nature. Contemporary quantum theory treats them as random variables in the sense that only the statistical weights of the jumps are specified: the actual choice of this or that event is not accounted for in the theory. This means that the way that the quantum state evolves is left basically unexplained. The occurrence or nonoccurrence of quantum jumps, and the choices they effect are entirely random with respect to the pre-existing possibilities. Such randomness is a major flaw, however, when it comes to extending quantum mechanics to macroscopic phenomena: it fails to give a coherent account of the progressive emergence of the transphysical levels of order in our experience. The kind of orders we now observe, as already noted in the Introduction, cannot have come about in a random universe — not even if random events interspersed the evolution of otherwise deterministic processes.

In the Heisenberg quantum universe the evolution of the highly ordered systems that populate the transphysical domains of experience

— life and mind, above all — is not explained. To explain it there would have to be a single, coherent dynamic for the alternative states that real world phenomena are said to assume prior to a 'detection event,' as well as for the selection among these states, with both aspects of the dynamic accounted for within the self — consistent structure of an overall theory. Stapp is confident that such a theory can be ultimately developed on the basis of quantum mechanics;[8] but whether or not this will be the case remains yet to be seen.

Prigogine's nonequilibrium systems

If an expanded concept of physics should prove insufficient to account for the emergence of order in nature, transdisciplinary theory would have to research the laws whereby such orders arise. General laws of a basically simple kind could suffice in principle: even a high degree of complexity can be generated by the constant iteration of very simple algorithms, as experience with cellular automata theory and similar mathematical simulations demonstrate.

In nature, elementary particles build into atoms and atoms build into molecules and crystals. Molecules in turn build into macromolecules and into still more complex cellular structures associated with life; and ultimately cells build into multicellular organisms and these again into social groups and ecologies. It is not necessary, nor indeed reasonable, that each of these processes of assembly should obey categorically distinct laws. The same basic laws, functioning as nature's algorithms, could create the interactive dynamics whereby complexity builds in the universe from the level of particles to that of organisms, and ecologies and societies of organisms. These would be the general laws of evolution in the natural realms; and the theories stating them would be general evolution theories.[9]

Until the last few decades, general evolution theories were produced by philosophers who complemented the lacunae of scientific knowledge with speculative insight. Although speculative, such works as Bergson's *Creative Evolution,* Herbert Spencer's *First Principles,* Samuel Alexander's *Space, Time and Deity,* and Alfred North Whitehead's *Process and Reality* stand as enduring milestones of evolutionary thinking. Recently, however, concepts and theories have been developed that promise to lift evolution as a general phenomenon from the realm of philosophical speculation into that of scientific investigation. Among these newcomers Ilya Prigogine's nonequilibrium thermodynamics — the thermodynamics of irreversible processes — merits special mention.[10]

Prigogine was among the first to realize the transdisciplinary implication of the study of evolutionary processes. A living system, he said, is not like a clockwork that can be explained by simple causal relations among its parts; in an organism each organ and each process is a function of the whole. A similar point of view, he added, is necessary in the social sciences. The theory of the irreversible evolution of thermodynamically open systems applies to physical chemistry, to biological systems, and also to human systems.

Classical thermodynamics was concerned with the transformation of free energy into waste heat in closed systems, with the consequent breakdown of order into randomness. In nineteenth century physics, the ultimate implication of this line of thought was the heat-death of the whole universe. But in the first half of the twentieth century, physicists have been exploring new approaches. Lars Onsager's 1931 study 'Reciprocal Relations in Irreversible Processes' was pointing in the direction of irreversible processes that move systems away from, rather than toward, thermodynamic equilibrium. In 1947 Prigogine devoted his doctoral dissertation to the behaviour of systems far from equilibrium, and in the early 1960s Aharon Katchalsky and P.F. Curran elaborated the mathematical basis of the new science of nonequilibrium thermodynamics. These investigators showed that by concentrating on gradual changes in closed systems, classical thermodynamics has failed to confront real world systems — nonequilibrium systems that evolve nonlinearly and are open to energy flows in their environment. Such systems are basic to life: as Schrödinger noted in mid-century, 'life feeds on negentropy.'

An open system far from thermodynamic equilibrium dissipates entropy as it performs work: in Prigogine's terms, it imports free energy from its surroundings and exports entropy to its environment. If such a system imports more negentropy than the entropy it dissipates, it grows and evolves. In open systems change in entropy is defined by the equation $dS = d_iS + d_eS$, where dS is the total change of entropy in the system, d_iS the entropy change produced by irreversible processes within it, and d_eS the entropy transported across the system's boundaries. In an isolated system dS is always positive, for it is uniquely determined by d_iS, which necessarily grows as the system performs work. However, in an open system d_eS can offset the entropy produced within the system and may even exceed it. Thus dS in an open system need not be positive: it can be zero or negative. An open system can be in a stationary state $(dS = 0)$, or it can grow and complexify $(dS < 0)$. Entropy change is then given by the equation $d_eS = (d_iS \leq 0)$, which means that the entropy produced by irreversible processes within the system is shifted into its environment.

Evolution — the negentropic complexification of a system — is triggered when a critical fluctuation pushes a far-from-equilibrium system still further from equilibrium. The new order arises in the interplay of critical fluctuations during the crucial phase-change of an instability. If the system is to evolve rather than devolve, at least one out of the many possible fluctuations must 'nucleate' — that is, diffuse rapidly throughout the system. If and when it does, the whole system undergoes a bifurcation: its evolutionary trajectory forks off into a new mode. The dynamic regime it then assumes defines the norm around which the system's typical values will thereafter fluctuate.

The evolutionary process as a whole depends critically on randomness in the system. 'Only when a system behaves in a sufficiently random way may the difference between past and future, and therefore irreversibility, enter into its description,' wrote Prigogine with Isabelle Stengers in *Order out of Chaos*.[11] 'The "historical" path along which the system evolves as the control parameter grows is characterized by a succession of stable regions, where deterministic laws dominate, and of unstable ones, near the bifurcation points, where the system can "choose" between or among more than one possible future. Both the deterministic character of the kinetic equations whereby the set of possible states and their respective stability can be calculated, and the random fluctuations "choosing" between or among the states around

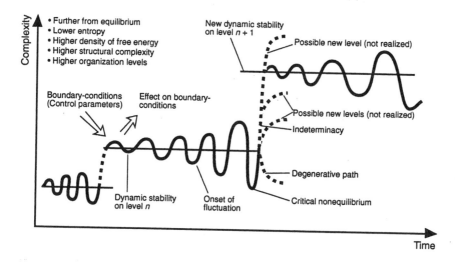

Figure 2. Bifurcations in a complex system far from equilibrium. Fluctuations beyond established boundary conditions produce a critical instability and consequent chaos. An indeterminate transition ('bifurcation' of the evolutionary trajectory) is resolved when the dynamic regime of the system is restructured on a new level of nonequilibrium.

bifurcation points, are inextricably connected. This mixture of necessity and chance constitutes the history of the system.'[12]

Perturbations, the random interplay of critical fluctuations, and the bifurcation that follows upon the nucleation of some of the fluctuations, are the key elements that define the interactive dynamics responsible for the evolution of far-from-equilibrium systems in nature (see Figure 2).

Prigogine's interactive dynamics links systems in all realms of observation: the physical, the chemical, the biological, the ecological, even the social. It offers a passport to transit from physics and chemistry to biology and ecology, and ultimately to the social sciences. But does the Prigoginian dynamics provide a full and satisfactory explanation of the orders that arise as a result of self-organization in nature?

Serious questions persist on this point. In the Prigoginian dynamics the specific developmental path of the evolving system is the prey of chance. The bifurcation process must be described by stochastic equations that allow a spread of probabilities in the outcome. Neither the past history of a system, nor the flows that reach it from its environment, decides which of the possibly numerous fluctuations will actually nucleate. This, however, creates a difficulty. If neither the past nor the environment determines the outcome of a bifurcation, then the dynamic regime that arises in a complex system is at the mercy of a random selection from among the many fluctuations that arose in the system. The way evolution unfolds in *one* system becomes fully unpredictable; and the way it unfolds in many systems is likely to be diverse. If systems were driven by the Prigoginian dynamics, they would tend to diverge and diversify rather than converge and unify. Even if two systems were to start in the same state and with the same initial conditions, they would still diverge in the course of their evolution as each system came to be exposed to a different set of external influences and different patterns of internal fluctuation. Prigogine spoke of a 'divergence property' basic to the evolutionary process — and with good reason.

This cannot be the whole story. If evolving systems were mainly to diversify over time, we should be surrounded by an uncoordinated welter of highly differentiated systems, instead of the consistent orders exhibited by the macrostructures of cosmology and the microstructures of physics, chemistry, and the life sciences. If theory is to be adequate to the facts, in addition to the dynamics of divergence, it must also describe the dynamics of convergence.

Sheldrake's formative causation

A bolder but also more controversial attempt to respond to the challenge of transdisciplinary unification is the work of plant-biologist Rupert Sheldrake. His theory of morphic resonance — also called 'hypothesis of formative causation' — was prompted by the need for a new approach in regard to the classical issue biologists call 'the problem of form.' Nature shows a great profusion of forms and structures, yet it also exhibits great consistency among them. To understand how the orders of living nature could have come about, one should know more about the generation of form in organic species. Some theoretical biologists suggested that, in addition to genetic programs, another factor may be at work in the organic realm. This factor, they said, could be a morphogenetic (that is, form-generating) field.

Morphogenetic fields were postulated as early as the 1920s by Alexander Gurwitsch, who used the concept to account for processes in embryology and developmental biology. A number of his contemporaries adopted this concept; it was likened at times to the field that surrounds the ends of a bar magnet. When a planarium (a type of flat worm) is cut in half, each half develops into a full organism. The morphogenetic explanation of this phenomenon was that the worm's regeneration is guided by its own biological field. Just as when a magnet is cut in half two new magnets form, each with their own complete field, so also the morphogenetic field of the worm splits into two identical halves when the worm is bisected. Each complete field then guides the worm halves to develop into complete organisms.

During the last fifty years, this initial insight underwent considerable development. In 1925 Paul Weiss applied the basic field concept to explain processes of regeneration in animals, and biologists as well as mathematicians picked up and elaborated the concept. D'Arcy Thompson produced his path-breaking work on the evolution of form in living species, illustrating it with transformations in fish, and Hermann Weyl demonstrated the remarkable transformations of symmetry in the form of living species. Geometrical forms and dynamical processes were connected by Conrad Waddington and René Thom by dividing the biofield into geometrical zones of structural stability.

There has been particular interest in bioenergy fields in the East, where they are associated with concepts handed down in the cultural tradition. Chi, yin and yang, Kundalini, and the energy flows associated with chakras and treated in acupuncture are as many expressions of cosmic and organic energy fields. Experiments at Lanzhou University and at the Atomic Nuclear Institute in Shanghai investigated the energy fields generated by the human body and found that they exist; moreover, they appear to vary with the mental powers of the subjects. Qigong Masters, for example, have a more pronounced energy field than other individuals. The human energy field has been also investigated in the former Soviet Union. Scientists at the A.S. Popov

Bio-information Institute reported that the field consists of frequencies within the range of 300 to 2000 manometers. Western researchers attempted to link it to the effect of natural healers (whose own bioenergy fields may interact with those of their patients) as well as with the bodily auras perceived by healers and other sensitives.

Within the more rigorous experimental domains, scientists such as Brian Goodwin could show that biofields are associated with growth processes in plants and animals. According to Goodwin, the forms of living nature develop when biological fields act on existing organic units. The biofield is the basic unit of organic form and organization; molecules and cells are but 'units of composition.' Life evolves, Goodwin claims, on the interface between organism and environment, in a 'sacred dance' generated in the interaction between organisms and the field that embeds them.[13]

As to the independent reality of biofields, opinions diverge. For mainstream biologists fields are merely heuristic devices called for when there are no better explanations. For Goodwin they are more: fields are as real as organisms, if not more so. V.M. Inyushin, unlike Goodwin, goes even further: he asserts the organism-independent existence of biological fields. Such fields, he claims, constitute a fifth state of matter, composed of ions, free electrons and free protons. In humans, the field is attached to the brain, but it may also project beyond the organism and produce telepathic phenomena.[14]

Also Sheldrake holds that biological fields have a reality of their own: though they do not carry any form of energy, they exist apart from the organisms on which they act. On his theory morphogenetic fields are continuously shaped and reinforced by previously existing organisms of the same kind. Living members of a species are linked with the forms of past members of the same species through a causal link that transcends space and time. The linkage occurs by means of morphic resonance, a phenomenon requiring similarity of form or pattern. Morphic resonance is not limited to living organisms: it shapes formative processes in the realm of crystals, molecules, and atoms. In consequence the theory of morphic resonance is not limited to biology but offers a universal principle of form and order in nature.

Since morphogenetic fields work through resonance reinforced by repetition, the more a given crystal has been synthesized the faster it will be synthesized in the future; the more a given behavioural routine has been learned by rats the faster other rats will learn the routine — and the more organisms of a given species have existed, the more likely it will be that organisms of that species will be generated again. In the latter regard morphic resonance is to explain why species breed true. Because the development of each organism is guided by its own species-specific morphic resonance, the morphology of the offspring becomes similar to the morphology of its progenitors.[15]

Morphogenetic fields create a causal connection between the past of the system, its milieu, and its evolution. Thanks to such fields, the forms and structures that emerge in nature are no longer at the mercy of chance: probabilities shift to favour results that approximate the already existing forms and structures. As a result the processes of evolution become biased in favour of consistency and order.

Sheldrake's concept of morphic resonance explains how consistent order can arise in nature. This is a major accomplishment, rectifying the factor of randomness that plagues the interactive dynamics described by Prigogine.

On a closer look, however, also Sheldrake's dynamics runs into difficulties. A major problem is its conservative bias. The morphogenetic field acts to preserve the past in the present — it is with good reason that Sheldrake entitled one of his books *The Presence of the Past*. But if it is indeed the case that the more a given structure or behaviour has occurred in the past, the more it will recur in the present, then it is difficult to see how a genuine innovation could establish itself. Things are as they are because they were as they were: the universe is a 'system of habits.' How new habits — new forms and new species — could come into being is something of a puzzle. With the passage of time, forms and routines would only become reinforced; evolutionary innovations would be squashed by the heavy hand of the past before they could develop an effective morphogenetic field of their own.

Sheldrake himself is keenly aware of the problem, as a conversation recorded in September 1989 testifies. He asks: if the universe is a system of habits, how do new patterns ever come into being — what is the basis of creativity? A theory of evolutionary habit, he affirms, demands a theory of evolutionary creativity. Unable to provide an answer within his theory, Sheldrake was led to more esoteric speculations. Could creativity on Earth be a product of the imagination of a Gaian mind? Could such an imagination, working throughout the natural world, be the basis of evolutionary creativity in nature the same as in the human realm?[16]

Another problem of Sheldrake's morphic resonance dynamics is its lack of consistency with the laws that govern physical phenomena. Resonance is a *bona fide* physical phenomenon (it is the reinforcement of the vibration of a body by the vibration of another body at or near its frequency), and in string and super string theory resonances have a major role. But there is no indication in physics that this phenomenon would act independently of some form of energy. Yet Sheldrake suggests that there is a non-energetic form-creating field for every atom, molecule, crystal, or organism that has ever come into being. This means that there is a morphogenetic field not only for rats and rabbits, but also for quarks, and for the fermions and bosons made of quarks, and for the asteroids, stars, planets, galaxies and galactic clusters made of fermions and bosons. In a mysterious non-energetic manner, the entire cosmos resonates with self-reinforcing fields.

Sheldrake's theory sheds light on the 'problem of form' in biology; its postulates, though bold, have considerable heuristic power. However, these postulates are incomplete. They do not account for creative divergence in nature, nor do they offer a credible mechanism for the transmission of the morphogenetic effect. Though it may well be (as we shall show in Part Three) that there is a universal field in the cosmos that shapes and informs organisms, molecules, organisms, and human brains, and reduces randomness in the evolutionary process, it is not likely that this field would merely reinforce established 'habits,' or that it would function without some — perhaps subtle — form of energy. Nor is it likely that such a field would transmit its effects by means of resonance. There are other ways in which a field in nature could code, store and transmit information; ways more distributed, potent and precise, and therefore more likely to be responsible for the creative dynamics whereby order emerges in space and time.

The missing factor

What is the current status of the perennial quest to find unity in nature? How far did physicists and transdisciplinary theorists get in their attempts to unify the scientific world picture? To answer these questions we should draw a preliminary balance sheet.

On the positive side, physicists have produced results that are remarkable both for their scope and for the mathematical precision with which they are stated. On the whole, physical scientists have given up trying to explain the world in terms of laws of motion governing the behaviour of individual particles. A coherent and consistent set of abstract and unvisualizable entities has replaced the classical notion of passive material atoms moving under the influence of external forces. This is important, because it is unlikely that phenomena of the level of complexity typical of life could be described by equations that centre uniquely on the motion of the universe's smallest building blocks, no matter how thoroughly these entities and their laws are explicated. A focus on a basic level of reality has proven to be unnecessary baggage left over from a classical theory that attempted to explain all things in reference to a combination of the properties of ultimate entities — which for long it has claimed to be atoms. Today physicists no longer maintain that nature can be explained in terms of groups of fundamental entities, even if the entities are not atoms but quarks, exchange particles, superstrings, or yet to be discovered, perhaps still more abstract entities.

A new picture of the world has been emerging; a highly unified picture. In this picture the particles and forces of the physical universe originate from a single 'super grand unified force' and, although separating into distinct dynamical events, they continue to interact. Spacetime has become a dynamic continuum in which particles and forces are integral elements. Every particle, every force, affects every other. There are no separate forces and things in nature, only sets of interacting events with differentiated characteristics.

This picture of an interacting and self-organizing universe is likely to remain valid, notwithstanding the high rate of attrition of the hypotheses that expound it. It is difficult to see how physics would ever progress backwards to a universe of separate material things and dynamical forces; to a mosaic of unrelated events in external equilibrium.

On the negative side, the emerging picture has been highly abstract, and it has not been sufficiently analysed. Scientists have been too intent to produce the mathematics that would unify the observed phenomena to venture deeper into the implication of their formulas, while philosophers, the traditional integrators of the knowledge of their times, have mostly kept away — with few exceptions, they have not caught up with the latest developments. The lack of deeper thinking is showing. In the first flush of success some physicists have been claiming that their grand unified theories are TOEs — theories of everything. This, however, is a considerable exaggeration.

As already noted, the problem with GUTs is that they cannot satisfactorily explain the progressive structuration of matter in space and time. Yet a theory capable of stating the laws that govern the progressive build-up of order and organization in the universe should be possible. The question is, whether such a theory can be formulated by enlarging the laws of physics, or whether it calls for transcending them in some way. Evidently, the higher domains of nature's self-organization are no longer domains of physical nature; theories in physics, as traditionally conceived, do not embrace them. However, as we have seen, there is a possibility that current theories in physics could be completed or generalized so as to satisfy this requirement.

Bohm, as already noted, attempted to complete quantum theory with a classical component. His factor Q functions as a pilot wave that removes the probabilistic indeterminacy of the quantum state. He traces this factor to a basic realm of the universe, the implicate order, from which all the orders emerging in the phenomenal realm of the explicate order are generated. The price he asks us to pay is the acceptance on faith of the 'separate reality' of the implicate order (to use an appropriately mystical term made popular by Carlos Castaneda). The implicate order is the primary dimension of reality and yet we have no direct knowledge of it; all our observations and experiments refer to the secondary reality which is the explicate order. In the explicate order, however, the origins and functions of the pilot wave are not explained; they remain *ad hoc* assumptions. Bohm needs the implicate order to remove the *ad hoc*ness of his classical component, even if in his theory that order remains an article of faith.

Stapp, in turn, following a lead of Heisenberg, generalizes the laws of quantum physics to macroscopic phenomena. The 'Heisenberg quantum universe' is a world where determinism and chance alternate. Deterministic laws create real alternatives, and the interaction of a device with indeterminately poised events selects one alternative and eradicates the others. This suggests a universal dynamic that promises to account for the behaviour not only of quanta, but of such complex systems as living organisms and conscious brains. There are vexing problems with this quantum universe, however.

One problem we have already noted: it is that there are no laws in the theory that would explain when and how the quantum event selects from among the available alternative possibilities. The selection process remains unexplained and thus entrusted to chance. There is also another problem: in the macrodomain to which the theory is said to apply, there would be an incessant process of selection. And if so, one may ask: selection among what? While one can readily allow that a photon travelling from the source that emits it to the counter that registers it is free of interaction — and hence in a probabilistic quantum state — how an organism or another macroscale system could be sufficiently isolated from its environment to be in a similar state is not easy to see. Yet, when such a system interacts with its environment — that is, with any part of the 'rest of the universe' — its wave function collapses. In the Stapp-Heisenberg quantum universe this would occur practically all the time. In matter-dense regions such as our world, the 'decision-events' are dense enough to prevent dynamical laws from creating the alternatives among which they are called upon to decide.

If expanding the theories of physics is not suited to explain the diverse yet consistent orders we meet with in experience, instead of elaborating GUTs we should turn to 'GETs' — general evolution theories. These theories moved from the field of philosophy to that of science with the development of the thermodynamics of irreversible processes in the 1960s. It was Prigogine's achievement to have disclosed the irreversible evolutionary dynamics of systems in dynamic regimes far from thermodynamic equilibrium. Systems in this 'third state' (neither at, nor near, equilibrium) behave in a highly specific manner: when destabilized by fluctuations they do not go to, or toward, equilibrium but may restructure their internal forces so as to take in, process and store more of the free energies present in their environment. As free energy represents negative entropy, third-state systems balance their inevitable internal entropy-production with 'imported' negentropy. In consequence they do not necessarily run down, but may wind up to reach increasingly dynamic regimes.

However, when it comes to accounting for the progressive emergence of ever higher levels and dimensions of order in the universe, the otherwise remarkable interactive dynamics of third-state systems has a flaw. The process by which the evolutionary trajectory of far-from-equilibrium systems bifurcates following critical instabilities is at the mercy of chance. The Prigoginian dynamics cannot account for the system's 'choice' of a new dynamic regime anymore than the Heisenberg quantum universe can account for the decision event that occurs when alternative possibilities are instrumentally or observationally registered. In consequence in Prigogine's universe, the same as in Heisenberg's universe, evolution remains punctuated by chance events. This, as we have noted, can explain progressive divergence in nature, but not the parallel and equally important process of convergence.

Sheldrake's theory of formative causation remedies this failing by suggesting that a resonating field conserves the form of living systems and ensures that their further evolution remains congruent with their already achieved form. Unfortunately, in regard to what we know of the universe, the morphogenetic field appears as an *ad hoc* postulate: its origins are not explained, while its functioning is quasi-miraculous — it is by pure resonance, without involving energy. Even more importantly, the interactive dynamics of formative causation overshoots the mark. Though it does give laws (even if *ad hoc* ones) for the consistency bias apparent in the probabilistic evolution of living systems, the laws tend to constrain diversity to the point where creativity is subordinated to repetition. If such laws actually held sway in the universe, we should find much more uniformity in nature; diversity should be exceptional.

There is as yet a 'missing factor' in current attempts to create unified theories of the observable and inferentially knowable universe. This factor is a sound interactive dynamics, capable of accounting for the progressive if nonlinear emergence of diverse yet consistent order in nature. This dynamics is not likely to be a deterministic process, derivable from causal interactions among individual atoms or mass points. It is more likely to be a systemic process, governed by laws that apply to entire ensembles; laws that create systemic processes that are frequently probabilistic, but never entirely random.

PART TWO

The Mysteries

– 4 –
Anomalies in Physics

The cosmological revolution is in full swing, but it has by no means run its course; a theory that would unify the many aspects and dimensions of experienced reality within a single and consistent framework still eludes contemporary scientists. Physicists are unifying the physical foundations of the universe, but have difficulty reaching beyond them to the higher spheres of complexity hallmarked by life and consciousness. And transdisciplinary theories that do tackle this ambitious task manifest significant lacunae in regard to their ability to provide a consistent explanation of the dynamics through which higher levels of order and complexity are generated in the physical universe.

We need to go beyond the grand unified theories of contemporary physics and follow up the attempts of leading-edge transdisciplinary thinkers to move beyond the universe's physical dimensions in search of a unitary concept of the experienced orders. The task is to seek the integrated, essentially unitary, dynamics through which the physical universe could bring forth the orders that underlie phenomena in the transphysical domains: the domains of life, and of mind and consciousness. This awesome task requires a fresh approach.

The approach taken here is to review the puzzles and paradoxes that crop up in the investigation of physical as well as biological phenomena, as well as the phenomena of mind and consciousness, in the expectation that they may provide significant clues for the factors that are missing in unified theories. The hypothesis is reasonable: if our search for unified understanding is not arbitrary but mirrors a deeper unity in nature, then whatever generates the puzzles in individual domains of investigation is likely to be precisely what is needed to integrate those domains within a unified concept.

The widespread assumption, that almost everything fundamental about the nature and workings of the universe is already known, ignores the depth and the breadth of the puzzles that face scientists in their investigation of diverse realms of experience. Puzzles, paradoxes and anomalies — we shall use these terms interchangeably — crop up in many regions of the current research landscape: in theories of physics, of biology, as well as of mind and consciousness. We shall review each of these fields in turn, beginning with the problems encountered in quantum physics.

The quantum paradoxes

Wheeler's dragon

Physicists view elementary particles as packets of matter-energy embedded in force-fields. These packets are quanta, and experiments show that they are strange beasts indeed.

As we shall see, the strange behaviour of quanta includes the corpuscle-wave duality, the Heisenberg uncertainty, as well as the phenomena of nonlocal and nondynamic interaction. All these remain acute paradoxes, thinly masked by the current injunction that physicists should content themselves with finding correlations between observations and not interpret what the observations actually refer to — that is, what quanta would be 'in themselves.'

The puzzles of the quantum world were the subject of probably the most famous, and certainly the most prolonged in-depth discussion of the ultimate nature of physical reality in the history of modern science. From 1927 to 1933, Albert Einstein and Niels Bohr met together and corresponded on the interpretation of the quantum observations. Einstein could not accept the indeterminacy that seemed inherent in the behaviour of quanta. He brought up idealized experiment after idealized experiment to show that quantum theory as currently formulated is logically inconsistent. Bohr, in turn, refused any interpretation that went beyond the range of actual observations. Nature, Bohr claimed, has not only placed an absolute limit on what can be measured and observed, but also on what one can speak about without ambiguity.

Einstein agreed to the Heisenberg uncertainty principle — that the position and the momentum of an elementary particle cannot be measured simultaneously — but did not concede that this would mean that elementary particles did not have a definite position and momentum at all times, independently of whether or not they were observed. Bohr disagreed: in his view it did not make sense to speak of a particle having a definite trajectory in the absence of observations; such trajectories are only defined *in* the act of observation. This, however, was not acceptable to Einstein. 'If a person, such as a mouse, looks at the world, does that change the state of the world?' he asked in Wheeler's relativity seminar. 'I find the idea quite intolerable' Einstein wrote earlier to Max Born. If Bohr's interpretation should prove correct, he continued, 'I would rather be a cobbler, or even an employee in a gaming house, than a physicist.'[1] In connection with quantum events, Bohr found himself restricted to the term 'phenomenon' in the final phase of his dialogue with Einstein. This term, John Wheeler later pointed out, is significant. It suggests that in speaking of quanta we are no longer dealing with an objective observer-independent reality. In Eugene Wigner's apt phrase, quantum physics deals with 'observations' and not with 'observables,' not to mention with the in-themselves unobservable physical realities John Bell termed 'beables.'

A divorce from substantive reality is always painful, and physicists did not agree to it lightly. They were forced to their phenomenalist conclusion by experiments that confounded all expectations of how chunks of matter should behave in the real world. The classic example is the famous double-slit experiment. Here a light is emitted from a source and is allowed to pass through a narrow slit in a screen. Another screen is placed behind the first, to register the rays that traverse the slit. Then, the same as if one allowed water to flow through a small hole, the light beam fans out and forms a diffraction pattern. The pattern shows the undulatory aspect of light, and is not anomalous in itself. But if a second slit is opened in the screen there is a superposition of two diffraction patterns, even if but a single photon was emitted. The waves propagating behind the slits form the characteristic interference pattern, with the wave fronts cancelling each other when their phase difference is 180° and reinforcing each other when they are in phase. It appears as if each photon would be passing through

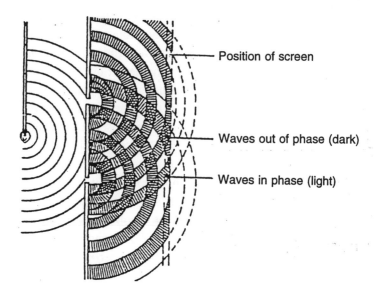

- Position of screen

- Waves out of phase (dark)

- Waves in phase (light)

Figure 3. Wave interference patterns in the double-slit experiment.

both holes at the same time. That, however, is not how a corpuscular object behaves in the real world (see Figure 3).

There are several variants of this basic experiment, each more puzzling than the other. In an experiment suggested by Y. Aharonov and David Bohm, a solenoid is placed between the electron beams exiting from the two slits. The phase-shift in the interference is then proportional to the flux of magnetic lines of force created by the solenoid, even though that region is not traversed by the particles (see Figure 4).

In another experiment, designed by Wheeler, photons are emitted one by one and travel from the emitting gun to a detector instrument that clicks or lights up when struck by a particle. A half-silvered mirror is inserted along the path of the photon. This splits the beam, giving rise to the probability that one in every two photons passes through the mirror and one in every two is deflected by it. To confirm this probability, photon counters are placed both behind the half-silvered mirror and at right angles to it. The expectation that on the average one in two photons travels by one route and the other by the

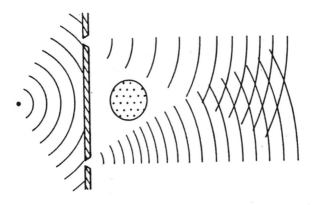

Figure 4. The so-called Aharonov-Bohm effect. A solenoid is placed between the electron beams exiting from two slits. The phase shift of wave propagations is due to the magnetic potential pointing generally parallel to the direction of one beam, and anti-parallel to the other.

second is confirmed by the results: the two counters register a roughly equal number of photons. Then comes the puzzle. A second half-silvered mirror is inserted in the path of the photons that were unreflected by the first. The angle of this mirror is such that the deflected and the unreflected photons would still arrive at one or the other of the two counters. Consequently one would expect to hear an equal number of clicks (or see an equal number of light signals) at both counters: the individually emitted photons would merely have exchanged destinations. But this is not the case. Only one of the counters clicks — or lights up — and never the other. All the photons arrive at one and the same destination (Figure 5).

The anomaly of the double-slit experiment recurs. The photons, emitted as individual particles, interfere with each other as waves. Above one of the mirrors the interference is destructive (since the phase difference between the photons is 180°) so that the photons, as waves, cancel each other. Below the other mirror the interference is constructive: the wave-phase of the photons is the same and they reinforce one another.

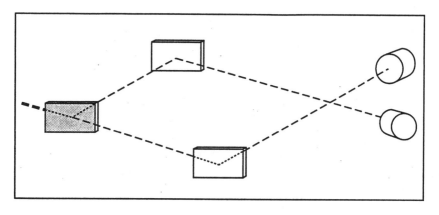

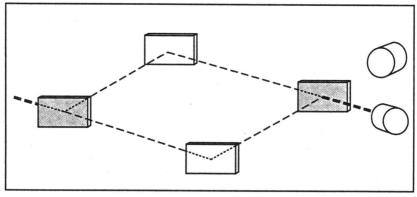

Figure 5. The split-beam experiment and two outcomes.
Above: The paths travelled by photons when only one half-silvered mirror is inserted.
Below: The paths when both mirrors are inserted.

There are many versions of this experiment, too, with results that are more and more mysterious. A second half-silvered mirror is inserted only *after* a photon has passed through the first mirror and is presumably on the way to its destination; the second stream will still interfere with the first and all the photons end up in one counter. If a barrier is then placed in the path of one of the photon streams, the experiment conforms to expectation: the single stream is split evenly between the two counters. But when the barrier is removed, all photons again arrive at one counter and none arrives at the other. Wheeler was forced to the curious conclusion that each photon somehow 'knows' what the others are doing and chooses its path accordingly.

This strange knowing is made stranger by the fact that time and space make little difference to it. In a 'cosmological' version of the split-beam experiment, photons are tested that originate in a distant galaxy, emitted thousands of years apart. The photons in one experiment were those emitted by the double quasi-stellar object known merely as 0957+516A,B. This distant quasar is now believed to be one object rather than two, its double image being due to the deflection of its light by an intervening galaxy situated about one-fourth of the distance from Earth. The deflection due to the gravitational lens action is large enough to bring together two light rays emitted by the quasar billions of years ago. Because of the additional distance travelled by the photons that are deflected by the galaxy, they have been on the way fifty thousand years longer than those that came by the direct route. But, although originating billions of years ago with an interval of fifty thousand years, the photons interfere with each other just as if they had been emitted seconds apart in the laboratory. The interference itself is puzzling enough, and the fact that it is not subject to space and time constraints confounds all expectations of how individual objects behave in nature.

In view of these and similar anomalies, the idea that we could know physical reality independently of our observations of it has been questioned. We have no basis, Bohr claimed, for speaking of what quanta are and of what they are doing between the observations that signal their emission and their reception. Whatever occurs in-between is, in Wheeler's picturesque phrase, a 'great smoky dragon.' Its tail is sharp where it is emitted, and its mouth is sharp where it bites the detector, but its body is 'smoky.' The 'quantum phenomenon,' said Wheeler, 'is the strangest thing in this strange world.'[2]

In Wheeler's definition, modern quantum theory represents a *state of* complete knowledge about a dynamic system by a probability *amplitude* which is a *complex* number (emphases in original).[3] The problem is, as Wheeler himself pointed out, a probability amplitude *of what*? No elementary quantum phenomenon is a phenomenon until it is a registered phenomenon, indelibly recorded; in Bohr's phrase, 'brought to a close' by an irreversible act of amplification such as the clicking of a Geiger counter or the blackening of a grain of photographic emulsion. There are observations of these acts of amplifications and assignments of probability amplitudes with complex numbers, but no answer as to what lies behind the amplitudes. Quantum physicists live in Alice's Wonderland where there are appearances of things but not their substance — the grin of Cheshire cats but not the cats themselves.

Einstein's experiment and Bell's theorem

Einstein did not concede that the Heisenberg uncertainty would be a physical factor; he was intent on showing that it could be overcome. The thought experiment he designed with colleagues Boris Podolski and Nathan Rosen — subsequently known as the EPR (Einstein-Podolski-Rosen) experiment — was designed to show that, in principle, *both* the momentum and the position of a particle can be determined; hence that it is meaningful to speak of particles as having both properties simultaneously.[4] The EPR experiment suggests that we take a reaction such as that produced by the collision of an electron and a positron. Here a pair of photons is produced in identical quantum states but propagating in opposite directions. We are to make a measurement of position on one of the photons; we can then use its results to predict the corresponding state of the other. On the second particle a complementary property is to be measured, such as momentum. In this way we would know *both* the momentum *and* the position of the second particle — a result forbidden by Heisenberg's uncertainty principle and incorporated in quantum theory. This would prove Einstein's point.

The EPR experiment was outlined in 1935, but it was not until 1982 that a version of it could be tested by physical instruments. The test, by Alain Aspect and collaborators, showed that, despite the spatial distance, the act of measurement on one particle collapsed the wave function also for the other. The same as in the split-beam experiment, two particles, though separate in space, turned out to be instantly correlated. This result was predicted already in the 1960s by John Bell.[5] Bell's theorem requires that a signal should pass instantaneously between spatially distant particles. It appears that signals (which are not information in the operational sense of the term) can travel across finite space without requiring finite time for their transmission.

Findings such as these prompted the invention of some other famous quantum thought experiments, including that which became widely known as 'Schrödinger's cat.' Erwin Schrödinger proposed that we take a cat and place it in a sealed container. We then set up a device which, entirely randomly, either does or does not emit a poisonous gas into the container. Thus when we open the container the cat is either dead or alive. Common sense would suggest that the cat died already when the gas was emitted — if indeed it was emitted — hence that it was either dead or alive before the container was opened. But this state of affairs is forbidden by quantum theory. As long as the container is sealed, there is a probabilistic superposition of states — the cat must be *both* alive *and* dead. It is only when the container is opened that the two probabilities collapse into one.

A similar thought experiment was proposed by Louis de Broglie. This time we take an electron rather than a cat, and place it in a sealed container. We divide the container, which is in Paris, and ship one part to Tokyo and the other to New York. This time common sense would dictate that if we open the half-container in New York and find the electron, then the electron must have been in that half already when the container was shipped from Paris. But this state of affairs, like that which decides whether Schrödinger's cat is alive or dead, is forbidden. Each half-container must have a non-zero probability of harbouring the electron. Then, the instant one of the halves is opened in New York — regardless of whether or not it contains the electron — the wave-packet defining the probability of the electron's existence is also reduced in Tokyo. But how does the hitherto probabilistically existing 'Tokyo-particle' find out just when, and with what result, the 'New York-particle' is being measured?

The instantaneous transmission of signals violates a basic law of relativity: that nothing in the universe can travel faster than the speed of light. But under certain conditions quanta seem to ignore this interdiction. Their correlation seems instantaneous, and it does not appear to diminish with distance.

Superconductivity and superfluidity

Instant correlations are more widespread in physical nature than is generally recognized. They also occur at extremely low temperatures, in the phenomena of superconductivity and superfluidity.

When various pure metals and alloys are supercooled to within a few degrees of absolute zero, their electrical resistance vanishes. The substances become superconductors: an electrical current passing through them is transported entirely without friction. This phenomenon was discovered by Kamerlingh Onnes in 1911, and its details, together with those of superfluidity (the lack of viscosity in a supercooled liquid such as helium), came to light in subsequent decades in research in low-temperature physics.

The vanishing of electrical resistance in a conductor is due to a remarkable degree of coherence among electrons. Normally, when an electrical current passes through a metal, it produces a drift in the electron gas — the electrons are scattered from vibrating atoms in the lattice structure of the metal. This retards the flow of electrons through the lattice and produces the friction that heats the metal: the phenomenon of electrical resistance. However, when the metal is supercooled, the vibrations of the atoms are reduced and the resistance of the metal is lowered. Since even at absolute zero on the Kelvin scale, zero-point energies keep the lattice vibrating, electrical resistance should actually be present even when metals or alloys are cooled to within a few degrees of absolute zero. Yet at these temperatures resistance vanishes entirely: the substances turn into superconductors. In a ring built of a superconductor an electrical current, once induced, keeps flowing indefinitely.

It turns out that as a metal or alloy is cooled to a critical temperature, electrons flow through it in a fully coherent manner. A similar phenomenon occurs in superfluids. Previously randomly colliding molecules cohere into a single quantum entity without apparent viscosity; such a fluid can flow through capillaries and cracks without resistance. In both cases a highly cohesive quantum state is generated. The Schrödinger wave function of the motion of all the electrons in a current, and of all the quanta that make up the molecules of a fluid, assumes one and the same form.

It appears that the electrons in a superconductor, and the particles that make up the molecules of a superfluid, are precisely and continuously correlated with each other. But how does one particle 'know' the state of another — there is no known form of energy or signal passing between them. Superconductivity and superfluidity are further instances of instantaneous correlation among entities at different (though in this case contiguous) locations in space and time.

Pauli's principle

While at extremely *low* temperatures nondynamic correlations issue in a form of extreme coherence, at extremely high temperatures they produce growing structural complexity. When at so-called 'nuclear cooking' temperatures atoms are subjected to high-energy radiation, nondynamic correlations among the electrons structure the distribution of the available energies within the atomic shells.

The atom's nucleus consists of various energy fields which define the energy levels that can be accommodated in the surrounding shells. Nuclear energies, however, do not define the *way* energy is accommodated in the shells: they do not determine the specific structure of the shells. That structure is determined by a peculiar correlation that occurs among the electrons within the shells themselves. These correlations are instant, and they do not occur among unassociated electrons and other independent particles. They occur only among electrons orbiting atomic nuclei.

The fact is, however, that electrons within the shells of an atom are not connected by any known form of energy. Yet the total pattern created by all electrons informs the behaviour of each and assigns the corresponding probabilities of their state. Here, too, it appears as if each electron 'knew' what all the others are doing.

The mathematical formula for the exclusion of electrons was given by Wolfgang Pauli in 1925. His 'exclusion principle' tells us that no two electrons around a nucleus or around several nuclei in a multi-atomic configuration — can be in a state of motion described by the same set of four quantum numbers. Exclusion follows an anti-symmetry rule. That is, if any two electrons are interchanged, their Schrödinger wave function ψ $(x_1, x_2, x_3, ... x_n)$, where the x's are the coordinates of the various electrons, including their spin) must change sign. The principle requires that electrons orbiting a nucleus must each occupy a different orbit. But how an atom — or molecule, metal, or other complex multi-atomic system — can obey this principle is not clear: there is no ordinary force or energy that would constrain their movement. The exclusion principle calls for precise correlation among electrons without involving a dynamical force. The same way as two electrons in the EPR experiment and two photons in the split-beam experiment seem to 'know' each other's quantum state without the exchange of energy, so too the electrons in an atom (or in a molecule or metal) are instantly and nondynamically interlinked.

The exclusion of electrons to unique states makes for the emergence of ordered atomic structures with specific properties. It is the basis of all complex orders in the universe. Yet the way exclusion operates is only described and not explained by the mathematics of Pauli's principle.

The cosmic paradoxes

Hoyle's hypothesis

Higher orders can emerge in the universe because matter can configure into more and more complex structures. This is made possible by electrons being constrained by the exclusion principle to occupy unique states around the atomic nucleus. For this process of structuration to reach higher levels of complexity, physical conditions in the universe would have to permit a sufficient number of electrons to enter the configuration field of neutral atoms. This calls for a harmonization of the energy levels of the respective nuclei: a phenomenon associated with resonance. Achieving the required resonance is not a simple matter: the fine-tuning required of the pertinent energy levels is colossally improbable. Here is where the paradoxes of the quantum domain aggregate into puzzles of cosmic dimensions.

In cosmic history, the first nuclei to form were those of hydrogen. The reactions that occurred subsequently in the early universe's intense radiation field fused some of the hydrogen nuclei into nuclei of helium. But a hydrogen-helium universe would not have been capable of creating additional kinds of atomic structures: both of these structures are inert, and the amount of nuclear energy required to make them combine into heavier elements would not have been available. The complex orders that now meet our eyes could not have evolved unless a way was found for moving beyond the hydrogen-helium gas. Nature did find a way: it was to create sufficient amounts of the element that could catalyse reactions leading beyond hydrogen and helium towards the synthesis of heavier elements. This element was carbon.

The puzzle is how large amounts of carbon could have been synthesized in the first place. The synthesis of carbon calls for a series of events that begins with the reaction helium + helium: this produces a nucleus of beryllium. The resulting beryllium nucleus is an unstable isotope: it disintegrates into helium almost as soon as it is created. In order to produce carbon, beryllium, rather than disintegrating into helium, would have to enter into reaction with it. This reaction, though it is *prima facie* improbable, does take place. The reason is that it is a 'resonance reaction' where the combined energy of the beryllium and helium nuclei (7.370 million electron volts [MeV]) is just slightly less than the energy of carbon, the product of the reaction (7.656 MeV).

It is not assured, however, that the carbon produced in this reaction would survive in the universe: a further reaction — with helium — would reduce it to oxygen. But it so happens that the carbon + helium reaction is not favoured by nature: the energy level of the reaction-product oxygen (7.1187 MeV), is below the energy level of the reactants carbon + helium (7.1616 MeV). As a result the nucleus of oxygen is relatively stable, and both carbon and oxygen are available in sufficient quantities in the universe to become elements in more complex molecular configurations, including those that on Earth give rise to the phenomena of life.

The probability that the energy levels of helium, beryllium, carbon, and oxygen should be fine-tuned to the required degree is extremely low. Nevertheless, Fred Hoyle proposed that it must be the case. Experiments carried out at the nuclear physics laboratory at Caltech proved Hoyle right. Nature does exhibit the most improbable fine-tuning of the energy levels of four entirely different elements. It is thanks to this apparent coincidence that orders could emerge in the universe more complex and interesting than those produced by random reactions of hydrogen and helium.

The tuning of the constants

There is yet another set of 'coincidences,' vaster than the fine-tuning of the energy levels of some atomic nuclei: they concern the values associated with the so-called universal constants.[6] Physicists discovered that not only are the processes of life precisely tuned to the physical processes of the universe — as well they might be, since life emerged out of the physical background — but also the physical processes of the universe, though they must have come first, are finely tuned to the processes of life. The facts are these:

— Massive particles (baryons) form but a thin precipitate in the universe; in terms of energy, they account for only about one-billionth of radiation. But this thin layer happens to be precisely the right thickness to permit the evolution of life. Were the 'matter-content' of the universe even slightly greater than it is, the higher density of stars would create a significant probability of interstellar encounters that would knock life-carrying planets out of safe orbits and would, in consequence, either freeze or vaporize all forms of life that may have evolved on them.

— If the strong force that binds the nucleons in the atom were merely a fraction *weaker* than it is, deuteron could not exist and the sun and other stars could not shine. If the strong force were slightly stronger than it is, the sun and other active stars would inflate and possibly explode.

— If the neutron did not outweigh the proton in the nucleus, the active lifetime of the sun and similar stars would be reduced to a few hundred years.

— If the electric charges of electrons and protons did not balance precisely, all material configurations would be unstable and the universe would consist of nothing more ordered than radiation and a relatively uniform mixture of gases.

— And, if the original explosion that gave birth to the universe did not include precise small-scale departures from the large-scale regularities, there would not be galaxies and stars today, and hence no planets on which conscious beings could wonder at all these coincidences.

The zero-point energies

Last but not least, there is a profound enigma associated with the so-called quantum vacuum, at the very roots of the universe. The world of matter-energy appears to float, rather as a thin precipitate, on a deep sea of almost infinite energies. These basic energies are not the same kind as those that go into the fermions that make up matter in the universe, or those in the bosons that are the units of force. The energies in question — also known as 'zero-point' energies, since experiments on black-body radiation show that they remain associated with particles even in their thermodynamically most probable non-dynamic ground energy state — are potential rather than actualized. They appear 'infolded' in the womb of physical reality. But the energies, though 'virtual' rather than 'real,' undoubtedly exist and, as we shall see in Part Three, cannot be safely ignored in the calculation of physical interactions.

The puzzle of the quasi-infinite zero-point energies of the quantum vacuum begins when we consider the source of energies in the electro-magnetic field. In the version of Maxwell's equations known as the vacuum field equations, one finds that, even though one describes electromagnetic waves propagating in a vacuum, there are no sources for the fields: the electron is a mathematical point and cannot be a field source. Yet the field in which the electron appears stores a very large, though not infinite, amount of energy. This paradox, as theoreticians have noted, has never been resolved in quantum field theory.[7]

The energy-density of the quantum vacuum constitutes a major anomaly in contemporary physics. It surfaces when we apply Heisenberg uncertainty principle to infinitely small domains. The principle specifies that it is not possible to measure the position and the momentum of a particle at the same time. In regard to electrons orbiting atomic nuclei, this means that the further one reduces the dimensions of the orbit, the more one specifies the position of the electron. It follows that as its position is specified, the electron's momentum becomes proportionately uncertain; at an infinitely small orbit it becomes infinite. In quantum electrodynamics this condition is described in terms of an infinite number of oscillators that define the energy of the electromagnetic field.

The energy-density of the vacuum is large, but it cannot be actually infinite because particles cannot be smaller than Planck-length nor exist for time intervals shorter than Planck-time. These Planck-limitations endow the vacuum with a finite and calculable amount of non-vectorial, so-called potential, energy. Wheeler calculated that if quantum laws hold all the way to the Planck-length of 10^{-35}m, the energy density of the vacuum must be 10^{94}g/cm^3. This magnitude, however, is a major puzzle. According to Einstein's celebrated mass/energy equivalence equation, energy is equal to mass at the square of the velocity of light; and gravitation, according to both classical and relativity physics, is proportional to mass. Consequently the gravitational potential in the universe must be proportional to its energy content. But if so, then the staggering energy density of the vacuum would create a gravitational potential that should have collapsed all matter in the universe to a singularity shortly after the Big Bang. Why the universe is spatially extended, and indeed continues to expand, remains a mystery.

The anomaly of the quasi-infinite zero-point energies of the cosmos is perhaps the most profound puzzle facing contemporary physics. It is not clear what role the energies that seem infolded in the quantum vacuum would play, not only in the genesis of the universe, but in its evolution in space and time. It is conceivable this puzzle is connected with the rest. The virtual energies of the quantum vacuum may be connected in some way with the strange way in which quanta act when measuring instruments interact with them; with the equally strange nondynamic exclusion of electrons around atomic nuclei; and also with the many 'coincidences' that make it appear as if the universe were predisposed for the evolution of life and complexity.

It is by no means inconceivable that the missing factor in laboratory investigations and in theoretical reconstruction is one and the same — that the factor that would clarify the persisting paradoxes of the physical world is the same factor that would make the interactive dynamics of general evolution theories capable of accounting for the way in which nature self-organizes to progressively higher levels of order and complexity. The assumption, as we said, is reasonable: a unified universe does not generate intrinsic puzzles when described in a unified conceptual framework.

– 5 –
Unresolved Puzzles in Biology

In order to explore the thesis that the missing factor in unified theories is the same factor of which the absence generates the puzzles in empirical investigations, we continue our review of the paradoxes that beset contemporary science with a look at the problems encountered in the sciences of life.

Biology and the related life sciences deal with phenomena more familiar than those of the subatomic world. Yet paradoxes and anomalies persist in this domain as well. The major puzzles concern the tempo and the mode of evolutionary processes, and the generation and regeneration of the morphology of living organisms.

The evolution of species

Mainstream biology accounts for the observed anatomical features of organisms in reference to the particular history of a given species, assuming that the vagaries of genetic mutation and natural selection mould the organism and create the organic form observed in nature. In this account Darwinism makes a categorical separation between the genetic information of a species — its germline — and the influences that act on its members — on the phenotype — in the milieu. Mutations occur in the highly shielded information pool of the species, and they are considered something like random 'typing mistakes' in the transmission of that information from parent to offspring. Mutations are produced by all species at a more or less constant rate. Most of the mutants produced by chance variations are likely to be faulty in some respect; hence they will be eliminated by natural selection. However, random mutations can occasionally hit upon a genetic combination that renders the phenotype more rather than less fit to live and to reproduce. Such an individual will then transmit its mutant genes to successive generations, and in the course of time the more numerous offspring produced by the mutant generations will replace the correctly reproducing lineage.

Some investigators, notably Richard Dawkins, appear perfectly satisfied with this account. According to Dawkins, genes propagate themselves through trial and error — living nature resembles a 'blind watchmaker' who in the course of time generates the entire panorama of order and diversity in the biosphere.[1] Others are less convinced. Michael Denton asked whether random processes could have constructed an evolutionary sequence of which even a basic element, such as a protein or a gene, is complex beyond human capacities. Can one account statistically for the chance emergence of systems of truly great complexity, such as the mammalian brain when, if specifically organized, just one percent of the connections in such a brain would be larger than the connections in the world's entire communications network? Denton concluded that chance mutations acted on by natural selection could well account for variations *within* given species, but hardly for successive variations *among* them.[2]

A similar position was taken by Konrad Lorenz. While it is formally correct, said Lorenz, to assert that the principles of chance mutation and natural selection play a role in evolution, by itself this cannot account for the facts. Mutations and natural selection may account for variations within given species, but the roughly four billion years available on this planet for biological evolution could not have been sufficient for chance processes to generate today's complex and ordered organisms from their protozoic ancestors.[3]

The problem is not new. Already in mid-century Hermann Weyl noted that, because each of the molecules on which life is based consists of something like a million atoms, the number of possible atomic combinations is astronomical. On the other hand the number of combinations that could create viable genes is relatively limited. Thus the probability that such combinations would occur through random processes is negligible. A more likely solution, said Weyl, is that some sort of selective process has been taking place, probing different possibilities and gradually groping its way from simple to complicated structures. Weyl himself was of the opinion that 'immaterial factors having the nature of images, ideas, "building plans" may be involved in the evolution of life.'[4]

Weyl's speculations were not accepted by the scientific community: scientists believe that nature creates its own designs instead of receiving them ready-made. Yet some sort of design does seem to be present. Jean Dorst, for example, though reluctant to admit final causes, was forced to admit that there is, after all, a design inscribed in nature: a design observed in the balance between different species as well as in some extraordinary adaptations, such as between plants and insects. These go far beyond the facts explicable by Darwinian theory.[5] Etienne Wolff, in turn, spoke of 'orientation' in evolution. There were ten or more precursors of the family of mammals between the end of the primary and the beginning of the secondary era, but only one among them gave rise to today's mammals. There were also many types of species that tried taking to the air, including dinosaurs, pterosaurs and reptiles, even the archeopteryx, but only one variety has succeeded. At every level of the hierarchy of animals there appeared to be a tendency in evolution to produce something new, more adapted, more complex. It is evident, Wolff asserted, that a chance process would not have evolved the kind of order and consistency that now meets the eye — if evolution had been at the mercy of chance, its course would have been entirely different.[6]

Living species are also remarkable for the consistency they exhibit relative to one another. For example, the wings of birds and bats are homologous with the flippers of the phylogenetically entirely unrelated seals and with the forelimbs of equally unrelated amphibians, reptiles, and vertebrates. While the size and shape of the bones show great variation, the bones themselves are similarly positioned, both in relation to each other and to the rest of the body. Diverse species exhibit common orders in regard to the position of the heart and the nervous system as well: in endoskeletal species the nervous system is in the dorsal (back) position and the heart in the ventral (front) position, while in exoskeletal species the positions are precisely reversed. Moreover some highly specific anatomical features are shared by species with widely different evolutionary histories. A striking example is the eye: its basic structure appears to have been invented independently by no less than forty phylogenetically unrelated species.

There are larger regularities to be accounted for as well, of entire families of species and of genera. As it happens, despite the staggering variety of organisms brought forth during the Cambrian period, the species that now populate the biosphere fall into about two dozen major taxonomic groups, and these exhibit striking regularities both within and among themselves.

There is also a puzzle connected with the time-scale of events at life's origins. Complex structures have appeared on Earth within astonishingly brief periods of time. The oldest rocks date from about four billion years, while the earliest and already highly complex life forms (blue-green algae and bacteria) are over 3.5 billion years old. How this level of complexity could have emerged within the relatively short time of about 500 million years lacks a satisfactory answer. Chance alone cannot account for the facts: a random mixing of a molecular soup would have taken incomparably longer to produce complex structures. Could it be, then, that life was imported to Earth 'ready-made' from elsewhere in the cosmos? In the last century Lord Kelvin thought so, and recently several scientists, including Francis Crick, revived the notion.

All this makes chance as a basic factor in evolution highly questionable. The improbability of evolution by chance is compounded by the fact that the environment in which species evolve is far from constant. What was once a suitable habitat may become less suitable in time, and may even threaten the survival of some species. In order to remain viable in a different milieu, living species have to modify their adaptive plan. But how such modification is accomplished is far from clear. The problem is that, if a species proceeded by random and stepwise mutations, it would risk maladaptation — and possibly extinction — before it could reach a new habitat.

This problem can be framed in terms of the 'evolutionary landscape' model used by evolutionary biologists (see Figure 6). We take a horizontal plane stretched like a sheet in two dimensions. The plane

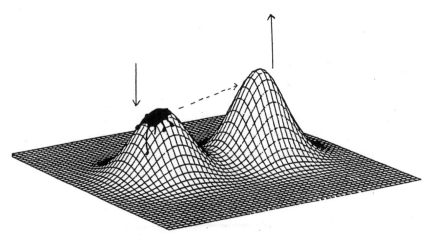

Figure 6. A segment of an adaptive landscape containing two fitness peaks. A species is shown occupying one of the peaks.

is not entirely flat; there are occasional hills projecting from it in the vertical (third) dimension. Every variation in the genetic heritage of the species moves it in one direction or another along the plain. The hills add the factor of fitness. The more a species is adapted to its environment, the higher it climbs on its hill — the top of the hill represents the point of maximum fitness.

Darwinian theory see species climbing gradually towards the top of their hill. Species climb upwards because they produce random variations in their genetic pool, and the resulting mutants are exposed to the test of survival. Since the mutants that happen to produce an improvement in the fitness of the species survive (the unfit mutants are weeded out by natural selection), the species moves progressively higher on its fitness slope. The question post-Darwinian theorists ask, however, is whether species can also move from their current hill to another, elsewhere on the adaptive landscape.

In a stable environment this question does not arise. Species can remain on their own hill, moving ever closer to the top. But in a changing landscape what was true fitness under one set of conditions may become a recipe for extinction under another — a transfer from one peak of adaptation to another becomes sooner or later necessary. But how do species manage this transfer? They do not have elevated

94

highways leading from their vanishing hill to more stable or newly rising ones. If they are to get to another hill they must first descend in the intervening valley. That, however, is forbidden in Darwinian theory. Random mutations are likely to produce a vast assortment of mutants, and the poorly fitting among them are eliminated by natural selection — and the ones producing an improved fit can only propel the species upwards on its current hill. No species can climb downward on a fitness slope. Natural selection chains them to the highest feasible point on whatever hill they happen to find themselves.

Some neo-Darwinians theorized that, when their hills began to shrink, the endangered species produces a large number of mutants, and some of the mutants act as exploratory arms, stretching down from the hill and across the valley to the next. But it is difficult to see how such a mutational arm could survive long enough to stretch from a shrinking hill to a rising one, even if, as Sewall Wright pointed out, in small populations random errors increase the importance of mutation relative to natural selection. The genetic space is vast, and given that mutations are produced randomly while the adaptive fit of a species is limited to a small subset of possible mutants, most of the mutants will be unfit. Unfit mutants will also occur on the way to a new hill. The small interbreeding populations (so-called demes) that, according to Sewall Wright, could accidentally 'stumble on to' a fitness slope — and thereafter be driven up on it by natural selection — seem more likely to stumble only into extinction.

Evidently, the ancestors of living species did not die out when their fitness peak vanished. They either managed to wander over the landscape and find another hill, or to produce the massively innovative 'systemic mutations' that would enable them to leap to another hill. The former assumption stretches the limits of credibility, while the latter fails to find explanation in Darwinian and neo-Darwinian theory.

Darwinism is wedded to a chance-driven process of continuous small-scale adaptation, and such a process is unlikely to have produced the observed dimensions of order in the known evolutionary time-frames. Both the randomness and the incrementalism of evolution are questionable factors. Indeed, 'phylogenetic incrementalism' is questioned by neo-Darwinists themselves. About a hundred years after the publication of Darwin's *Origin of Species* (where Darwin declared: 'Natural selection ... can produce no great or sudden modifications; it can act only by short and slow steps'), Jay Gould and Niles Eldredge formulated the theory of evolutionary leaps: the theory of 'punctuated equilibria.'[7]

The contrast between classical Darwinian evolutionary theory and the theory of punctuated equilibria was summed up by Gould and Eldredge in reference to the transformation that occurs as new species emerge. For Darwinian theory such transformation:

— concerns an ancestral population that evolves into its descendants by means of gradual modifications;
— is even and slow;
— involves large numbers, usually the entire ancestral population;
— and occurs over all or a large part of the geographic range of the ancestral species.

If so, the fossil record should consist of a long sequence of continuous, insensibly graded intermediate forms linking ancestor and descendant, with morphological breaks in this sequence due only to imperfections in the geological record.

This does not appear to be the case. The fossil record is discontinuous, and the 'missing links' are not due to imperfect knowledge, but to nature. In view of these facts, the theory of punctuated equilibria asserts that new species:

— arise following the splitting of lineages;
— develop rapidly;
— come about in a small sub-population of the ancestral form;
— and originate in a small part of the ancestral species' geographic extent, in an isolated area at the periphery of the range.[8]

As Gould and Eldredge remarked, the paleontological record shows that 'speciation' is a rapid process: new species burst on the scene within time periods of the order of 5000 to 50000 years. Not only individual species but entire genera make their appearance in sudden epochs of creativity. For example, the Cambrian explosion brought forth in the span of a few million years most of the invertebrate species that now populate the earth.

Evolution, punctuated equilibria theory claims, acts on species and populations, and not only — or even mainly — on individual reproducers. Individual variations do not contribute significantly to the emergence of new species; the classical Darwinian mechanism works mainly to adapt individuals to their existing niches. When the milieu changes and the existing niches disappear, species often die out. Then the 'peripheral isolates' invade the centres of dominance and take over as the new dominant species.

The rejection of gradualism in favour of evolutionary bursts does not remove the factor of randomness from evolution. The Gould-Eldredge theory merely shifts the element of chance from individual survivors and reproducers to an entire hierarchy that includes species and populations. As Gould himself pointed out, the new theory advances above all two sorts of proposal: a widened role for non-adaptation and for chance as a source of evolutionary change; and the construction of a hierarchical concept based on the interaction of selective (and other) forces at numerous levels from genes to entire population groups, rather than almost exclusively upon selection among organisms.[9]

Chance, however, even in the currently conceptualized form of 'non-adaptive and non-selective drift,' remains a questionable factor in evolution. How could evolution by chance produce the kind of changes in DNA that could assure the viability of a new species? As we have seen, it is not enough for mutations to produce one or a few positive changes in the organism; they must produce a full set. The evolution of feathers, for example, does not produce a reptile that can fly: radical changes in bone structure and musculature are also required, along with a faster metabolism to power sustained flight. Each innovation by itself is not likely to offer evolutionary advantage; on the contrary, it is likely to be unfit and hence eliminated. It is not easy to see how evolution could have proceeded by a random stepwise elaboration of the genetic code of the surviving species.

M. Schutzenberger noted that one would need an almost blind faith in Darwinian theory to believe that chance alone could have produced in the line of birds all the modifications needed to make them high-performing flying machines, or that random mutations would have led to the line of mammals after the extinction of the dinosaurs — given that mammals are a long way from dinosaurs along the axis that conduces from fish to reptiles. Evolution, Schutzenberger concluded, contradicts categorically Gould's thesis on chance.[10] Giuseppe Sermonti concurred: it is hardly credible, he said, that small random mutations and natural selection could have produced a dinosaur from an amoeba.[11]

Chance may not be as dominant in the evolution of species as Darwinists are wont to assume: it appears that under certain conditions genetic mutations are not entirely random. The separation of the germ-line from the vicissitudes of the phenotype is not watertight; it appears that 'directed' genomic changes can take place under certain conditions. Both plants and insects can mutate so as to detoxify the chemicals that enter their environment and create resistance to toxic substances. Especially puzzling is the ability of certain bacteria to mutate in ways that can ensure their immediate survival.

That bacteria would mutate randomly has been known since the 1940s, but experimenters have looked only at mutations occurring under favourable conditions, in populations of rapidly dividing bacteria. In 1982 Barry Hall of the University of Rochester experimented with wild type *Escherichia coli* bacteria in which he had cut out the β-galactosidase gene which it needs to metabolize lactose. When he placed *E. coli* in a solution consisting solely of lactose, many bacteria mutated so as to produce a substitute enzyme, *ebg*. How *E. coli* could perform this feat is not clear. John Cairns and colleagues had similar results in their 1988 experiments at the Harvard School of Public Health. They investigated genetically defective bacteria that were likewise incapable of metabolizing lactose. They, too, restricted their specimens to a lactose diet and found that a significant number mutated back to the normal genetic form.

The way bacteria can mutate with such level of selectivity under stress is not understood. Originally, it was believed that under stress the entire bacterium will mutate, including all or most of its genes. (This is possible in principle: the experimenters may have noted only those mutations that concerned the defective genes.) But if many genes had mutated under stress, most of the bacteria would have died: alterations in the functional genes are likely to have been negative on the whole, and fatal in the overall effect.

Subsequently Hall could show conclusively that bacteria are able to mutate solely their defective genes. He tested specimens in which two of the five genes needed to synthesize *tryptophan (Trp)* were defective, yet some bacteria survived the test by recovering the ability to synthesize this substance. It turned out that they mutated precisely and exclusively the two genes that were needed to metabolize *Trp*. This level of specificity, as Hall concluded, is truly incredible. Certainly, purely random mutations could never have led to the rectification of only those strands of information in only those two genes that happened to be defective.[12]

Darwinian theory, to use Michael Denton's term, is in crisis. The case against it was summed up by Roberto Fondi in reference to the following postulates of the theory:

(1) life is spontaneously generated in assemblies of different molecules;

(2) life has been subject to a process of gradual transformation that allowed it to move from simple forms to ever more complex organisms; and

(3) the generation and transformation of life were due purely to the action of natural forces, such as electromagnetism, chemistry, and gravitation.

According to Fondi, recent findings have falsified all of these tenets. A spontaneous assemblage of molecules driven by chance cannot account for the emergence of complex organisms — even the oldest algae and bacteria are too complex to have resulted from chance processes in the observed time frames. The second postulate is refuted by paleontology. The fossil record, as Gould and Eldredge noted, is full of sudden leaps: species appear suddenly, often in entirely different forms, and remain substantially unchanged during millions of years. Then just as suddenly they become extinct and are immediately followed by other species, entirely different from them. Fondi, himself a paleontologist, held that the discontinuities are too radical to allow the Darwinian interpretation: new species could not have arisen by one species transforming into another. In consequence the Darwinian conception of the tree of life — a tree that grows in continuous incremental steps from roots to crown — could never stand upright: it has only leaves and branches, not a continuous trunk. According to Fondi, natural forces cannot explain the observed course of biological evolution — living matter must be informed by basic patterns, something like Jungian archetypes.[13]

Fondi's suggestion may be surprising, but it is not new: over a century and a half ago, Wolfgang Goethe proposed a similar hypothesis when he traced the form of living plants to a common ancestral form he called the *Urpflanze*. Few biologists have accepted such explanations — until recently. Today, as the current Darwinian explanation exhibits ever more lacunae, renewed interest focuses on ideas of recurrent forms. More and more scientists are coming to the realization that there is more to the dynamics of biological evolution than random mutation and natural selection.

The generation and regeneration of organisms

Once a species has evolved, how do its members manage to generate their species-specific form? This is the puzzle that confronts biologists on the ontogenetic level of the individual organism. Single-celled organisms can reproduce by division, transferring the DNA of their chromosomes to new cells by splitting. More complex species, however, reproduce from their reproductive cells. Presumably, each of these cells has the full set of instructions to build the entire organism. But does it?

The fact that species breed true — that out of a chicken egg comes a chicken and not a pheasant — calls for explanation. Explanation is usually given in terms of DNA: it is assumed that the genetic code of each species contains the blueprint for the whole organism. There are problems with this assumption. To begin with, the genetic code is often closely similar among widely divergent species, and divergent among relatively similar ones. The DNA in the chromosome of the chimpanzee is 98.4 percent the same as that of humans, while amphibians that share many morphological features turn out to have widely differing genetic information.

It is likewise a puzzle how DNA could account for the complex development processes of embryogenesis. In the case of mammalian species, the development of the embryo requires the ordered unfolding of myriad dynamic pathways in the womb, involving the coordinated interaction of billions of dividing cells. If this process were entirely coded by genes, the genetic program would have to be miraculously complete and detailed. It would also have to be flexible enough to ensure the differentiation and organization of a large number of dynamic pathways under a potentially wide range of conditions. Yet the genetic code is the same for every cell in the embryo. It is by no means clear how this code could conduct and coordinate the full range of developmental interactions.

François Jacob asserted that very little is known about regulatory circuits and embryonic development. Aside from as yet vague notions of epigenetic landscapes and biological fields, the only logic that biologists really master is linear and one-dimensional. If molecular biology was able to develop rapidly, said Jacob, it was largely because information in microbiology happens to be determined by linear sequences of building blocks. And so everything turned out to be one-dimensionally linear: the genetic message, the relations between the primary structures, the logic of heredity, and so on. Yet, in the development of an embryo, the world is no longer linear. The one-dimensional sequence of bases in the genes determines the production of two-dimensional cell layers that fold in precise ways to produce the three-dimensional tissues and organs that give the organism its shape and properties. According to Jacob, how this occurs is still a complete mystery. The principles of the regulatory circuits involved in embryonic development are not known. For example, while the molecular anatomy of a human hand is understood in some detail, almost nothing is known about how the human organism instructs itself to build that hand.[14]

A similar problem arises in regard to organic regeneration pheno-mena. Obviously, self-repair by the organism has distinct survival value: one may assume that natural selection would have favoured mutations that ensure effective repair programs in the organism. The puzzle is that organisms possess programs of repair that could not have been naturally selected: the kind of damage which they repair is not likely to have befallen their progenitors in the entire history of a species. There are, for example, organisms that can grow back entire organs or limbs; and some — like marine sponges and sea-urchins — can reconstitute themselves from their constituent cells. Yet ordinarily nature does not remove organs and limbs and dissect living organisms down to their cells — it takes scientists in laboratories to do so.

The case of the marine sponge is especially remarkable. The sponge is a true multicellular organism consisting of several different types of cells, closely coordinated in specialized functions. When sponges are cut up and their parts squeezed through a sieve fine enough to break apart intercellular connections, the separated cells can reassemble themselves into the full organism. It appears that the cells are guided by an orientation system that functions even when separated from one another.

Marine sponges are not alone in regard to such feats of regenera-tion: sea-urchins perform analogously. These are more complex organ-isms, complete with digestive tracts, vascular systems, tube-like feet for locomotion, and a ring of plates surrounding the skeletal scaffold. When they are deprived of the calcium required for their skeletal frame, their parts disassemble and they dissolve into a mass of sepa-rate cells. But as soon as the required level of calcium is reintroduced, the cells reorganize themselves into complete sea-urchins.

In more complex species such forms of regeneration are not poss-ible, but there are cases of partial regeneration that are almost as remarkable. Scientists can divide the egg of a dragonfly into two, and destroy one of the halves: the other can still develop into a complete dragonfly. A flatworm can be cut into several pieces, and each segment can grow into a complete worm. One can cut off the leg of a newt and the newt — unlike the otherwise closely similar frog — will grow a new leg. It will even regenerate the lens of its eye: when it is surgically removed, the tissues at the edge of the iris reassemble into a new lens.

Although recent years have witnessed great breakthroughs in genetics and more are likely to be forthcoming in the future, it is not likely that a complete genetic answer will be forthcoming to the puzzle of the generation and regeneration of the morphology of living organisms. Many investigators have come to the conclusion that morphological organization must rely on as yet unknown extra-genetic, in addition to the known genetic, factors.

Goethe spoke of an *Urpflanze* after which all plants are patterned, and Hermann Weyl of 'immaterial factors' in the living world, in the nature of ideas, images or building plans. More recently Alister Hardy speculated about a 'psychic blueprint' that would be shared by all members of a species; Jean Dorst suspected a basic design in evolution; Gordon Rattray Taylor claimed that there must be a built-in tendency to self-assembly in the biological sphere already at the most elementary level; and the idea of intrinsic forms or archetypes has been resuscitated in biological theory.[15] But there is no clear conception as yet of the nature of the extra-genetic factors in biological evolution, nor of the way they would interact with genetic programs. Yale biologist Edmund Sinnott's mid-century assessment remains valid. Genetic models are too simplistic to account for the facts: something fundamental remains still to be discovered about form-generating processes in biology.[16]

Is it inconceivable that this 'something' will turn out to be the interactive dynamics that lifted the evolution of order in the universe from the realm of atoms and molecules into that of living cells — and then evolved living cells into the diverse yet coordinated range of organic species that now inhabits the biosphere?

– 6 –
Uncharted Domains of Mind and Consciousness

The sciences of the brain assume that underlying the phenomena of mind and consciousness there are complex functions performed by the brain. 'Mind-events' must thus be explained in terms of — or at least in correlation with 'brain-events.' Yet, even if the brain and the mind are but different aspects of the same reality, we have more familiarity with the mind-aspect than with the brain-aspect; after all, what we experience is the mind and not the brain. Brain-events must be theoretically reconstructed, much like events in any other sphere of nature. Consequently the relationship between brain and mind — physiological grey matter and lived, conscious experience — is as yet imperfectly understood.

Knowing the brain is not an easy matter: the grey matter we carry in our cranium is a highly integrated system topped by a cortex constituted as a six-layered sheet of some ten billion neurons with up to a million-billion connections. Contemporary brain theory is not able to decode the full workings of this staggeringly complex system and is thus not able to clarify the neurophysiological processes underlying the major varieties of conscious mental experience. Neurophysiologists are only now beginning to understand such basic elements of mental function as object and event categorization, concept-formation, and self-recognition.

Not only are many elements of human experience as yet poorly understood in physiological terms, often even psychological explanations are missing, or are vague and controversial. This is true especially of the farther reaches of human experience, such as intuition, inspiration, extrasensory perception, foresight; even long-term memory. The brain-events that would correlate with such mind-events are only vaguely known, even if, as we shall soon see, promising insights have surfaced lately.

We shall review the problems and insights within contemporary investigations of mind and brain in view of the possibility that they may provide further clues as to the dynamics by which order in nature could emerge, and reach beyond the biological level to the level of the human brain and mind.

Long-term memory

The evidence for long-term — and possibly even permanent — memory is impressive, yet how such memory would function is not well understood. The brain, it appears, can store its impressions both temporarily and in the long run. Short-term memory can be relatively well understood in reference to the formation and reformation of neuronal networks in the cortex, but long-term memory remains a puzzle. It seems to call for some variety of traces or 'engrams' that modify the synapses between neurons. John Eccles, for example, wrote that 'we have to suppose that long-term memories are somehow encoded in the neuronal connectivities of the brain. We are thus led to conjecture that the structural basis of memory lies in the enduring modification of the synapses.'[1]

However, the search for engrams, or other enduring synaptic modifications through which experiences would be permanently stored, has proved fruitless. The search began in a systematic fashion in the 1940s with the celebrated series of animal experiments of neurosurgeon Karl Lashley. Lashley was trying to find permanent engrams in the brain of rats by the expedient of teaching the rats specific behavioural routines and then cutting out various parts of their cortex to see where the instructions for the routines would be stored. He cut out larger and larger segments of brain tissue, but found no correlation between brain area and recall of the routine: the test animals' recall degenerated proportionately to the amount of tissue removed, but never ceased entirely.[2] The puzzle as to where the traces of the routines are stored, has not been solved to this day. J.Z. Young conceded that, even if most neuroscientists believe in a theory of synaptic change, there is little direct evidence of the details of it.[3]

Despite the puzzle of neural storage, long-term memory in humans cannot be ignored. In addition to introspective recall, two further strands of evidence have surfaced in recent years: one comes from so-called NDEs (near-death experiences), and the other from regression analysis conducted by qualified psychotherapists.

Since Elisabeth Kübler-Ross' classic studies, NDEs have been systematically investigated by clinical psychologists and specialized researchers. It appears that people who come close to death undergo a remarkable experience. Raymond Moody, Jr., who pioneered the systematic study of NDEs, concluded that it is now 'clearly established' that the experience of a significant proportion of the people who are revived following close calls with death is quite similar from case to case, regardless of the patient's age, sex, religious, cultural, educational or socioeconomic background.[4] The experience itself is more widespread than is generally recognized; a survey conducted by George Gallup, Jr. in 1982 found that some eight million adults in the US alone have undergone them.[5] The near-death experience alters the subsequent course of people's lives: they are no longer fearful of death but focus on the importance of the present with enhanced love and concern for others.

Memories of one's lifetime form an important element of the near-death experience: thirty-two percent of the eight million people reported in the Gallup poll said that 'life-reviews' were a part of their experience. NDE researcher David Lorimer distinguished two kinds of lifetime recall: panoramic memory, and the life-review itself. Panoramic memory, he noted, consists of a display of images and memories with little or no direct emotional involvement on the part of the subject; while life-review, although superficially similar, also involves emotional involvement and moral assessment.[6] The clarity of mental processes is noteworthy in both. Recall is especially vivid in panoramic memory, where there is a remarkable speed, reality and accuracy in the images that flash across the mind. Lorimer noted that the time-sequence of the memories may vary: some start in early childhood and move towards the present; others start in the present and move backwards to childhood. Still others come superposed, as if in a holographic clump. To the subjects it appears that everything they have ever experienced in their lifetime is being recalled; no thought, no incident, appears to have been lost.

NDEs demonstrate the possibility of a quasi-total recall of a person's prior experiences. Such recall would be staggering: John von Neumann calculated that an individual accumulates some 2.8×10^{20} 'bits' of information during his or her lifetime. There is evidence, however, that people have access to a store of information that is even larger than this. The credible strands of evidence come from practising psychotherapists who, by 'regressing' patients to early childhood, find that they can proceed still further back in time, to experiences of the womb and of birth, and sometimes still further, to apparent prior lifetimes. Jungian and transpersonal psychotherapists engage in 'regression therapy' not for the intrinsic interest of the memory flow, but because the images and events recalled by patients can frequently relieve their traumas and neuroses. The technique no longer requires patients to be hypnotized; a deeply relaxed meditative state suffices to start the flow of images.

Therapists find that many of their patients can recall several past lives covering a vast time span. According to Thorwald Detlefsen, a famous if controversial therapist in Munich, Germany, the series of 'reincarnations' runs into the hundreds and may encompass 12000 years. Stanislav Grof, a likewise famous and controversial investigator in the United States, claims to have hypno-regressed subjects to the state of animal ancestors.

Independently of large claims by some therapists, the findings are clearly impressive. Ian Stevenson has had scores of children recount past-life experiences, many of which have proved to refer to the lives of actual personages.[7] Patients of all ages tell stories of prior life-experiences, often associated with present problems and neuroses. Detlefsen's case histories include the story of a patient who could not see in an otherwise functional eye; he came up with the memory of being a medieval soldier whose eye was pierced by an arrow. A patient of pioneer investigator Morris Netherton, suffering from ulcerative colitis, re-lived the sensations of an eight-year-old girl shot at a mass grave by Nazi soldiers. And New York therapist Roger Woolger's patient, who complained of rigid neck and shoulders, recalled committing suicide by hanging as a Dutch painter.

Such images and experiences often have a therapeutic effect. Many psychic and some bodily ills seem to be the result of traumas that appear as if they were experienced in previous lifetimes. To recall and re-live such events releases so-called 'karmic bonds': feelings of guilt and anxiety carried over from prior lifetimes. But it is not clear whether the images and experiences themselves are products of the subjects' imagination, or come to them paranormally from an external source.

Some investigators uncovered evidence that in certain cases subjects who recalled a particular image or event had prior information about the given persons, times, and places. The possibility arises, then, that in a deep meditative (or hypnotic) state the imagination of the subjects elaborates these kernels of information, at times into veritable historical novels. On the other hand in some cases the information produced by regressed subjects contained elements that are not likely to have been previously available to them, such as obscure (but subsequently verified) historical and geographical particulars. The cases most difficult to account for are those in which a subject began to speak a previously unknown foreign tongue. The phenomenon, known as xenoglossy, cannot be explained by assuming a chance acquaintance with some elements of the given language; in several recorded cases hypnotized and regressed subjects engaged in prolonged and fluent conversations with persons who spoke that language.[8]

Some paranormal information does seem to surface in the process of regression, but that it does is not in itself an assurance that individuals who produce such information reincarnate previously living persons. Reincarnation is one interpretation of the phenomenon but, as we shall see, it is not the only one. There is not much agreement on the reincarnation hypothesis even among investigators who have had extensive experience with the relevant phenomena. Detlefsen is categorically for reincarnation: everybody should be clear, he wrote, that any explanation of the findings that does not affirm reincarnation is absurd.[9] Also Stevenson believes in reincarnation, but he is not dogmatic about it: if genetic variation and environmental influences cannot satisfactorily explain certain attributes in some persons, he noted, then reincarnation deserves consideration as the third factor.[10] Woolger is more cautious. He stresses that what matters is the therapeutic effect and not whether one believes in reincarnation or not. Even when the conscious mind is sceptical, the unconscious mind will almost always produce a 'past life story' if invited in the right way.[11]

Simultaneous insights

Another puzzling dimension of experience is the sharing of entire cultural patterns among people who live — or have lived — in different places and at different times. Simultaneity among distinct and distant events is a frequent occurrence in cultural history. Aside from cases of reputed 'synchronicity' — which struck psychologist Carl Jung as having a deep significance — there are well-documented occurrences that cannot be dismissed as simple coincidence.

Strikingly similar achievements have surfaced among populations that were unlikely to have been in communication with each other, or even to have known of the other's existence. The 'invention' of fire may have been the first of this strange series. *Homo erectus*, our direct forebear, seems to have tended fires in distant locations. On a historical time-scale, a number of unrelated populations appear to have evolved the art of igniting, tending and transporting fires almost simultaneously. The archeological finds speak clearly: there were humanly laid fires at such diverse sites as Zhoukoudien near Beijing, Aragon in the south of France, and Vértesszöllős in Hungary.

Different cultures also developed a wide array of similar tools. The Acheulian hand axe, for example, was a widespread tool of the Stone Age, and it had a typical almond or tear-shaped design carefully chipped into symmetry on both sides. In Europe the axe was made of flint, in the Middle East of chert, and in Africa of quartzite, shale, or diabase. Its basic form was functional, yet the agreement in the details of its execution in virtually all known cultures cannot be readily explained by the coincidental discovery of utilitarian solutions to shared needs — trial and error is unlikely to have produced such similarity in these far-flung populations.

Other artifacts, too, seem to have leaped across space in history. Giant pyramids were built in ancient Egypt as well as in pre-Colombian America, with remarkable agreement in design. Crafts, such as pottery-making, have taken much the same form in all cultures. Even the technique of making fire brought forth implements of the same basic design in different parts of the world. Although each culture added its own embellishments, Aztecs and Etruscans, Zulus and Malays, classical Indians and ancient Chinese, all fashioned their tools and built their monuments as if following a common basic pattern or 'archetype.'

More than physical artifacts, entire culture patterns emerged more or less simultaneously, yet independently of each other. The great breakthroughs of classical Hebrew, Greek, Chinese, and Indian culture occurred in widely scattered regions, yet they occurred practically simultaneously. The major Hebrew prophets flourished in Palestine between 750 and 500 BC; in India the early Upanishads were composed between 660 and 550 BC and Siddharta the Buddha lived from 563 to 487 BC; Confucius taught in China around 551-479 BC; and Socrates lived in Hellenic Greece from 469 to 399 BC. Just when the Hellenic philosophers created the basis of Western civilization in Platonic and Aristotelian philosophy, the Chinese philosophers founded the ideational basis of Oriental civilization in the Confucian, Taoist and Legalist doctrines. While in the Hellas of the post-Peloponnesian Wars period, Plato founded his Academy and Aristotle his Lyceum, and scores of itinerant sophists preached to and advised kings, tyrants and citizens, in China the similarly restless and inventive 'Shih' founded schools, lectured to crowds, established doctrines, and manoeuvred among the scheming princes of the late Warring States Period.

Simultaneous cultural achievements are not limited to classical civilizations: they also occur among modern individuals. Even within the disciplined domain of science, there are documented cases of insights occurring at the same time to different investigators who did not know of each other's work. The most celebrated of these cases concerns the simultaneous and independent discovery of calculus by Newton and by Leibniz, the likewise simultaneous and independent elaboration of the fundamental mechanisms of biological evolution by Darwin and by Wallace, and the concurrent invention of the telephone by Bell and by Gray.

There have been cases where insight and discovery leapt across different branches of a culture. As Newton was using a prism to break down the shafts of light that entered the windows of his Cambridge lodgings, Vermeer and other Flemish artists were exploring the nature of light entering through coloured window- and door-panes. While Maxwell was formulating his electromagnetic theory, according to which light is produced by the reciprocal revolution of electrical and magnetic waves, Turner was painting light as swirling vortices. In recent years physicists have been exploring many-dimensional spaces in grand unified theories, and simultaneously, and apparently entirely independently, avant-garde artists started to experiment with visual superposition on their canvases, representing as many as seven spatial dimensions.

Space and time, light and gravity, mass and energy have all been explored by physicists and by artists, sometimes at the same time, sometimes one preceding the other, but seldom if ever in conscious knowledge of each other. Leonard Shlain explored these 'coincidences' in detail and provided stunning illustrations of the power of artists to mirror, and frequently to anticipate, the conceptual breakthroughs occurring in the minds of physicists without knowing anything about physics and the concerns of its investigators.[12]

Researchers of synchronicity point out that coincidences of this kind are legion.[13] Some can be dismissed as illusory; others may have been due to pure chance. But there still remains a hard core of simultaneous insights among individuals as well as cultures that goes beyond the established frontiers of science. It is in recognition of this that Hegel formulated his celebrated concept of *Zeitgeist,* the spirit of an age that infuses the minds of its contemporaries, and Jung advanced the concept of the 'collective unconscious,' the sharing of mythic symbols and archetypes in different cultures.

Extra-sensory perception

Telepathy and related forms of extrasensory perception (ESP) constitute further puzzling aspects of the human mind. Until recently, ESP has not been taken seriously by the scientific community: it was considered paranormal and its investigation was relegated to parapsychology. This attitude is no longer justified. While there are esoteric aspects of experience that do not merit investigation, some varieties of ESP do. Telepathy, for example, has been experimentally investigated, and there can be little doubt that something like an extrasensory transference of thoughts and images does occur. Explanations in terms of hidden sensory cues, machine bias, cheating by subjects, and experimenter error or incompetence have all been considered, but they were found unable to account for a number of statistically significant results.

Telepathy may have been fairly common among so-called primitive people. To this day, Australian aborigines seem to be occasionally informed of the fate of family and friends, even when out of sensory communication range with them. Anthropologist A.P. Elkin noted that a man, far from his homeland, 'will suddenly announce one day that his father is dead, that his wife has given birth to a child, or that there is some trouble in his country. He is so sure of his facts that he would return at once if he could.'[14] It appears that in many tribal societies shamans were able to communicate telepathically, using a variety of techniques to enter the altered states of consciousness that seem required for it, including solitude, concentration, fasting, as well as chanting, dancing, drumming, and the use of psychedelic herbs.

Aside from anthropological data, largely anecdotal and unrepeatable, scientific evidence for various kinds of telepathy comes from laboratory research based on controlled experiments. The scientific investigation of ESP dates back to J.B. Rhine's pioneering though controversial experiments at Duke University in the 1930s. More recently experimental controls became rigorous; physicists often join psychologists in the design of experiments. In fact, in the 1970s two physicists, Russell Targ and Harold Puthoff of Stanford Research

Institute, carried out some of the best known experiments on thought and image transference.

Targ and Puthoff wished to ascertain the reality of telepathic transmission between different individuals, one of whom would act as 'sender' and the other as 'receiver.' They placed the receiver in a sealed, opaque and electrically shielded chamber, and the sender in another room where he or she was subjected to bright flashes of light at regular intervals. Electroencephalograph (EEG) machines registered the brain-wave patterns of both. As expected, the sender exhibited the rhythmic brain waves that normally accompany exposure to bright flashes of light. But, after a brief interval the receiver also began to produce the same patterns, although he or she was not exposed to the flashes and was not receiving sense-perceivable signals from the sender.

The investigators went on to design so-called remote viewing experiments. In these experiments sender and receiver are separated by distances that preclude any form of sensory communication between them. At a site chosen at random, the sender would act as a 'beacon'; the receiver would then try to pick up what the receiver saw. To document his or her impressions, the receiver would give verbal descriptions, at times accompanied by sketches. Judges found that the descriptions of the sketches matched on the average 66% of the time the characteristics of the site actually seen by the beacon.[15]

Remote viewing experiments reported from other laboratories involved distances from half a mile to several thousand miles. Regardless of where they were carried out, and by whom, the success rate generally was around fifty percent — considerably above random probability. The most successful viewers appeared to be those who were relaxed, attentive, meditative. They said that they received a preliminary impression as a gentle and fleeting form which gradually evolved into an integrated image. They experienced the image as a surprise, both because it was clear and because it was clearly elsewhere.

Images can also be transmitted while the receiver is asleep. Over several decades, Stanley Krippner and his associates carried out 'dream ESP experiments' at the Dream Laboratory of Maimondes

Hospital in New York. The experiments followed a simple yet effective protocol. The volunteer, who would spend the night at the laboratory, met the sender and the experimenters on arrival and had the procedure explained. Electrodes were attached to the volunteer's head to monitor brain waves and eye movements; there was no further sensory contact with the sender until the next morning. One of the experimenters threw dice that, in combination with a random number table, gave a number that corresponded to a sealed envelope containing an art print. The envelope was opened when the sender reached his or her private room in a distant part of the hospital. The sender then spent the night concentrating on the print.

The experimenters, who took turns in monitoring the volunteer's sleep, woke him or her by intercom when the monitor showed the end of a period of rapid eye-movement (REM) sleep. The subject would be asked to describe any dream he or she might have had before awakening. The comments were recorded, together with the contents of an interview next morning when the subject was asked to associate with the remembered dream contents. The interview was conducted 'double blind' — neither the subject nor the experimenters knew which art print had been selected the night before.

Using data taken from the first night each volunteer spent at the dream laboratory, a series of experiments that took place between 1964 and 1969 produced 62 nights of data for analysis. The result was a significant correlation between the art print selected for a given night and the recipient's dreams on that night. Dividing the results into four categories, ranging from 'high hit' to 'low miss,' there were a total of 18 high hits, 29 low hits, seven high misses, and eight low misses.[16]

There have been other controlled, hospital-based experiments on the extrasensory transmission of information, and at times the results proved still more puzzling. In some experiments not thoughts or images, but healing effects seemed to have been transmitted. 'Distance healing' is a well-known phenomenon among natural healers and other adepts, but it has seldom been systematically tested. Cardiologist Randolph Byrd, a former professor at the University of California, attempted to rectify this situation. He carried out a ten-month computer-assisted study of the medical histories of patients admitted to the coronary care unit at San Francisco General Hospital. Byrd formed a group of experimenters made up not of known healers, but of ordinary people whose only common characteristic was a habit of regular prayer in Catholic or Protestant congregations around the country. The selected people were asked to pray for the recovery of a group of 192 patients; another set of 210 patients, for whom nobody prayed in the experiment, made up the control group. Rigid criteria were used: the selection was randomized and the experiment was carried out double blind, with neither the patients, nor the nurses and doctors knowing which patients belonged to which group.

The experimenters were given the names of the patients, some information about their heart condition, and were asked to pray for them every day. They were not told anything further. Since each experimenter could pray for several patients, each patient had between five and seven people praying for him or her. The results were statistically significant. The prayed-for group, it turned out, was five times less likely than the control group to require antibiotics (three compared to sixteen patients); it was three times less likely to develop pulmonary edema (three versus eighteen patients); none in the prayed-for group required endotracheal incubation (while twelve patients in the control group did); and fewer patients died in the former than in the latter group (though this particular result was statistically not significant). It did not matter how close or far the patients were to those who prayed for them, nor did the manner of praying make any difference. Only the fact of concentrated and repeated prayer seemed to have been a factor, without regard to whom the prayer was addressed and to where the prayers took place.[17]

The above findings are not unmatched in the landscape of current experimentation with distance effects: there is also the so-called 'Maharishi-effect.' This concerns the statistically significant effect of meditation (or of meditators) on a community. In 1974 the Maharishi Mahesh Yogi revived an ancient Hindu notion when he suggested that, if but one percent of a population were to meditate regularly, the remaining 99 percent would also be notably affected. Subsequent statistical studies, by Garland Landrith and David Orme-Johnson among others, showed that the classical insight was sound. There appears to be more than random correlation between the number of meditators in a community and community crime rates, incidence of traffic fatalities, deaths due to alcoholism, and even levels of pollution.[18]

The above examples point in a definite direction. They furnish evidence that the human mind is more widely 'informed' than has been generally recognized. Our sources of information are not limited to the bodily sense organs; there are also items entering our consciousness that exceed the range of sensory perception: they can leap, it seems, across wide reaches of space and time. These items can no longer be ignored; their occurrence is relatively frequent, and is in part demonstrated in controlled and repeated experiments. Confounding mid-century optimistic assessments, that everything knowable about the mind can be ultimately inferred from the observation of behaviour and referred to corresponding cerebral structures, scientists are now forced to acknowledge the reality of elements in conscious experience that, though analysable in principle to correlated brain structures, are not reducible to inputs by eye and ear, and the other sensory organs.

The realization we have come to in regard to the physical world and the world of the living applies also to the world of mind and consciousness. Here, too, something fundamental remains yet to be discovered. The question is, whether the factor that is as yet missing in theories of mind and consciousness could be the same factor that is missing in general evolution theories. Because, if so, finding this factor would at one and the same time improve our understanding of the workings of mind and brain, and clarify the nature of the dynamics whereby order emerges in the universe.

PART THREE

Emerging Insights

– 7 –
Towards a Unified
Interactive Dynamics (UID)

When assembling a jigsaw puzzle, the task becomes easier as one goes along. More of the image appears, and fewer of the unassembled pieces are left. One can match the remaining pieces with increasing ease against what is still missing in the picture.

Something similar is happening at this stage in our search for a unified science of the experienced world. We know what is still missing in the contemporary scientific world picture: it is a correct grasp of the interactive dynamics whereby diversified yet consistent order builds up in nature. We also have some bits and pieces of uninterpreted puzzle on our hands; these are the persistent paradoxes we have reviewed of the physical and the living world, and the world of mind and consciousness. The hypothesis we wish to test is whether a sound interpretation of the paradoxes would put into our hands a piece of the jigsaw puzzle that would 'fit' the evolutionary dynamics, and thus bring us closer to the unified science we are seeking.

In order to explore this possibility, we shall summarize the main thrust of the above noted paradoxes, and then elucidate their meaning.

In the physical world:

— the anomaly that results from the testing of the EPR experiment concerns the quantum state of jointly originating and then spatially separated particles: these states turn out to be instantaneously correlated;

— in double-slit and split-beam experiments, sequentially emitted photons interfere with one another, whether they originated

119

seconds ago in a laboratory or thousands of years ago in distant galaxies;

— in the shells surrounding atomic nuclei, electrons exclude one another to successive energy levels in accordance with Pauli's antisymmetry principle, even though there is no dynamical force exchanged between them;

— the resonance frequencies of four different elements (helium, an unstable isotope of beryllium, carbon, and oxygen), though highly improbable, are precisely tuned so that sufficient carbon can be produced in the universe to build towards the heavier elements, essential for the evolution of life;

— the physical constants of the universe are also improbably finely tuned to each other, seemingly in view of giving rise to life. This includes the precise amount and distribution of 'matter' (baryons) in the universe, the values of the universal forces, and the respective charge of neutrons, protons, and electrons.

In the living world:

— high levels of diversity and consistency have come about regarding both the morphology of individual organisms and their ordering within embracing taxonomical groups, even though evolution within its finite time-frame is believed to have been governed by random processes of mutation and natural selection;

— within the strands of order that evolved, individual organisms can reproduce their complex multicellular structures although each of their cells contains an identical set of genetic instructions which, moreover, are not likely to have come about through random mutations exposed to the serendipity of natural selection;

— some organisms can regenerate limbs and organs, and in a few cases the full organism, although such repair programs exceed requirements in nature, and are thus beyond the pale of natural selection.

In the sphere of mind and consciousness:

— individuals appear able at times to recall nearly all their experiences, and even experiences that appear as if they belonged to a previous lifetime, or to some other person;

— information seems to be occasionally transmitted from person to person beyond the range of direct sensory perception. And such information transfer occurs not only among individuals but among entire cultures, and not just among primitive peoples but also in modern society; even in the disciplined domains of science.

What shall we make of these paradoxical findings? We cannot simply dismiss them, for many of them occur under repeatable conditions and some in rigorously controlled experiments. Instead, we should attempt to elucidate their meaning.

— *The puzzles of the physical universe* concern the transmission of information among particles and other physical systems, as well as the coordination of their properties. Under certain circumstances one particle is instantaneously informed of the state of another particle, even if the two particles do not exchange known forms of energy and are at different points in space and time. Moreover, the properties of the principal varieties of particles, and of the forces of nature that embed them, are precisely coordinated throughout space and time.

— *The puzzles of the living world* concern the limitation of randomness in the evolutionary process and the need for some factor that would bias variational probabilities in favour of outcomes of order and consistency. In processes of generation and regeneration a factor is required that would inform cells in multicellular organisms of the morphology of the whole organism. On higher organizational levels an analogous informational factor is needed to explain the observed fit of individual organisms within the topology of their adaptive landscape.

— *The puzzles of mind and consciousness* imply the transmission of information among individuals and groups of individuals beyond the known limits of space and time.

These findings have a common thrust: they suggest that the things and events of this world are linked more intimately than mainstream science can allow. A space- and time-connecting factor appears present in all domains of nature, the physical, the biological as well as the cognitive. In the absence of connectedness we could not expect anything more interesting to have come about in the physical universe than hydrogen and helium; the presence of complex systems such as those required for life would have to be ascribed to an unfathomable stroke of luck, if not to the will of an omnipotent Creator. Likewise the evolution of biological systems, and their generation and regeneration, would require explanation in terms of mysterious 'building plans' or other metaphysical factors instead of *bona fide* scientific concepts rooted in the observable characteristics of nature. And many of the remarkable phenomena of mind and consciousness that come to light in recent investigations would have to be relegated to the extra-scientific domains of parapsychology, if not simply dismissed as superstition.

Space- and time-connections in nature

What means are there at our disposal to account for the implied space- and time-connections? There may be several; yet the simplest and most logical is that of a field with the required space- and time-binding properties.

Field is the indicated concept to understand how event *A* at one point in space and time is connected with event *B* at a different point. A field connecting the two events may not be observable in itself; it is enough that its effects be observable. It is as if we had knots on an imaginary fishing net. Our net may be so fine that we cannot see it; we may only see the points where its strands have been joined in knots. Yet we know that when one knot moves this means that the net itself has moved. Since the net is continuous, motion at any one point is communicated to all other points: when we move one of the knots, knots everywhere along the net will be brought into motion. The net, though invisible in itself, interconnects its visible knots. (See Appendix for note on *Fields*).

In a somewhat more apt simile, we can think of a series of springs each of which is connected to its neighbours (this is the case already in the ordinary inner sprung mattress). As one spring is depressed, all other springs are affected — they are expanded, depressed, or bent. The entire surface moves coherently, though not uniformly. The same holds true when the springs are vibrations occurring in spacetime at specific frequencies. If local vibrations are interconnected (for example, by force fields), a change in the frequency of one produces corresponding changes in the frequencies of the others. This is basically how string theories conceptualize elementary particles: in these theories, particles are localized vibration-patterns in continuous vibratory fields.

Space-binding in nature is likely to occur by means of a field: the real continuum that, according to physics, underlies and interconnects all phenomena. What about time binding, then? Space and time form a continuum in the current conception, and the principle that enables us to account for space-binding should also give us the key to explain time-binding.

In classical science time-connections between phenomena were believed to be clearly understood. In the deterministic concept of Newtonian physics, the linkage of the past with the present was furnished by an unbroken chain of causes and effects. Universal laws of motion combined with rigorous causal transmissions enabled physicists to trace effects to prior causes with mathematical precision. For example, when a ball rolls down on an inclined plane, the speed and acceleration of the ball is determined by the law of gravitation plus the size and weight of the ball (assuming negligible friction between ball and plane). The law of gravitation is a constant, entering into all things the same way. The size and the weight of the ball are variable: they define the specific initial conditions of the process. The combination of constant gravitation with variable initial conditions makes possible the precise description and accurate prediction of the motion of the rolling ball.

The linkage of past and present through dependence on initial conditions extends logically to the very beginning of time: the initial conditions of every process may be seen as the effects of prior causes that, in turn, are the effects of still prior causes. Consequently there should be an unbroken causal chain stretching back to the hypothetical first instant when the universe was set in motion. Given that the laws of motion themselves remain space- and time-invariant, the initial conditions that reigned at that hypothetical instant must have predetermined everything that took place thereafter.

This form of time-binding is no longer affirmed in science. By the first decades of this century the determinism of classical mechanics was discarded, and time linkages through chains of processes with initial-condition dependence had to be rejected. A probabilistic universe cannot be 'caused' by its past; at the most, specific events could leave traceable impressions on a limited range of subsequent events.

However, contemporary science knows forms of time-binding other than deterministic causal links. The relevant concept is *memory*. If one event is linked with another over time, then the former is in some sense 'remembered' by the latter. Although in humans memory is associated with mind, memory can exist independently of mind and consciousness. The simplest of living organisms conserves some impressions of its environment: it has some form of memory although it does not possess a nervous system capable of consciousness. Even an exposed film has memory: it 'remembers' the pattern of light of various intensities that reaches its surface through the camera lens; and the computer that processes the text now being written also has memory — and even a form of logic and intelligence — though it is not likely to have mind and consciousness. It is, however, the type of memory that is associated with the hologram that furnishes the most likely principle for understanding time-binding in nature.

The holographic principle has been known since 1946 when Dennis Gabor discovered it in his search for a more efficient microscope.[1] As used by scientists and engineers, holography is an artificial process, created for specific purposes. The process rests, however, on a physical principle that could also be realized in nature. If it occurred in association with a universal field, it would endow that field with the potential for memory.

The principle itself is simple. A hologram consists of a wave-interference pattern produced by two intersecting beams of light stored on a photographic plate or film. One beam reaches the plate directly, while the other is scattered off the object to be reproduced. The two beams interact, and the interference patterns encode the characteristics of the surface from which one of the beams was reflected. As the interference pattern is spread across the entire plate, all parts of it receive information regarding the light reflective surface of the object. Thus in a hologram information is recorded in a distributed fashion.

Holographic information storage has properties that are directly relevant to the possibilities of time-binding in nature. First of all, because all parts of the holographic plate receive information from all parts of the photographed object, the full 3-D image can be retrieved by reconstructing the wave interference patterns stored on any part of the plate — although the smaller the part used in reconstructing the information the fuzzier the resulting image. In practice this means that, since two or more parts of the holographic plate can be viewed simultaneously, observers on different locations can retrieve the same information at the same time.

Second, in addition to being distributed, holographic information storage is extremely dense. A small portion of a holographic plate can conserve an enormous variety of wave interference patterns. According to some estimates, the entire contents of the US Library of Congress could be stored on a holographic medium the size of a cube of sugar.

These properties of holographic information storage suggest that space- and time-binding in nature is likely to function as some variety of holographic process. Space-binding calls for the simultaneous availability of information at different spatial locations; and the distributed nature of holographic information storage responds to this requirement. Time-binding, in turn, calls for the enduring conservation of a staggering amount of information, and the holographic process satisfies this requirement as well.

125

The emergence of order

A universal field with holographic properties would constitute a medium with distributed read-out potential and quasi-unlimited information-storage capacities. Would it also produce the interactive dynamics by which the observed orders arise in nature within the observed timeframes?

We can respond to this question by framing it in the context of two intriguing metaphors. One was outlined by Fred Hoyle, and the other — though in a different context — by John Wheeler.

Suppose, said Hoyle, that a blind man is trying to order the scrambled faces of a Rubik cube. As the experience of anyone who has tried it shows, matching the colours on all six faces of the cube can be a lengthy process; even a bright and physically non-handicapped person can spend hours groping a way towards the solution. A blind man would take much longer, since he is handicapped by not knowing whether any twist he is giving the cube brings him closer to or further from his goal. In Hoyle's calculation his chances of achieving a simultaneous colour matching of the six faces of the cube are of the order of 1 to 5×10^{18}. Consequently a blind man is not likely to live to see success: if he works at the rate of one move per second, he will need 5×10^{18} seconds to work through all possibilities. This length of time, however, is not only more than his life expectancy: it is more than the age of the universe.[2]

The situation changes radically if the blind man receives prompting during his efforts. If he receives a correct 'yes' or 'no' prompt at each move, he will unscramble the cube on the average in 120 moves. Working at the rate of one move per second, he will need two minutes, rather than 126 billion years, to reach his goal.

Hoyle's metaphor illustrates the difference that the feedback of relevant information makes in an otherwise random process. If the feedback is both perfect and compelling, the reduction of the number of decision-points needed to reach a goal can be as dramatic as above. If it is neither perfect nor compelling, the time-reduction would not be as dramatic, but it could still be significant. Even an occasional and non-compelling 'prompt' could speed up randomly groping developmental processes. It could, for example, make the evolution of organic species fall within acceptable time-frames.

Injecting information into a random process could not only speed up its unfolding: it could also give it direction. A striking example, suggested this time by Wheeler, makes this second key point.

The Wheeler metaphor (originally suggested to show that an ongoing process can determine its own initial conditions — an assumption needed to understand how a particle, at the time it is measured, can decide in what state it was emitted) concerns the popular parlour game known as 'Twenty Questions.' In this game the object is to identify a particular object or person agreed upon by a group of players by means of a series of twenty questions to which only yes or no answers can be given. One person leaves the room while the others think up the object or person he or she is to guess. The guessing proceeds first by asking general questions such as 'Is it vegetable?' and then proceeding to more specific ones such as 'Is it larger than an elephant?' before reaching the final stage where a definite question can be posed, such as 'Is it the lamp on the street corner?'

In the usual variant, the game is goal-oriented: the players establish the thing or person to be guessed. But the game can also be played in a nonteleological way. In this 'Wheeler variant' the players conspire not to think of any thing or person to be guessed, but not to disclose this to the one who does the guessing; he or she will ask questions as if there was something definite to find out. The game would end in utter confusion were it not for a simple rule that the players decide to obey: any answer they will give must be consistent with the answers they have given before. If, for example, the answer to the question 'Is it vegetable?' happened to be yes, all further answers must be given as if the thing to be guessed were a plant. As the questions move from the general to the particular, the range of permissible answers becomes progressively more limited. A skilled interlocutor can arrive at a specific question to which the other players, bound by the non-contradiction rule, will be obliged to answer 'yes.' The game moves towards a specific goal, even though none was set at the beginning.

This particular example shows that games that remember their own past states and feed back the relevant information achieve a seemingly goal-oriented consistency. Thus processes in which there is a dependable feedback of information are not only incomparably *faster* than random processes; they are also vastly more *self-consistent*.

Unconstrained randomness, as we have seen, can produce only divergence and not convergence: for the latter there must be some bias that reduces the probabilities to mutually consistent dimensions. A 'prompt' that would constrain the play of probabilities in favour of future outcomes that are consistent with outcomes achieved in the past would introduce order into the process. If such a prompt occurred in nature, it would limit the random play of probability in the bifurcations that mark the evolution of complex systems, thereby speeding up developmental processes and rendering them more self-consistent. The 'divergence property' noted by Prigogine would be complemented with a 'convergence property.'

A caveat has to be entered, however: the above examples do not map all essential elements of the self-ordering process in nature. Prompts that make the future unfolding of a process consistent with its past can only point towards a definite outcome, such as the colour-matching of the six faces of the Rubik cube or the guessing of a particular object in 'Twenty Questions.' Evolution, however, is an open process where each step opens up more alternatives than it closes. It must, therefore, involve more than the feedback of its own past. Such a 'creative feedback' is possible in a holographic process where multi-dimensional signals fit not only each system to its own past, but an entire hierarchy of evolving systems to one another. Thus parts can evolve consistently with wholes, and wholes consistently with parts. The entire hierarchy can move towards increasing order within multiple levels of mutually-tuned organization.

It appears, therefore, that if there is a holographic pattern-conserving and transmitting field in nature, its effect would be to speed up evolutionary processes and make their products self-consistent as well as innovative. Evolution in the cosmos and in the biosphere would shift from unacceptably long to empirically acceptable time-frames, and acquire the characteristics of consistently ordered diversity we meet with in experience. We may find ourselves in possession of a key element of the unified interactive dynamics by which we could account for the sequential emergence of order in nature.

The fifth field

Does a holographic field actually exist in nature? Certainly, the field concept is important: Einstein's comment about fields transforming our concept of reality is to the point. Though they are not observable in themselves, fields are just as real as any other physical entity. In Einstein's own theory, four-dimensional spacetime is a structured continuum that is more than a geometrical abstraction: it is a fundamental field of which the reality can no longer be in question.

The world concept of contemporary physics is furnished with four specific varieties of field: the gravitational, the electromagnetic, and the strong and the weak nuclear fields. As we have seen, according to current super-GUTs all four fields of interaction originated as a single 'super-grand-unified force' in the very early universe: the currently observed four fields separated out by spontaneous symmetry-breaking in the expanding and cooling universe. But are these fields sufficient to account for the kind of spacetime connections we have noted? This is by no means clear. The nuclear fields are local forces of interaction; they could not interconnect phenomena across wide stretches of spacetime. Gravitation and electromagnetism are both cosmically extended fields, yet the kind of connections we have noted constitute anomalies in regard to received theories of gravitational and electromagnetic fields. Is there, then, an as yet unidentified 'fifth field' in nature?

We should examine this question in reference to what is already known about the physical universe. The quantum vacuum, a feature that is known to exist but is little understood, is a meaningful place to begin.

Despite the great interest generated by this almost infinite energy field in particle physics and cosmology, the quantum vacuum remains one of the most puzzling phenomena in the physical world. When it comes to the calculation of interaction effects, physicists tend to ignore the vacuum's intrinsic energies: they 'renormalize' the phenomena. The mathematics of doing so are effective: the values derived through renormalization show significant agreement with observations. Thus the mathematics of renormalization is accepted, even though it obliges scientists to chose values for masses and forces to fit their observations, rather than deriving the values from the theory. Renormalization, however, does not remove the puzzle of quasi-infinite zero-point energies; it just sweeps it under the rug.

One reason why the science community is ready to neglect the quasi-infinite energies of the vacuum is that these energies generate infinities in the mathematics. But this entailment, while vexing, is not the whole reason: if physicists were convinced that the energies of the quantum vacuum are an important factor in physical interactions, they would find a way to take them into consideration. But they are not convinced, and why this is so has much to do with the history of the ether.

The precursor of today's quantum vacuum was the luminiferous ether. In its time, the ether concept made eminent sense: it explained how objects can influence each other beyond direct physical contact. The idea of an invisible medium that would fill space and convey effects over distance was proposed already by Descartes, who used it to explain the propagation of light and heat. Subsequently the ether was held to transmit not only light and heat, but also gravitational, electric, and magnetic forces. Solid objects were assumed to move through it, and in so doing to produce some level of friction. A.F. Fresnel produced detailed and experimentally testable calculations of the 'ether-drag,' and in 1881 Albert Michelson began a series of experiments to test Fesnel's drag-coefficient. The series of ingenious experiments, concluded in 1887 with E.W. Morley, showed no ether-drag whatever.

At first the physics community was reluctant to surrender the ether concept and sought alternative explanations: some spoke of a 'conspiracy of natural law' that would prevent the observation of motion relative to the ether. Then Einstein's theory of relativity permitted the calculation of physical effects without taking into account an ether drag: the computations referred to changes in the relative position of points in spacetime rather than to the motion of single points. The place of a universal reference frame, filled with a mechanistic medium, was taken by relativistic spacetime, described in geometrical terms.

Subsequently physicists replaced the notion of an ether-filled plenum with that of a cosmic vacuum. They reasoned that the ground state of the universe is free of matter and gravitation: it must therefore be seen as a vacuum. This conclusion, however, went beyond the implications of the negative results of the Michelson-Morley experiments. In a paper written as early as 1881, Michelson pointed out that the experiments did not call into question 'the existence of a medium called the ether, whose vibrations produce the phenomenon of heat and light, and which is supposed to fill all space.'[3] The fact that the interpretation of the ether produced by Fresnel was disproved, said Michelson, should not be taken as proof that there is no medium that fills space and time and transmits a variety of effects gravitational, electromagnetic, and possibly still others.

Michelson may have been right. Spacetime, it turned out, is by no means empty: it is reasonable to view it as an energy-filled plenum. Einstein did not make the mistake of throwing out the concept in favour of his own relativistic spacetime: as he said in 1924, 'In a consequent and coherent field theory, elementary particles constitute particular state spaces ... In this way all the objects are included again in the ether concept.'[4]

A new generation of physicists is now exploring this concept. Like Manfred Requardt of the University of Göttingen and Ignazio Licata of the University of Sicily, the new physicists consider quantum mechanics as a 'coarse-grained' theory of a more fundamental level of physical reality. The investigators attempt to clarify the puzzling aspects of the quantum state by viewing quanta as embedded in a dynamic sub-quantum field. (In Licata's view this field — 'reticular spacetime' — functions as an ultra-referential structure in which absolute deformations are described by the stochastic metric tensor and express deviations from isotropy and homogeneity in the Lorentz-invariant background. Thus for Licata, Lorentz transformations are actual physical effects created by the spacetime motion of matter.)[5]

Thomas Bearden, a US nuclear scientist and military strategist who developed a 'scalar electromagnetics' based in part on intelligence reports of Soviet research on the military applications of scalar waves, considers the electrostatic scalar potential as an n-dimensional stress in the quantum vacuum, where n is equal to, or greater than, four. Thus in Bearden's theory the vacuum is equal to energy-filled spacetime: a highly charged cosmic medium. In his view the virtual state of this medium determines all that emerges into physical reality as vectorial and matter-bound energy.[6]

Independently of speculative theories at the frontiers of physics, there are significant elements within physical cosmology that suggest that the quantum vacuum is an active energy field. It is now well established that it was this energy field that gave birth to the observable universe when the 'Minkowski vacuum' became unstable and split into matter and gravitation; and also it was this field, in the subsequent Robertson-Walker universe, that synthesized all matter that now exists in space and time. And the quantum vacuum continues to create pairs of particles/antiparticles whenever fluctuations within its gas of virtual particles exceed a critical threshold.

The vacuum, moreover, is not only the source of matter in the universe: it is also its sink. Hawking's theory calls for incessant vacuum fluctuations: at the 'event horizon' of the superdense stellar objects known as black holes, one particle of the pair of particles synthesized in the vacuum escapes into surrounding space, while its antiparticle twin is sucked into the black hole, where it decays — ultimately back into the vacuum.

The quantum vacuum is even more than the source and the sink of matter in the universe; recent evidence indicates that it can also influence the spacetime motion of matter. There is the so-called Casimir-effect and the Lamb-shift, where the electron in a hydrogen atom is subject to the fluctuation of virtual particles in addition to the usual Coulomb potential. A gas of virtual particles, it appears, can interact with 'real' particles and produce spontaneous emissions of radiation from atomic nuclei as well as from entire atoms.

Vacuum fluctuations act on particles as a stochastic force, similarly to Brownian motion in a fluid. In an isotropous and homogeneous field, these fluctuations permeate spacetime uniformly. On the universal scale this implies that the higher the velocity of a given particle, the greater the number of collisions it is likely to suffer with pairs of virtual particles. As a result particles will diffuse in spacetime from higher to lower concentrations.

If the vacuum energies are not entirely potential — that is, if they are not entirely 'infolded' in the vacuum — they interlink the motion of particles. In that event the movement of quanta is no longer Markovian. (In a Markov-chain the elements x_1, x_2, ... x_n are defined by mutually dependent random variables in such a way that predictions about the next link in the chain $[x_{n+1}]$ can be made uniquely on the basis of a knowledge of the last link $[x_n]$; in a non-Markovian chain, on the other hand, such prediction requires a knowledge of all links x_1, ... x_n.) And if the motions of quanta are interlinked, physicists will have to undertake a dynamic analysis of the internal structure of spacetime, for example, in terms of the 'infinitely small neighbourhoods' of mathematical non-standard analysis. Wheeler's remark will take on fresh significance: 'vacuum physics' will indeed 'lie at the core of everything.'[7]

If the quantum vacuum is an energy-filled plenum of which the potential energies interact with the vectorial energies of the material universe, we have good reasons for identifying the fifth field with the interactive face of that vacuum. The fifth field could then take its place in our knowledge of physical reality, joining the fields of gravitation, electromagnetism, and the weak and strong nuclear interactions.

– 8 –
UID: The Conceptual Foundations

We are seeking for the simplest possible scheme of thought that will bind together the observed facts.
Albert Einstein, *The World As I See It* (1934)

Binding together the observed facts in the simplest possible scheme is a perennial goal of systematic thought in science as well as in philosophy. It is also the goal of this study. We attempt to elucidate the unified interactive dynamics (UID) through which the facts investigated in physics, biology, and the sciences of mind and consciousness could be simply and coherently bound together.

Before we lay the conceptual foundations for the UID we seek, we should note that in light of our foregoing considerations that this dynamics is rooted in the quantum vacuum, a domain of physical reality that is intrinsically inaccessible to direct observation and experimentation. Does this condemn the entire venture to mere speculation?

At this stage, a sceptical conclusion would be premature. Science can deal with intrinsically unobservable domains of reality without loss of cogency, and this for several reasons. First, because there is no assumption that the observable domains of the universe would make up the universe in its totality; second, because there are scientifically legitimate ways of investigating domains of reality that are intrinsically unobservable.

Making use of legitimate methods of inference, in themselves unobservable phenomena can be investigated with considerable rigour. Astronomers, for example, infer from the anomalous motion of

134

observed stars and planets the presence of observationally unavailable stellar bodies. In the same way, other branches of natural science refer unexplained phenomena to postulates that account for them in reference to intrinsically (rather than accidentally) unobservable forces and processes.

Intrinsically unobservable forces and processes are not to be introduced, however, except where there is definite warrant for them. Would all phenomena be capable of explanation in terms of directly or instrumentally observable domains, Occam's razor ('theoretical entities are not to be multiplied beyond strictest necessity') would forbid making inferences to unobservable realities. If, however, anomalies persist within the directly or instrumentally observable domains, an inference beyond these domains becomes permissible, and indeed warranted. Only in this way can we proceed from *observations* to *observables,* and even to *'beables.'*

The anomalies that prompt inference to the sub-quantum level are the following:

— In *quantum physics*, progress beyond the 'phenomena' of laboratory observations to the 'beables' of the physical universe requires a reasonable explanation *inter alia* of nonlocal interactions, nondynamic correlations, and simultaneous wave and particle properties. Such explanation can be furnished by a holographically pattern-conserving sub-quantum field, interlinking quanta beyond the limits of relativistic spacetime and ordering their trajectories.

— In *biology*, going beyond what some investigators call 'the problem of form' in a theory that would give an acceptable account of species evolution, as well as of the generation and regeneration of complex organic structures, requires postulating randomness-limiting interconnections between the organism and an ambient form-conserving and transmitting field.

— In *brain and mind research*, a coherent explanation of an entire range of esoteric — but observationally repeatedly confirmed and in part also experimentally tested — phenomena calls for a closer than generally acknowledged connection between the conscious brain and the manifold dimensions of the information that reach the organism from its environment.

The above anomalies suggest the existence of a space- and time-connecting field in nature. This field, we have suggested, is best traced to the quantum vacuum. Consequently the interactive dynamics through which diversified yet consistent order emerges in nature must be rooted on the sub-quantum level. We shall now attempt to lay the conceptual foundations for the thereby indicated 'vacuum physics.'

The sub-quantum postulates

Quanta as solitons

We can map out the dynamic properties of the sub-quantum 'fifth field' in reference to what we know of pertinent phenomena in the observable universe. We begin by noting that the interactions of quanta show an amazing degree of complexity. Either quanta are themselves compound entities, with an internal structure that accounts for the specific complexity of their interactions, or the structure of the field in which they are embedded has the required degree of complexity. Both of these approaches are currently explored by theoretical physics. As there is no independent evidence for assuming that quanta themselves are complex entities, in this exposition we choose the second option. After all, the field in which quanta are embedded could well have a substructure; it is filled with an almost infinitely energetic gas of virtual particles. Quanta may be singularities — nodes or condensations — within that gas.

In this view, quanta, the basic units of the observable domain of the universe, merely *seem* like independent entities; in reality they are part and parcel of the information-rich sub-quantum field in which they appear. They approximate what in the observable domain we know as solitary waves: so-called solitons.

Solitons are nonlinear waves appearing in certain turbulent media. While they disclose characteristics that make them appear as discrete entities, they are part of the medium in which they subsist. As a number of physicists have found, they are a good dynamic metaphor for quanta.[1]

The first known report on solitons was filed by J. Scott Russell for the British Association for the Advancement of Science in 1845. He recounted riding beside a narrow channel of water and observing a wave rolling with great speed, 'assuming the form of a large solitary elevation, a rounded, smooth and well defined heap of water, which continued its course along the channel apparently without change of form or diminution of speed.'[2] Similar phenomena have since been observed in a variety of cases involving turbulent and nonlinear substances. Solitons appear in impulses in the nervous system and in complex electrical circuits. They have been observed in tidal bores, in atmospheric pressure waves, in heat conduction in solids, and in superfluidity and superconductivity. The Great Red Eye of the planet Jupiter, though seemingly a detached object, is in fact a soliton produced by Jupiter's turbulent surface. Solitons move along defined trajectories, and if their trajectories meet, they have been known to deflect one another.

While solitons are as yet imperfectly understood, their apparent behaviour qualifies them as a useful dynamic metaphor for the better grasp of the nature of quanta, a phenomenon of which the true nature is still less understood. The metaphor discloses that, although some observed entities appear as distinct corpuscular entities, they may still be waves within a subtending medium. Such phenomena are part of the medium in which they arise rather than separate entities. Quanta are phenomena of this kind. Their 'embeddedness' in the subtending vacuum is highlighted in current experience with particle accelerators.

When in a high-energy experiment a proton is accelerated almost to the speed of light and is then 'smashed' against an antiproton, the two particles annihilate each other and a variety of strange particles appear in their place. These particles are not, as physicists have originally suspected, 'contained' in some way in the particles that were annihilated: there is no independent evidence that protons and other quanta would be compound entities. Rather than quanta breaking open and spewing forth their highly diverse contents, the unit energy bound in

137

them is released into the vacuum. There it creates a fluctuation that exceeds the critical threshold which, when transgressed, creates 'real' (that is, instrumentally observable) particles from the virtual gas of the vacuum. Hence in a particle accelerator if anything 'breaks open' it is not the colliding particles, but the locally energized vacuum. This suggests that in the last count quanta are not separate entities, but critical singularities — captive local energy nodes — propagating in the vacuum.

Quanta are solitary waves within a nonlinear medium and not ordinary waves within a linear medium. The distinction is essential. The waves familiar in everyday experience consist of a number of molecules and atoms — hence of quanta — whereas quanta do not consist of other quanta. This makes for some crucial differences. When an ordinary wave moves in a medium such as the sea, the molecules of water are not displaced along with it; only their up-and-down motion is transmitted to those contiguous to them. As a result the waves of the sea move over the water surface without the water molecules moving along with them. But quanta are not compound entities moving within a linear medium but part of a sub-quantum (and hence also submolecular) medium, and their motion does not consist of the transmission of movement among other quanta. Rather, quanta are soliton-like propagations *within* the vacuum: nonlinear flows within the virtual-particle gas that fills cosmic spacetime.

As a first approximation we shall define quanta as instrumentally observable soliton-like flows within an otherwise unobservable sub-quantum medium. If we take only quanta into account and ignore (or 'renormalize') the energy values of the subtending medium, the description we get is that of a wave packet moving in empty space. If we take only the field into account, we obtain a description in terms of a flow in a sub-quantum virtual energy field. In a sound approach we take *both* the quanta and the subtending vacuum into account. A future science based on this approach will give a balanced description: it will describe the behaviour of quanta in reference to wave-mechanics, and the behaviour of the vacuum in terms of fluid-dynamics.

Vector waves and scalar waves

Following up the above approximation of quanta as solitary waves in the vacuum, we can take a more penetrating and technical look at the likely dynamics of the pertinent sub-quantum field.

In the light of contemporary physics, the quantum vacuum is a dense structure of virtual energy: it consists of a continuous but variable-density gas of fluctuating virtual particles. If we follow quantum geometrodynamics, we find that at the Planck-length of 10^{-35}m, the oscillations of the vacuum become so energetic as to break up the structure of the spacetime continuum, giving rise to sporadic-ally connecting and disconnecting distinct 'spacetime segments.' This veritable 'quantum foam' — Wheeler called it *superspace* — consists of a pure massless charge-flux. Theory claims that when fluxes in the virtual gas of the vacuum do not breach the level where quantized particle/antiparticle pair-creation occurs, they remain massless (virtual-energy) charges.*

In the view propounded here, the quantum vacuum is a 'virtual-particle' (rather than a 'material') ether, that is, a structured virtual-energy field. This field, we maintain, produces two kinds of wave. Quanta are soliton-like vectorial waves: charged masses propagating in spacetime. Another kind of wave propagating in the vacuum is non-vectorial, that is, 'scalar.'†

In regard to scalar wave propagations, the quantum vacuum is a cosmically extended scalar field, a continuum of which each point is

---

* Ordinarily, charge is defined as a virtual particle flux on and off some mass, where it is assumed that charge does not exist in the absence of mass. In the virtual energy field of the vacuum, however, this is the condition that prevails. Massless charge fluxes are real, even if they are not observable by means of devices that detect ordinary gravitational and electromagnetic phenomena.

† A scalar, in ordinary vector analysis, is a quantity that is completely defined by magnitude alone, without reference to displacement. Scalar waves, discovered by Nikola Tesla at the turn of the century, are longitudinal waves, somewhat like sound-waves, rather than the transverse waves of classical electromagnetic theory. In the absence of charged mass particles with specific spin-states, Tesla waves do not form classical electromagnetic waves but remain 'shadow vector' waves, that is, waves in the virtual state.

defined by a corresponding magnitude. In this continuum the magnitude at a given point is an n-dimensional virtual-state flux. Consequently at each point of the field the flux is a local scalar wave within a massless charge-field.

In this concept the quantum vacuum is identical with a realistically interpreted spacetime. It is a field of virtual energies expressed as a continuum of stresses and potentials. Its stress energies can be expressed in terms of geometrodynamics as electric potentials, more exactly, as the electrostatic scalar potential ϕ (phi). The quantity ϕ_0 measures the amount of work that needs to be performed against a unit charged mass in order to push it in from infinity against the charged field potential. The electrostatic charge of the vacuum, we should note, unlike the energy-density calculated by Wheeler, is not an anomaly: a massless charge does not correlate with finite gravitational potential and hence its accumulation in the vacuum does not interfere with the expansion of the universe.

Since the two kinds of waves propagating in the vacuum constitute distinct kinds of energies, we distinguish two basic energies in the universe. One is the energy 'trapped' in mass — that is, the vectorial-energy defined in Einstein's mass-energy equivalence relation; the other is the massless electrostatic scalar charge-energy of the vacuum. The two energies, while distinct, originate from the same source: mass is created as a standing scalar wave in the vacuum, trapped by local spin and vortex action.

Vector-wave and scalar-wave propagations

Vector-waves and scalar-waves propagate in the vacuum at different velocities. Quanta constitute vectorial waves, and their velocity in the vacuum is limited to the value of c (currently estimated at $299\,748 \pm 15$ km/sec). Such limitation may be ascribed to the finite electromagnetic permeability of the vacuum: c is then inversely proportional to the square-root of the product of the vacuum's electric and magnetic permeability $(c = 1/\sqrt{\mu_0 \varepsilon_0})$. Scalar waves, however, being massless charge propagations rather than massive charge flows, are not limited by this factor. Consequently while quanta particles such as photons propagate in the vacuum at the finite value of c, scalar waves (which are neither 'matter,' 'light,' nor 'force') propagate at speeds superior to c. Their velocity can be inferred as directly proportional to the local mass-density of the vacuum, that is, to the vacuum's local electrostatic scalar potential. This is variable: it is higher in regions of dense mass, in or near stars and planets, and lower in deep space. (The variation is due to the increase in vacuum flux intensity by the accumulation of charged masses.) It follows that scalars, longitudinally propagating virtual-particle fluxes, travel faster through matter-dense regions than in deep space, much as sound waves travel faster in a dense medium such as water than in a thin medium such as air. We may assume that in regions of superdense mass, the velocity of scalar-wave propagations is extremely high. It may approach infinity in regard to measurements with physical detection devices.

Vector-wave/scalar-wave interaction

We shall next consider the dynamics of vector-wave and scalar-wave interaction. This amounts to interaction between the matter-energies of the observable world and the unobservable virtual energies of the quantum vacuum.

Quanta, massive charge propagations travelling within the vacuum similarly to solitons, are not likely to flow without triggering secondary effects in the vacuum's virtual particle gas. If we do not fully separate the dynamics of the vacuum from the dynamics of quanta — a separation that, we have seen, is counterindicated both in theory and in the light of empirical evidence — we shall recognize that the laws of action-reaction hold also in regard to the motion of quanta and the virtual particle gas of the vacuum.

Vacuum/quantum interaction can be reconstructed in its essentials. We note first, that the finite speed of light in the vacuum is not an arbitrary constant but an effect of the finite electric and magnetic permeability of the vacuum. This indicates that the vacuum has some level of 'viscosity': it offers positive resistance to the displacement of quantal particles, including photons. The reaction to this action is a flux within the virtual particle gas of the vacuum. The minute fluxes created by the motion of quanta do not exceed the threshold of pair-creation; they remain virtual.

Second, we note that the fluxes created by the motion of quanta are massless charges (scalar waves), of which the propagation is not limited by the vacuum's electric and magnetic permeability. Consequently virtual scalars can travel at speeds higher than c. In a matter-dense region such as ours at the surface of the Earth, the secondary scalar wave-propagations created by the motion of quanta may reach speeds unmeasurably close to infinity. We thus have c-velocity limited vector-waves triggering supra-c velocity scalar-waves.

Third, we add that the laws of action-reaction hold also in the reverse case: the virtual scalar-waves propagating in the vacuum affect in turn the soliton-like vector-waves that triggered them. A complete feedback cycle evolves between the universe's two basic energies. The motion of quanta triggers secondary waves, and the secondary waves affect the motion of quanta.

Due to the higher velocity of the quanta-triggered virtual flux propagations, the above feedback affects the motion of almost all quanta present within a matter-dense region. While beyond such a region the Weyl spacetime cone — of the causal effect propagating from the past of the universe to its present — assumes dimensions that are close to those determined by the speed of light in the vacuum, in a matter-dense region the Weyl cone opens up. It embraces all quanta in that region up to the last infinitesome fraction of a second. Thus the secondary wavefronts created by quanta in such regions spread quasi-instantaneously throughout those regions.

The interference patterns created by the motion of quanta in a region modify the local topology of the vacuum, thus modifying the spacetime trajectories of the quanta. Regions densely populated with quanta are highly modulated: ever more virtual fluxes propagate and intersect in them, creating ever more interference patterns that constrain the quantal trajectories.

By creating secondary wavefronts that encode their evolutionary trajectories, matter creates a record of its own evolution. This record is likely to be enduring. While in the unfolded vectorial energy realm of the observable world no wave pattern remains indefinitely conserved — sooner or later it is cancelled by succeeding waves or by erosive forces — scalar virtual waves in the vacuum are not subject to temporal attenuation. Such a wave, once created, becomes part of the foregoing waves. As wave after wave interacts with those that preceded them, the interference pattern that results builds towards higher and higher dimensions of superposition.

The interaction postulates

We can now move from the abstruse and intrinsically unobservable sub-quantum domain to the more familiar world of observable phenomena. The unobservable and the observable domains are interlinked: feedbacks from the unobservable vacuum field produce subtle yet observable effects. These include the nonlocality and nondynamic interaction of quanta, as well as the space- and time-linkages of macroscale systems.

Since quanta are soliton-like flows *in* the vacuum, microscale systems — that is, systems whose action is of the order of Planck's constant — are directly exposed to the feedback effects. Macroscale systems, on the other hand, are governed by classical dynamical laws and they are thus generally independent of vacuum fluctuations. Nevertheless, macroscale systems may on occasion assume ultrasensitive states in which vacuum feedback effects become manifest. These are the states that contemporary dynamical systems theory describes as 'states of chaos.' (See Appendix for note on *Chaos.)*

The trajectories of complex macroscale systems are governed by several types of attractor at the same time, and these include chaotic attractors as well (see Figure 7). Thus, whether the evolutionary trajectory of such a system is stable or chaotic depends not so much on the exclusive presence of one or another type of attractor, but on the relative dominance of a particular type of attractor in the system's phase portrait. Given the presence of chaotic attractors in the dynamics of complex systems, many systems in the real world are likely periodically to evolve a level of sensitivity that extends even to vacuum-level fluctuations.

The secondary waves that carry vacuum fluctuations — and thus affect micro- as well as macro-scale systems — superpose in the

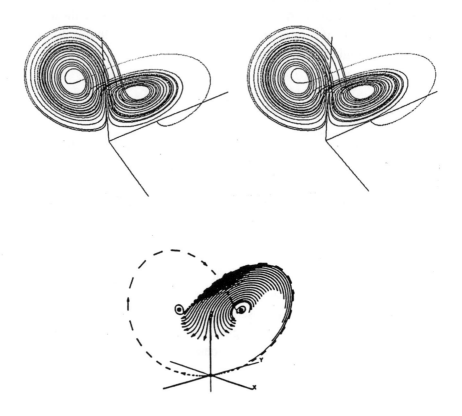

Figure 7.
Above: A chaotic attractor of a weather system, originally discovered by Edward Lorenz in the 1960s. Such attractors act like an asymptote: while the trajectory of the system never repeats, no trajectory falls outside the limiting form of the attractor, and the longer the trajectories are traced, the more completely is the attractor's limiting form approximated. (Stereo view from Paul Chernoff, Dynamics Newsletter, Sep 1988.)
Below: A chaotic attractor showing diverging orbits. In these attractors, the orbits of the various trajectories can come arbitrarily close, yet it can be mathematically shown that they never touch. Orbits that are immeasurably close may nevertheless explode into wide divergences, contradicting the classical assumption that an equation based on closely similar variables will produce closely similar solutions. (From Thompson and Stewart, Nonlinear Dynamics and Chaos, *Wiley, New York, 1986.)*

course of time, but are not likely to attenuate. The quantum vacuum, after all, is not subject to the action of dissipative forces; there is nothing other than the vectorial energies of the universe that could act on it. These energies, however, do not destroy the scalar wave-interference patterns of the vacuum: they merely retranscribe them in multiple dimensions. And in a multi-dimensional superposition the information encoded in each component wave is not destroyed but integrated.

Consequently we can claim that the observable matter-energy domain evolves through a unified interactive dynamics that involves reference to its own spectral record. While this record is unobservable in itself, interaction with it produces observable effects. The effects amount to that subtle but necessary bias that is called for to reduce randomness in the evolutionary process, and create consistency among its diversified products.

The conceptual intricacies of matter-energy/vacuum interaction can be made more transparent through the use of a suitable dynamic metaphor. Such a metaphor is offered by the familiar features of the ordinary sea surface. This is because interaction between matter and vacuum amounts to a two-way translation process that is analogous in some respects to the translation that occurs between sea-going vessels and the surface of the sea.

Acquaintance with waves on the sea surface shows that these waves are remarkably information-rich. When H.C. Yuan and B.M. Lake subjected the highly modulated surface to mathematical analysis, they found that wave patterns disclose information on the passage of ships, the direction of wind, the effect of shorelines, and other factors that have previously perturbed the surface.[3] Wave-patterns may be conserved hours, sometimes for days, after the vessels themselves have disappeared. Though ultimately the patterns dissipate, eroded by the combined action of gravity, wind, and shorelines, as long as they persist, waves created in heavily travelled seas provide information on the events that occurred at the surface of those seas.

The waves created by passing vessels not only inform observers of the vessels that catalyzed them: they also affect the motion of the vessels that pass over that part of the sea. These effects are ordinarily minor: in a large ship one can hardly notice the pitch or roll induced by the wake of another vessel. (This is not the case, though, when a small craft sails close behind an ocean liner: the effect, as anyone who has tried it can testify, can be dramatic.) But, whether noticeable or not, the passage of one vessel creates effects that feed back to influence the passage of other vessels. This feedback is crucial for understanding the subtle effect of the quantum vacuum on quanta, organisms, and other matter-energy systems.

Although the sea, unlike the quantum vacuum, is a linear medium, interaction between vessels and sea can serve as a dynamic metaphor of the interaction that occurs between the two kinds of energies in the universe. There is, in both cases, a two-way translation process: from spacetime trajectories into waveforms, and from the spectral domain of the wavefronts back to spacetime trajectories. The details of such translations are known: the mathematics expounding them was the work of Jean-Baptiste Fourier in the late nineteenth century. Fourier showed that any pattern in space and time can be analysed into a set of regular, periodic oscillations that differ only in frequency, amplitude, and phase. Specific waveforms can become exact representations — 'Fourier-transforms' — of three-dimensional objects.

Fourier-transforms are widely used in quantitative analysis; they are basic also to holography. In creating a hologram, a pattern in space and time is transformed into a series of waves, where each wave has a characteristic frequency and amplitude. Unlike a photograph, the holographic process does not map the three-dimensional outlines of objects on to the holographic film or plate: it maps the coefficients of the interference patterns created by the wave transforms. The coefficients represent the reinforcements and occlusions that occur at the intersections of the wavefronts. The sites of the intersections are nodes of various amplitudes, and the recorded pattern consists of these nodes.

When a vessel creates waves on the surface of the sea, it creates Fourier-transforms of its impact on the waters of the sea. This is also what happens when objects trace their evolutionary trajectory in space and time: they leave their Fourier-transforms in the virtual particle gas that fills spacetime.

The virtual-gas substructure of the vacuum, much as the sea's surface, encodes the coefficients of the interfering wavefronts produced by the objects that traverse it. In encoding the trajectories of material objects, the vacuum carries out nature's equivalent of the forward Fourier-transform: it translates a pattern from the spatiotemporal to the spectral domain. Then, in the inverse transform (from the spectral to the spatiotemporal domain) the interference patterns encoded in the vacuum affect the trajectories of objects in space and time. With some simplification, we may say that in the forward transform three-dimensional objects produce a spectral imprint in the vacuum, and that in the reverse transform the vacuum produces a dynamic effect on three-dimensional objects.

The vacuum, a cosmically extended holographic medium, encodes the adventures of objects throughout space and time. As a result the hologram-like substructure of the vacuum co-evolves with the quanta, and the macroscale configurations of quanta, that are the furnishings of the observable universe.

The psi-field

The sub-quantum and interaction postulates of our unified interactive dynamics enlarge the standard concept of the universe. The universe now includes *both* the sphere of actualized matter-energies *and* the virtual energy fluxes of the quantum vacuum. Given that the energies contained in the latter are larger by several magnitudes than all the actualized vectorial energies, their continuing neglect in the study of real world processes would be like insistently disregarding the depths of the high seas while studying the dynamics of the ripples that play on its surface.

This enlarged concept of the universe calls for a suitably revised terminology. The self-modulating vacuum field must not remain a mere abstraction: though virtual in itself, it does, we claim, produce manifest effects. This in-itself unobservable, yet observable-effect creating field deserves to become part of our repertory of basic notions about the world. For this reason we shall forego the technicalities that were required to expose the physical basis of this field, and henceforth refer to it simply as 'ψ (psi)-field.' In turn, we shall name the effect that the field produces on observable phenomena as 'ψ-effect.'

This choice of a Greek symbol is not arbitrary. First, given that the field in question is a major — though hitherto neglected — aspect of nature, it deserves a scientific name of its own. Second, the name in question, even if meriting a Greek symbol, should be pertinent to the properties of the field it names and to the effects the field produces. The meanings currently and traditionally associated with the symbol ψ — standing for the Schrödinger wave function as well as for *psyche* (soul, intelligence, or generally principle of life and mind) — satisfy this requirement.

Indeed, our use of ψ for the space- and time-connecting field has a threefold rationale:

First: In regard to the realm of the quantum, the field completes the description of the quantum state — it further specifies the wave function of the particle. According to the postulates of UID, the physical universe complete with ψ-field satisfies Schrödinger's equation $\psi(x,t)$, much as the geometric structure of spacetime satisfies Einstein's gravitational constant and the electromagnetic field satisfies Maxwell's equations.

Second: With respect to the living world, the field is a factor of self-referentiality. It 'in-forms' organisms consistently with their own and their milieu's morphology and may thus be viewed as a kind of intelligence — a generalized sort of 'psyche' operating in the womb of nature.

Third: In the domain of mind and consciousness, the field creates spontaneous communication between human brains as well as between human brains and the environment of the organisms possessing the brains. Though the field's effects are not limited to ESP and other esoterica, they convey the kind of information that has been traditionally subsumed in the category of 'psi-phenomena.'

We thus have good reasons for speaking of 'ψ-effect' in regard to the strange (but henceforth no longer entirely anomalous) behaviour of quanta, as well as with respect to the remarkable coordination of living organisms, and the no less remarkable information gathering and transmitting capacity of human brains.

In Part Four we shall make use of this simplified terminology as we review the earlier noted anomalies and paradoxes in reference to a subtle interaction between virtual wave fluxes in the quantum vacuum and matter-bound vectorial energies: the unified interactive dynamics that co-evolves the observable universe with the ψ-field.

PART FOUR

Explorations

– 9 –

Rethinking the Puzzles
of Physics

As Einstein often pointed out, the basic concepts of our theories of the world are products of the imagination. Scientific imagination, of course, must be disciplined: first by a testable hypothesis as to what is likely to be the case, and then by the exploration of that hypothesis in regard to its power to demonstrate what actually is (or seems to be) the case. Verification is never complete and final: as Popper has shown, there are no 'crucial experiments' that could decide once and for all whether any given theory is true or false. Progress in science is assured by the disciplined invention of working hypotheses and their systematic exploration in regard to their power to explain, and if possible to predict, relevant phenomena.

The postulates of the above outlined interactive dynamics, the same as other theories in physics, biology, and the cognitive sciences, are creations of disciplined imagination. When developed into explicit hypotheses, they become available for testing in regard to their capacity to shed light on patterns of empirical observation and experience. Hypotheses that prove to be 'the simplest possible scheme of thought that binds together the observed facts' can be considered verified until such a time that the observed facts prove to be capable of being bound together by yet simpler schemes of thought.

Here simplicity is understood as a specific property of a theory or hypothesis. That theory or hypothesis is optimally simple which postulates the smallest number of unanalysed premises from which to draw consistent inferences as to the nature of observed facts. In consequence in science simplicity is the very opposite of simple-mindedness: the simplest possible scheme of thought is usually the most abstract — a fact amply corroborated by theoretical innovations in most disciplines, above all in cosmology and in quantum and field physics.

In this Part we undertake to develop the unified interactive dynamics outlined in Part Three as specific hypotheses, explored in regard to their ability to shed light on the anomalies that beset the physical, the biological, and the psychological fields of investigation. We begin with the problems encountered in research on quanta.

The quantum reality problem

For the greater part of this century, quantum physics has had a serious reality problem. In 1900, Planck showed that energy radiates from a body in discontinuous packets called quanta; in 1905, Einstein proved that light, in addition to its known undulatory properties, possesses a corpuscular character; in 1913, Bohr demonstrated that electrons move from one orbital trajectory around a nucleus to another without passing through intermediate stages; in 1923, de Broglie postulated that quanta have irreducible corpuscular as well as wave properties; and in 1927, Heisenberg formulated the principle of uncertainty by which effective limits are set to our knowledge of an observer-independent quantum reality. Ultimately Bohr was forced to the Copenhagen interpretation according to which the quantum world is an elementary phenomenon that cannot be known, and should not be speculated upon, beyond observations in the laboratory.

The accumulating anomalies of the quantum world created a practically incomprehensible concept of reality on the subatomic scale; small wonder that the Copenhagen school refused to speculate on it. But, while many quantum physicists abided by the Copenhagen interdiction, some theorists did hazard explanations of what might, after all, underlie the 'elementary quantum phenomenon.' It became evident that the Copenhagen interpretation is not logically compelling: contemporary physicists have several alternatives when it comes to interpreting the nature of the quantum world. The 'decision-tree' suggested by Jean Staune maps out the major issues together with the available choices (see Figure 8).

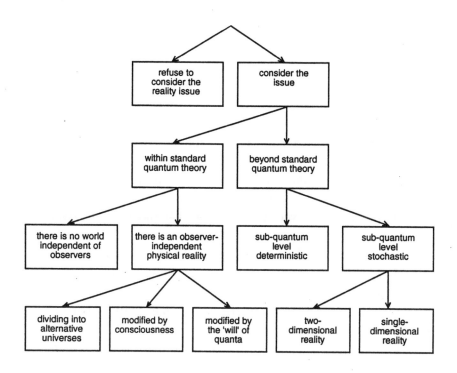

Figure 8. The quantum reality decision-tree, mapping the choices available to contemporary physics in attempting to interpret the nature of the quantum world. (After Jean Staune, "La révolution quantique et ses conséquences sur notre vision du monde," in 3e Millénaire, *Vol.15, 16, 1989/90.)*

There is, first of all, a fundamental choice: should we inquire into what Bernard d'Espagnat called 'the veiled reality' and Wheeler 'the great smoky dragon,' or should we ignore the entire issue? If we opt to ignore it, we can proceed with experiments and observations without further ado (we must, however, tolerate living in Alice's Wonderland where cats have grins but not substance — i.e., where there are *observations* but not *observables*). If, on the other hand, we take the option to confront the reality issue, we find several alternatives.

The first alternative is to move within the confines of quantum theory proper. In that case we can deny that there is a world independent of the observer — and if so, only the observer has reality: the rest is folded into his experience. But we can also opt to strike out beyond such radical phenomenalism and allow for an observer-independent reality. In that case we are logically obliged to clarify why this reality appears to be affected by our observations of it.

We may answer that the conscious mind of the observer acts on the quantum event: the position espoused among others by John von Neumann and Eugene Wigner.[1] We may also answer, however, that it is not the observer of the event, but the observed event itself, that decides the outcome: for example, the electron chooses its own state, as asserted by R.G. Jahn and B.J. Dunne.[2] A third alternative is that the observed universe divides into as many alternative universes as there are possible observed states; a view championed by H. Everett.[3]

If none of the above is satisfactory, we can retrace our steps along the decision-tree and take another branch. The alternative branch leads beyond the horizons of the Copenhagen school along the lines maintained by Einstein: it views current quantum theory as essentially incomplete. This position was reaffirmed more recently by Dirac, who was quoted as saying, 'present quantum mechanics is not in its final form. Further changes, about as drastic as the changes which we made in passing from Bohr's orbits to quantum theory proper, will be necessary. It is very likely that in the long run Einstein will turn out to be correct.'[4]

In mid-century David Bohm explored this branch of the decision-tree in his famous, if controversial, theory of hidden variables. Since then an entire array of field theories replaced the local determinism of hidden variable theory with the interactive determinism intrinsic to the ensemble of relations in which quanta are embedded. In S-matrix, bootstrap, and quantum field theories the state of quanta is referred to the ensemble of interactions that characterize the totality of the universe.

The question we confront at this point concerns the nature of this totality. Bohm, who in the 1980s moved beyond the local determinants of hidden variable theory to the holistic determinism of the implicate order, suggested that there is another, non-temporal and non-spatial sphere where all that ever took place, and all that ever will, is given completely and permanently. This, however, is not the only alternative at this bifurcation of the decision-tree: we can also choose the UID option. If we do, we encounter a single-dimensional reality where the interaction of matter with the quantum vacuum — the fifth field of the universe — defines the quantum state.

To reach this branch of the quantum reality decision-tree, we must begin by choosing to consider the reality issue, and proceed then to pursue the issue beyond the bounds of mainstream quantum doctrine. We have to continue with a choice to view the whole-universe as determining the quantum state; and must finally select the option of adopting a single-dimensional view of reality where field/quantum interactions generate the observed phenomena.

A fresh look at the quantum paradoxes

The postulates of a unified interactive dynamics may throw fresh light on the problems that beset the investigation of the quantum world. To test this assumption, we need first to state the 'quantum ψ-field hypothesis' and then to explore it in regard to its heuristic power.

In its simplest form, the quantum ψ-field hypothesis maintains that the quantum state is defined in the interaction of quanta with the ψ-field. The observed peculiarity of quantum behaviour, including particle-wave duality and nonlocality, is due to the resulting 'ψ-effect.'

Similarly to solitons, quanta appear to observers as independent entities even though they are part of the subtending medium: the virtual-energy filled quantum vacuum. The displacement velocity of the soliton-like quantal flows is determined by the vacuum's electro-magnetic permeability: this limits velocities to the speed of light. The flows of quanta, however, create secondary wavefronts that are not limited to the value of c: scalar virtual-wave propagations diffuse quasi-instantaneously throughout matter-dense regions of the vacuum. The interference patterns produced by these propagations modify the parameters of the quantal flows, so that the motion of quanta produces effects that feed back to the quanta themselves.

Because the wavefronts created by quanta propagate faster than the quanta themselves, the feedback from the vacuum 'in-forms' the trajectories of quanta not only in regard to their own motion, but in regard to the concurrent motion of other quanta in a given region. Consequently almost the entire state of a matter-dense region is reflected in each feedback from the ψ-field.

It is, however, not the totality of the information contained in the wave-pattern fed back from the vacuum that produces the ψ-effect: each quantum is in-formed only by that waveform component of the pattern which corresponds to its own spatiotemporal trajectory. In the case of multiparticle systems, this 'in-formation' amounts to the $3n$-dimensional configuration-space of the whole system (where the wave-function of the system is represented as a configuration-space in which there are three dimensions for every particle, so that in a system of n-particles, the configuration-space of the system is $3n$-dimensional).

The above hypothesis is to account for the indeterminacy and non-locality of quantum behaviour in reference to a continuous inter-action between quanta and the substructure of the quantum vacuum. Every interference pattern in the vacuum feeds back to the correspond-ing spatiotemporal trajectory or configuration-space, obeying the principle that the inverse of the transform that translates from the spatiotemporal into the spectral domain translates back from the spectral to the spatiotemporal domain. Consequently within a matter-dense region of spacetime — where secondary secular waves propa-gate almost instantaneously — every atom, every photon, and every electron and every nucleon within every atom, is continually in-formed by the wavepattern that corresponds to its own $3n$-dimensional con-figuration-space.

We can test the above hypothesis by applying it to the already fa-mous quantum paradoxes. We can summarize them again as follows:*

— photons emitted one by .one as seemingly distinct corpuscles interfere with one another as waves;
— the measurement of the probabilistic state of one particle deter-mines ('collapses the wave-function') of the state of the other;
— electrons, when flowing through superconductors, are in fully

* The paradox of the universal constants will be considered in Chapter 12.

coherent motion, and when they orbit atomic nuclei they exclude
one another without the exchange of manifest forms of energy;
— the energy levels of carbon, helium, an isotope of beryllium and
  oxygen are improbably finely correlated;
— and the physical constants that govern the evolution of matter in
  the universe are likewise astonishingly finely coordinated.

Since Alain Aspect's testing of the EPR thought experiment in
1982, that a measurement on one particle could determine the state of
another can no longer be doubted.[5] Yet quantum theory's explanation
of the phenomenon stretches the limits of credibility. If particles are
in a state of probabilistic superposition until one of them is observed,
and if at that instant both shift into a deterministic nonsuperposed state
— and if the instruments of observation do not interconnect them in
any way — then a signal faster than light must pass between them.
Should this conclusion be rejected, one is forced either to assume that
the two particles are intrinsically inseparable as elements in a common
system of coordinates (in which case we need to discover the nature
of this system) or we must accept that the observed particle somehow
moves back in time to inform its twin of the measurement carried out
on it.[6]

The quantum ψ-field hypothesis furnishes a realistic explanation of
the system of coordinates in which the particles are integrated. A
quantum is a soliton-like wave flowing in the vacuum, and it creates
scalar wavefronts that, not breaching the threshold of particle pair-
creation, remain in a virtual state. The wavefronts travel at velocities
superior to the value of c and interact with the trajectories of individual quanta. As quantum-trajectories trigger secondary wavefronts in
the vacuum, the resulting modulated virtual energy field creates connections among individual trajectories that are quasi-instantaneous in
matter-dense regions of the field. In our simplified terminology we can
say that, through the ψ-field, each quantum is instantly 'in-formed' of
the spacetime trajectory of other quanta in its cosmic region. The
result is the observed nonlocality: a vacuum-transmitted feedback of
one particle's state to the other.

In the double-slit experiment photons, emitted as corpuscular

159

particles, interfere with each other as waves. To account for this phenomenon we do not require a pilot wave to accompany corpuscle-like particles and inform their motion. Photons, electrons, and other particles are themselves soliton-like waves propagating within a universal energy field. That field conserves, and feeds back, the spectral transform of the trajectory of the particles, giving rise to the observed wave-interference phenomenon.

The quantum ψ-field hypothesis also applies to nondynamic correlations among electrons within atomic shells. We can renounce the myth that each electron 'knows' in some way the quantum state of the others and adopts the corresponding antisymmetric wave-function; instead, we can assert that electrons are connected by a continuous, instantly signal-transmitting field. In the case of entire configurations of particles, this field conserves and feeds back the $3n$-dimensional configuration-space of the ensemble.

The phenomena of superconductivity and superfluidity can be tackled as well. As noted in Chapter 4, the vanishing of electrical resistance in a superconductor is due to the high degree of coherence among the electrons whose movement creates the current. At ordinary temperatures, the vibratory motion of the atoms in the lattices disrupts the coherence of the electron flow and produces the phenomenon of electrical resistance. But when the conductor is supercooled, the Schrödinger wave function ψ assumes one and the same form for all the electrons; consequently the current passes through the metal without resistance. Due to such coherence, supercooled helium and similar superfluids penetrate without resistance through narrow capillaries and other channels.

The ψ-field hypothesis suggests that the coherence of quanta in these phenomena is an indication that contiguous electrons in the vacuum move as flows. Given some degree of viscosity in the vacuum (suggested by the finite electrical and magnetic permeability that limits the speed of quantal propagations), particles in mutual proximity entrain each other. Hence electrons in a supercooled fluid create a single, globally coherent flow. Such global coherence cannot be limited to supercooled fluids but must characterize all flows in the vacuum. This is not apparent, however, because at all but lowest temperatures 'thermal noise' (the Brownian motion of particles within atomic lattices) perturbs the flow's coherence. Supercooling removes the thermal perturbation and exhibits the coherence that is intrinsic to all quantal flows within the vacuum.

As we remove the vacuum field from the sphere of mathematical abstraction and allow it to interact with events in the real world, we recognize a two-way interaction between this field and the motion of quanta. When thoroughly researched, a due consideration of this interaction can provide a basis for transforming the shadow-world of the quantum into a world that obeys coherent laws, the same as the macroworld of familiar phenomena.

– 10 –
New Horizons in Biology

On Earth, and possibly on some other planets, evolution produced a Chinese box-like sequence of systems-within-systems. Planetary ecologies, the largest of the terrestrial structures, consist of continental and smaller-scale ecologies which in turn consist of populations of organisms within particular physical, chemical and biological environments. The individual organisms are made up of cells, cells are made up of proteins, proteins consist of a combination of molecular groups, molecules consist of atoms, and atoms are configurations of nucleonic and electronic particles.

How is it that biological evolution could attain such levels of complexity? How does the complexity it has already attained reproduce and maintain itself? Evidently, something more than chance must be at work in nature, and the additional factor is not likely to reduce to purely genetic information. Sequences of DNA in the chromosomes of cells cannot by themselves account for the differentiation and organization of a great variety of cells under a great variety of conditions; random mutations cannot account for the leaps that hallmark the emergence of new species, and body chemistry alone cannot furnish a full explanation of the regeneration of bodily form.

François Jacob noted that what distinguishes a butterfly from a lion, a hen from a fly, or a worm from a whale is much less a difference in chemical constituents than it is in the organization and distribution of these constituents. Among vertebrates, the chemistry is the same; differences between different species cannot be traced to structure, they are a matter of regulation. Minor changes in the regulatory circuits during the development of the embryo can deeply affect the final result. A substantially different animal can be produced just by changing the growth rate of different tissues, or the time of synthesis of the various proteins. Is DNA, which is the same in each cell of the developing organism, alone responsible for such regulation?

The programs that execute the regeneration of damaged organisms pose similar problems. How is it that the loss of the lens from the newt's eye can be made good by the newt even if such loss is extremely unlikely to occur in nature? How can the artificially disaggregated cells of a marine sponge reassemble into the complete organism?

The survival of species in a changing environment creates a further set of problems. From time to time, in order to survive, species have to shift from one niche to another. It is by no means clear how they could do so. If evolution relied entirely on random mutations, mutants that happened to be adapted to a new niche would not survive long enough for the species to reach that niche: given that they are less adapted to the current niche than the non-mutant lineages, they would be eliminated by natural selection.

The discontinuous nature of evolution is yet another puzzle: its leaps defy Darwinian explanation in terms of a gradual and continuous transformation of existing species. Faced with such findings, biologists such as Brian Goodwin and Rupert Sheldrake called for biological fields; others appealed to more esoteric explanations. Alister Hardy spoke of the likely existence of psychic blueprints; Hermann Weyl postulated the presence of immaterial guiding factors such ideas, images, or building plans; and Roberto Fondi speculated that archetypes or similar spiritual factors must inform living organisms.

These and related 'problems of form' find a coherent explanation when we refer them to the biological derivative of our basic hypothesis. This suggests that living organisms interact constantly, if not always measurably, with the ψ-field. The interaction can be described as a continuous 'read-in' of the dynamically changing $3n$-dimensional configuration-space of living organisms into the ψ-field, and the equally continuous but only occasionally manifest 'read-out' of the corresponding multidimensional wave-pattern from the field.

The two-way translation process involved in this interaction unfolds as the Fourier-transform of the $3n$-dimensional configuration-space of a given organism diffuses in the vacuum in the form of a secondary wavepattern, and the reverse transform feeds back to organisms characterized by a matching configuration-space. The wavepatterns, being multidimensional, encode the configuration-space of individual organisms within the still higher-dimensional configuration-space of their environment. Thus, thanks to the multidimensionality of the wavepattern, organisms are in-formed both with their own species-specific morphological pattern, and the pattern of the milieu in which they find themselves. Periodically, this 'in-formation' produces manifest effects due to the ultrasensitivity of chaotic states.

Living systems are highly complex and inherently unstable; thus they are governed by a variety of attractors, including chaotic ones. Periodically, chaotic attractors dominate their phase-portraits. Even under relatively stable conditions, when turbulent states are not manifest, chaotic attractors could be present in a latent form, somewhat like recessive genes. However, periodically entire populations, organisms, and particular organs or organ systems enter prevalently chaotic states. Even the heart, a paradigm of stable regularity, 'dances' when it is healthy: its beat is interspersed with subtle irregularities. There is danger of malfunction only when the irregularities escape control, as, for example, in fibrillation. But when all traces of chaos vanish and the heart beats with monotonous regularity, the organism is not in good health — it is, on the contrary, close to death. Also the neural nets in the neocortex are in predominantly chaotic states. Investigators in the new field of neural nonlinear dynamics note that in many physiological areas 'the more chaos the better' — although they cannot say why.[1]

There are chaotic processes on the level of entire species and populations as well. First and foremost among them is the variability of the genotype. Although the genome is subject to a variety of external influences and its variability is not unconstrained, the mutations it produces approximate a random-variation generating system. As a result the genotype, much like the brain and the biological organism itself, is sensitive even to minute changes in its relevant environment.

Given that entire species and populations, as well as individual organisms and organ systems, find themselves periodically in significantly chaotic states, we can explore these states for evidence of information conveyed through subtle vacuum fluctuations. We look for ψ-effects first in morphological generation and regeneration in the context of ontogenesis, and then in the species-evolving processes that make up phylogenesis.

The psi-effect in ontogenesis

In higher organisms ontogenesis — the development of individual organisms — begins with the growth and development of the embryo. Embryogenesis is known to constitute a chaotic, that is in some respects ultrasensitive, system. Enormously intricate processes are involved in cell-division and differentiation, calling for detailed and accurate regulation. Such regulation cannot be mapped by stable attractors, and it is not likely to be governed alone by genetic information. Regulation is more likely to result from an interaction between DNA-coded cells and an 'epigenetic' landscape, with numerous chaotic (but not necessarily random) features.

In the context of embryogenesis, the concept of epigenetic landscape was originally intended by Waddington to refer to the complex milieu formed by genes, environment and the organization of the morphogenetic field. This milieu defines the attractors available to the embryo, enabling it to choose the chreods (dynamic pathways) required for its development. In the context of our unified interactive dynamics, the morphogenetic field includes fluctuations in the quantum vacuum. Given that the cellular growth-system is significantly chaotic — hence ultrasensitive — the information encoded at the vacuum level may account for the precise regulation of the growth and differentiation of the embryo as an interaction between DNA-coded cells, the biochemistry of the womb, and in-formation transmitted through the ψ-field. The logic of this assumption is as follows.

The cells that make up the developing embryo constitute a dynamic configuration of atoms and molecules with significantly chaotic dynamics. As all chaotic systems, this dynamically indeterminate ensemble is highly sensitive to minute variations in its internal and external parameters. Unmeasurable vacuum fluctuations reaching the system may produce measurable — in fact, decisive — effects on its evolution. We allow, then, that the embryo's ultra sensitive growth-system is in continuous interaction with the multidimensional waveform translated into the vacuum by generations of organisms of its particular species. The embryo's chaos dynamics retranslates this minute input through the inverse Fourier-transform, enlarging it into precisely biased selections of evolutionary trajectories. Thus feedback from the ψ-field can effectively guide otherwise indeterminate choices among the various pathways of cellular differentiation. It can govern the growth rate of different tissues, the time of synthesis of various proteins, and orient the interplay of the pathways of differentiation. As a result the embryo can develop consistently with the morphology of its species.

The biological ψ-field hypothesis supplements the genetic theory also in regard to the puzzle of how species can breed true. In the perspective of the hypothesis the fact that another hen evolves from the hen's egg and not a pheasant, and that a human being forms in the mother's womb and not a chimpanzee, is because the hen and the human being are in interaction with their own species-specific ψ-field pattern. The read-out of this pattern from the field guides the chaos dynamics underlying the differentiation of the fertilized cells, enabling the processes of ontogenesis to generate the species-specific morphology.

Our hypothesis can shed light on the puzzles associated with morphological regeneration as well. All organisms leave their species-specific imprints in the ψ-field, and organisms that 'match' these imprints are constantly affected by them. The results become manifest in chaotic states. Hence whenever the ultrasensitive dynamics of chaos come into play, the ψ-effect guides not only processes of generation, but also processes of regeneration. For example when, having been separated by a sieve, the cells of a marine sponge enter a chaotic state, the feedback of the species-specific $3n$-dimensional pattern of the marine sponge in its ensemble provides the subtle 'prompt' that the attractors of chaos inflate into an effective intercellular guide for the re-assembly of the complete sponge.

Basically the same dynamic is at work when the cells that make up the lens of a newt reassemble, and when in other species entire organs and limbs regenerate.

The psi-effect in phylogenesis

Interaction between organisms and the quantum vacuum cannot be limited to the read-out by organisms of their own $3n$-dimensional configuration-space; it must comprise the read-out of the higher-order configuration-space of the milieu in which given organisms are embedded. The latter can explain how species produce the massively innovative mutants that are periodically required to ensure their survival.

The topological model of the adaptive landscape outlined in Chapter 5 highlights the problem of survival in a changing environment. Populations that are well adapted to their present niche can only climb upwards on the slope of their hill; mutations that would produce a contrary movement are eliminated by natural selection. This, however, chains living populations to their existing hill — into their current niche. How species within a vanishing niche can evolve mutants that are capable of surviving in a different niche is not explained in the classical theory. Evidently, such significant evolutionary events as the emergence of new species cannot be accounted for on the assumption that macro-evolution is the sum of the set of randomly produced and naturally selected micro-evolutionary modifications.

The insight that is dawning on many biologists is that new species could not have arisen by the stepwise modification of previous species. The fossil record itself testifies that evolution has been not piecemeal and continuous but saltatory and discontinuous. It is both extremely unlikely, and entirely contrary to the evidence, that major evolutionary novelties should have resulted from the gradual accumulation of minor changes.

Because the variational possibilities are too vast and the observed leaps between species too great, random variation in the species genotype cannot explain the observed course of evolution. New species are produced by massive, systemic innovations in the geno-type, not by incremental steps exposed to natural selection.

Yet Darwinian and neo-Darwinian theories state that life has evolved by the natural selection of random mutations. The theories are based on Weismann's doctrine of the separation between soma and germline, and the assumption of randomness in the germline's varia-tions. Weismann's doctrine is usually interpreted to mean that physio-logical interactions with the environment during the lifetime of the organism do not have heritable effects — they do not produce changes in germline DNA.[2] In turn, the randomness of mutations is to ensure that genetic changes in the germline are influenced neither by the state of the phenotype nor by conditions in the environment. Adaptive evolution, Darwinists tell us, proceeds by an *a posteriori* selection of randomly produced genetic variants that happen to 'fit' particular environments. However, as Ho, among others, pointed out, these assumptions — the randomness of mutations and the insulation of genes from environmental influence — have both been falsified by empirical findings in molecular genetics.[3]

Regarding the insulation of the genome, alterations occurring in DNA both during development and in evolution turned out to be sufficiently large to have prompted molecular geneticists to coin the phrase 'the fluid genome.' DNA appears to be structurally and func-tionally as flexible as the rest of the organism. Recent findings suggest that, even if some nucleotide changes in the DNA are fortui-tous, the resulting variations in the organism are not random but occur within the context of a highly structured epigenetic system. The dynamical structure of this system shapes the variations in the germ-line of species in such a way that variations result not only from the random variability of the genome, but also from environmental factors that act on the genome's variability. Indeed, many germline changes are found to have been produced as the result of specific environ-mental perturbations; the resulting changes are then passed on to subsequent generations. Such basically Lamarckian evolution is exhibited by directed genomic changes occurring in flax and other plants following treatment with fertilizers, and by various insect species that, exposed to insecticides, produce heritable amplifications of specific genes that detoxify the chemicals and create genetic resistance to the toxins.

The ability of bacteria to mutate under particularly stressful conditions is perhaps the most striking evidence for environmentally influenced genetic variation. We have already noted that 'starving' bacteria can selectively mutate the precise strand of information in the precise genes in precisely such a way as to metabolize the food it is fed. But how bacteria could detect which information in which gene is incorrect and what is the correction necessary to rectify the condition, is beyond mainstream biological theory.

The explanation of directed mutation requires reference to the pattern that codes the bacterium's normal functioning, that is, its particular $3n$-dimensional configuration-space. If the stressed and therefore strongly chaotic bacterium is significantly in-formed with this pattern, its otherwise random mutations become subtly oriented towards producing the right mutations at the right time. This bias would not save all bacteria in a threatened population, but it would save a sufficient number of them to produce the actually noted — and statistically significant — result.[4]

Germline stability, it seems, is not due to the insulation of the genotype from the phenotype, and continued fitness is not the result of random mutations exposed to the test of natural selection. Natural selection does exist and does play a role in evolution: variations that are distinctly disadvantageous do not persist, and this contributes to the observed fit between organism and environment. But natural selection, as Saunders argued, could not even have led to the bisexual mode of reproduction: such a mechanism, while offering an obvious long-term advantage (the more rapid spread of advantageous mutations) does involve an equally obvious short-term disadvantage (the reduced average number of descendants due to males failing to produce offspring).[5] Selection in nature is a negative rather than a creative factor: it weeds out the unfit mutants, but it does not ensure that there should also be mutants that are fit.

It follows that genetic variation in a population is not a matter of selection from among fully random mutations. Instead, as Ho said, 'the dynamic structure of the epigenetic system ... organically "selects"

169

the "response" or action that is appropriate.' Organism and environment are closely interconnected, from the sociocultural level right down to genomic DNA.[6]

The factor of interconnectedness is acknowledged by some neo-Darwinian biologists. Gould, for example, defined one of the two basic proposals of punctuated equilibria theory as the attempt to construct a hierarchical concept based on the interaction of selective (and other) forces at various levels, from genes to entire population groups. Eldredge, in turn, spoke of two process hierarchies each of which, plus their interaction, produce the events and patterns of evolution. One hierarchy is concerned with the development, retention and modification of genetic information; and the other — a nested hierarchy of ecological individuals — reflects the economic organization and integration of living systems. The latter includes proteins, organisms, as well as populations, communities, and regional biotal systems.[7]

Though neo-Darwinists now contemplate and occasionally affirm the effect of environmental systems on the evolution of species, they cannot give a detailed account of it. How systems at a high level of one hierarchy, such as populations, communities and regional biotal systems, could interact with systems at a low level of another hierarchy, such as genes, organisms, and the genetic information encoded in the genome, is not explained on Darwinian premises alone.

Under pressure of such anomalies, Darwinian theory itself exhibits something like a directed mutation. In the emerging post-Darwinian biology the milieu that is relevant to the functioning of the organism and the survival of the species is extended to include the physical, the ecological, the social, and on occasion even the sociocultural, environment.[8] In the new biology the organism is, in Ho's words, an integrated whole that is 'transparent' to its environment.

Such 'transparency' cannot be accounted for in physical and biochemical terms alone; a remarkably precise and complete set of signals links the organism with the rest of its adaptive landscape. This suggests that there is a multidimensional signal-transmitting field 'informing' the organism. (A one-dimensional signal, we should note, such as morphic resonance, would only depress the variability of the genome: it would make nature, as Sheldrake remarked, a 'system of habits.') The wave interference pattern postulated in the biological ψ-field hypothesis satisfies this requirement. The multidimensionally pattern-coding and transmitting holofield is capable of in-forming the organism and its genome in regard to several levels of organization at the same time.

The signal transmitted through the ψ-field focuses the otherwise indeterminate variability of the genome on the subset of variations that can fit the species to its changing environment. It enhances the probability that massively innovative mutants should appear in a population, leading in the course of time to functional transformations in the germline of the species.

In this perspective the categorical disjunction of classical Darwinism, between a mutating population and its changing environment, is replaced with a subtle but effective chaos-based information link between organisms and their milieu. The biosphere as a whole becomes thoroughly interlinked with quasi-instantaneously propagating signals. This relates evolution in the living world to physical events in the quantum realm — and, as we shall see, also to psychological and neurophysiological phenomena in the realm of brain, mind, and consciousness.

– 11 –
Decoding the Mysteries of Mind

The question we pose in this chapter is how the human brain, a supercomplex system of matter-energy, relates to the structured virtual energy field we call ψ-field. The question is meaningful: it is known that the brain's sensitivity range is unexpectedly vast; it may extend to fluctuations in the quantum vacuum.

That the brain would be sensitive to the ψ-field, the interactive face of the quantum vacuum, follows from the postulates of our unified interactive dynamics. Quanta interact with that field and, in chaotic states, so do macroscale biological systems. It is not likely that the neural networks of the human brain, a chaotic and extremely sensitive signal-analysing system, should be an exception.

The cognitive variant of the basic ψ-field hypothesis suggests that the human brain interacts with the ψ-field in a significant and re-searchable manner. We conceive of this interaction as a 'read-out' from, and 'read-in' to, the ψ-field. The read-in — the way the neural nets of the brain produce spectral transforms in the quantum vacuum — is spontaneous and need not penetrate consciousness. The read-out, on the other hand — that is, the effect of subtle vacuum wave propagations on the brain — may produce effects that reach consciousness. These effects we shall identify as elements of 'ψ-field perception.' However, the origins of these read-outs are not necessarily identified as such: we may view them as fantasy, illusion, or strange bits of sensory experience.

In examining the above hypothesis we should keep in mind that there are as yet numerous uncharted domains of mind and conscious-ness. The phenomena that populate these domains suggest precisely the kind of space- and time-connections between brains that the ψ-field would supply. We shall proceed, therefore, to examine the

172

assumption according to which in experiences where items of consciousness transcend the ordinary bounds of space and time, the chaos-dynamics of the brain's neural networks is in-formed by signals transmitted through the ψ-field.

Sensory perception

According to the Western philosophical and scientific tradition, everything that we perceive comes to us through the senses. This, however, is not necessarily true. Even if the brain is the key organ in our traffic with the external world, that it would be limited to the flow of data transmitted by our five exteroceptive senses does not follow. While it is clear that the principal varieties of distance-perception originate either in the electromagnetic field (the visual data) or in the atmosphere (the acoustic data), this does not mean that the brain must be entirely limited to these sources of information. It need not be the case that all contents of mind and consciousness that are not conveyed by eye, ear, and the other bodily senses would be either inferences from sensory data, or products of the imagination.

The Western empiricist tradition further assumes that the entire world of consciousness is built stepwise from sensory inputs. Sensory data are inscribed as of birth on the initially clean slate of the mind. Yet the mind, as it turned out, is not a passive slate upon which sensory experience can inscribe the full story of experienced reality. It is far more active in perception than it was earlier believed. William James remarked that just as a sculptor carves a particular statue out of a slab of stone and just as different sculptors would carve different statues out of the same stone — so each human mind constructs its own image of reality out of the mass of data that reaches it throughout a lifetime. Perception, psychologists are discovering, is a creative process.

Neurophysiologists, in turn, find that the brain generates much of the information involved in ordinary perception. In fact, there is more information prefigured in the brain than there is coming to it from the exteroceptive senses. For example, nerve impulses from the eye reach the part of the thalamus known as the lateral geniculate nucleus (LGN). Here there are more than eighty input fibres from the rest of the brain for each fibre conveying signals from the eye. And the areas of the cortex where visual information is processed contain several hundred times more neurons than those that are connected with the LGN. These cortical areas are directly linked with the limbic system and have additional connections to motor areas responsible for the movement and the focusing of the eyes. Thus the brain does more than passively receive information from eyes and ears and other exteroceptors: it integrates the incoming signals with signals already circulating within, and adjusts the receptors consistently with the results of that integration.

Even the ear, long held a passive receptor of sound waves carried in the air, has turned out to be a highly sophisticated signal-interpreter. A linear and passive mechanical pattern analysis cannot explain the ear's power of discriminating among frequencies — a power that extends down to the atomic range. Indeed, the inner ear amplifies mechanical vibrations smaller than the diameter of a hydrogen atom into yes/no responses so that, transformed into basilar membrane vibration, the incredibly minute amplitude of 10^{-11}m can produce a sensation. For this reason the basilar membrane cannot be a passive vibratory system like a microphone driven by a sound signal; additional mechanisms must be present, sharpening minute excitation patterns sufficiently to be discriminated. Although the details are still not fully understood, it is believed that the ear is set in a passive resonance mode only at high signal levels, while at low levels it 'locks on' to the signal by producing a vibration of its own. As a result the mechanism of auditory perception is an interaction between signals produced by the ear and signals reaching it from the outside. Hearing is the product of the analysis of the phase coherence between the external and the internal oscillators.[1]

The eye does not create its own light waves to interact with those falling on the retina, but it, too, is an actively interpretive system with a signal discrimination capacity extending to small sets of photons. The analytical functions of the eye are all the more remarkable as the radiant energy that reaches the retina is not organized into ready-made images. The so-called optical array is literally 'broadcast': broadly scattered like radio waves in the electromagnetic spectrum. It takes a sophisticated instrument to integrate this array into coherent patterns. The visual centres of the brain perform this feat: they function like sophisticated radio or television receivers, decoding and re-encoding the broadly scattered light picked up by the eye.

The notion that the eye would act as a passive self-contained camera, taking snapshots of a flat and structureless visual field, has been demolished by J.J. Gibson in his 'ecological approach' to perception.[2] Gibson showed that the optical array is composed of the totality of the ambient light reflected from different surfaces, and in perceiving this array the activity of the whole organism is involved. Perception depends on the visual system and not just the sense of sight; it embraces the eyes, the visual cortex, and the entire nervous system. The visual system as a whole consists of moving eyes with a light-sensitive retina and neural connections, linked with a nervous system endowed with other sensory faculties as well as with a body equipped with feet and able to explore the environment from different positions.

Ongoing experiments on visual perception confirm the active interpretive function of the visual system and specify its nature. It appears that the visual system operates similarly to the optical image processing taking place in holography. Experimentalists have found that the cortical regions responsible for visual perception perform a Fourier analysis on the incoming light signals, decoding their elements into waveforms of specific frequency and amplitude. Neurons in the visual areas respond to these well-defined waves, and not only to changes in light intensity corresponding to the outlines of objects. Russell and Karen DeValois have shown repeatedly that neurons in the visual areas fire most readily when stimulated by patterns that correspond to the orientation of the Fourier-transforms of the optical array. They used checkerboards and plaids to stimulate the visual system, and found that the response of the neurons is poor when described by the orientation of lines that drift across the visual field of the subjects, whereas it is accurate when described in terms of the orientation and spatial frequency of a grating presented to them.[3]

Holographic functions are not limited to the eye; they characterize basic cognitive operations in the brain. This has been shown in the quanta field theory of the brain developed by Karl Pribram. His research indicates that the best mathematical description of certain brain processes is by analogy with what is known as a 'patch hologram.' In a patch hologram the overall receiving surface is made up of patches of individual holograms that are spatially ordered with respect to one another. The process-logic of such a system is 'holonomic' — a term that was first used by Hertz to describe linear transformations when extended into a more encompassing domain. In Pribram's use, the term covers the entire domain of wave phenomena. In his holonomic brain theory *holos* refers to the spectral (waveform) domain and *nomos* to the generalization of the wave concept in a theory.

Pribram's work shows that holograms of the type involved in brain processing are composed by converting successive sensory images into their spectral 're-presentations' and patching these micro representations into orderly spatial arrangements. These correspond to the original temporal order of the successive images. In the spectral domain information becomes both distributed over the extent of each holographic receptive field, and enfolded within it. As a result the reconstruction of sensory images can occur from any receptive patch within the total receptive field. The brain has a holistic aspect.

Much as a holographic device converts a jumble of interference lines on a holographic plate into an ordered stereoscopic image, the receptive patches in the holographic field of the visual areas of the cortex decode the distributed information in the optical array into the 3-D images of familiar things and events. Thus when we open our eyes we perceive not diffuse light patterns, but the furnishings of the everyday world.

Perception by means of a system of receptive assemblies means that in the brain an image is assembled much as it is in the eye of an insect: from composite elements transmitted by various individual receptors. Although this system operates like a mosaic, it is able to produce the perception of motion: a sense of continuous movement is conveyed when changes in the perceived patterns sweep through the receptors. Motion, as all elements of perception, is not localized: it derives from the behaviour of the whole system.

Holonomic brain theory, unlike the more mechanistic classical theories, gives a 'top-down' rather than a 'bottom up' account of the relevant brain functions. Pribram emphasises that both kinds of processes occur in the brain. There are distributed (holistic) as well as localized (structural) processes, and it is the job of the brain scientist to discern which processes are distributed and which are localized.[4]

Processes of perception are mainly distributed. What is perceived depends more on the overall pattern of the synaptic microprocesses than on the action of individual neurons or networks of neurons. Holonomic theory maintains that it does not matter which particular cortical receptors are stimulated; the system of receptors reacts as a function of the *content* of the stimulus and not of its *location*.[5]

Because information is distributed throughout wide areas of the brain and is decoded by a system of receptive assemblies, rather than assuming that the brain 'constructs' information from the input of a sensory nerve, we should suppose, as Gibson said, that the centres of the nervous system 'resonate' to this information.[6]

Psi-field perception

The thrust of current theories of sensory perception is that, when we perceive the world beyond our body, the brain performs complex analyses on signals reaching it in the form of nerve impulses. Classical empiricism maintained that all the information that reaches the brain originates in nerve impulses, and that all nerve impulses originate in the exteroceptive organs. Recent theories cannot offer such categorical restrictions. The brain turned out to be far more than a passive analyser of information conveyed by the senses: it produces much of the information on which it operates. And its interactive analysis of incoming information extends all the way to the quantum level.

The cognitive ψ-field hypothesis complements current theories of perception by asserting that, in addition to sense-organ-transmitted nerve impulses, the information processed by the brain includes signals transmitted through the ψ-field. The theoretical basis for this assertion is the interaction postulate of unified interactive dynamics: according to this postulate the relationship between the human brain and that field is a special case of the general relationship between matter-energy systems and the quantum vacuum.

Like other matter-energy systems, the brain continually interacts with the energy-field of the vacuum. The $3n$-dimensional configuration-space of neural networks in the brain is ongoingly read into the field, and the corresponding multidimensional wave-transform is read out. The read-out can produce manifest effect due to the receptivity of the cerebral hemispheres to scalar wave-propagations and the sensitivity of the chaos dynamics of the neural networks. Observers have noted that vast collections of neurons shift abruptly and simultaneously from one complex activity pattern to another in response to extremely fine variations. Within the ten billion neurons of the brain, each with an average of twenty thousand interconnections, the action potential of the smallest neuronal cluster creates a 'butterfly effect' that triggers massive gravitation towards one or another of the chaotic attractors. Chaotic attractors amplify the fluctuations and produce observable effects on the brain's information-processing structures.

Action potentials within the neural nets may be significantly affected by fluctuations in the quantum vacuum. As in the brain a staggering number of dendrites fire ions, each of which constitutes a minute electric field vector, the cerebral hemispheres act as specialized scalar interferometers. It is thus likely that the neural nets of the brain are affected by scalar waves propagating in the virtual-particle gas of the vacuum. These waves alter the initial conditions of the nets, and the alterations are amplified by the chaotic attractors governing the pertinent cerebral processes. In this way the ψ-effect becomes a factor in the brain's information processing — a factor that, under favourable (that is, non-filtered and non-repressive) circumstances penetrates to the level of consciousness.

There is now some evidence regarding the likely physiology of vacuum-triggered — that is, essentially extrasensory — signal-processing in the brain. As Pribram noted, the contents of consciousness are not exhaustively described by the 'qualia' of feelings of familiarity and novelty, which are the basis for episodic and narrative consciousness, and by the data of extra-corporeal and corporeal consciousness. There are many instances of uncommon states that produce uncommon contents, and Pribram noted that the way the brain processes these contents differs from the processing modes of ordinary perceptions and feelings. More specifically, Pribram suggests that such uncommon contents — the 'spiritual content of consciousness' — is the effect of an excitation of the frontolimbic forebrain on the dendritic microprocess characterizing the cortical receptive fields.[7]

Holonomic brain theory may shed light on the way the brain is amplifying and processing fluctuations originating in the vacuum. It appears that the gross as well as micro-organization of the cortical neurons in the extrinsic systems resembles the organization of a multiplex hologram. In ordinary perception a Gaussian envelope constrains the otherwise unlimited Fourier-transforms and yields the patchwork Gabor-transforms. (Dennis Gabor showed that the information encoded in a holographic pattern is specifically delimited. The transforms that impose a specific limitation on the Fourier infinities are the so-called Gabor-transforms.) Pribram's experiments demonstrate that the electrical excitation of frontal and limbic structures relaxes the Gaussian constraints. While during ordinary levels of excitation of the frontolimbic system, signal processing creates the usual narrative consciousness, when the excitation of this system exceeds a certain threshold, conscious experience is dominated by unconstrained holographic processes. The result is a timeless, spaceless, causeless, 'oceanic' sensation. Pribram found that in these states the nervous system becomes, as he said, 'attuned to the holographic aspects of — the holograph-like order in — the universe.'[8]

It seems that, when highly stimulated, the frontolimbic formations are the locus of the chaos-dynamics that amplify unmeasurably fine vacuum fluctuations into inputs that may penetrate to consciousness. This is at variance with the common-sense assumption that frontolimbic stimulation would *produce* the holographic variety of experience, much as fantasies and other images are produced when certain areas of the cortex are electrically stimulated. An unprejudiced analysis of the facts suggests that frontolimbic stimulation does not produce, but rather *conveys* the information embedded in the holographic variety of experience: it creates a state of heightened chaos in which the frontolimbic regions become responsive to scalar wave propagations of vacuum-fluctuation magnitude. The excitation of these regions relaxes the Gaussian constraints on the neural networks that constitute its receptive patches and produces the heightened sensitivity of a chaotic scalar interferometer.

If the above analysis is basically correct, our brain should be receiving ψ-field transmitted information on an ongoing basis. Why, then, does our consciousness not display the results? Our waking states of awareness should be permanently infused with space- and time-transcending contents. But they are not ordinarily so infused.

The absence of holographic-type experiences in our ordinary waking states may be due to a number of reasons. First of all, we should note that there are various fields and propagations in our environment that affect our nervous system without our having conscious knowledge of them. The conscious brain registers electromagnetic waves only in the relatively small visible range; above and below there is no conscious perception of the existing wave propagations. Yet modern medicine is discovering that many frequencies beyond the visible range have a pronounced effect on the nervous system, including the extremely low frequency ELF waves emitted by TV sets, computer monitors, electric transformers, and high power lines.

Thus our brain could be receiving ψ-field signals without waking consciousness registering them. This is a strong possibility in regard to ψ-field information: the linear logic of the left cortical hemisphere suppresses perceptions that are anomalous to common sense. Indeed, space- and time-transcending experiences tend to occur mainly in altered states of consciousness, where the censorship of the left hemisphere is lifted.

Second, some ψ-field signals may actually penetrate to consciousness without our recognizing them as such. The fact is that the signals analysed by the brain do not come with tags of origin attached. Wave-interference patterns that would bypass the optical sensory system and proceed directly to the cortical region where visual signals are processed would be decoded as objects in the perceptual image space regardless of whether they originated in the electromagnetic spectrum or in the sub-quantum field. Consequently we may be actually experiencing events and images that come to us through the ψ-field without our realizing their surprising origins.

We should not forget, however, that even if in ordinary states modern western consciousness ignores or suppresses information that does not have an evident sensory origin, other forms of consciousness in both East and West have been keenly aware of them. Terms used to describe such experiences range from the prosaic 'ESP' to the esoteric 'third eye,' while the subtle energies thought to be conveyed in the experiences have been described on the one hand as scientifically researchable bodily auras and bio-energies, and on the other as auric force fields, or etheric, Chi, prana and vortex energies.

Permanent memory

It is entirely plausible that the puzzling phenomena at the farther reaches of mind and consciousness should be products of the information of the brain with signals transmitted through the ψ-field. A case in point is memory.

Since the finding of surprisingly distributed memory in rats by Lashley, few neuroscientists would maintain that memory is coded by localized engrams in the brain. Lashley's own conclusion was that, without regard to particular nerve cells, behaviour must be determined by 'masses of excitation' within general fields of activity. He likened these fields to the force fields that determine form during embryogenesis: similar lines of forces, he speculated, could create patterns in cortical tissue.[9]

Lashley may have been on the right tack, but few neuroscientists have taken up his suggestion. Instead of fields of force, memory is currently referred to the formation and reformation of neuronal networks. For example, in Gerald Edelman's theory of neuronal group selection (TNGS), cognitive functions are explained in terms of structurally distinct neuronal groups that range anywhere from one hundred to one million cells. Such groups are said to respond as a unit to a signal conveyed to them. Each group responds to a specific subset of signal types; these are the subsets that generate attention-responses in mental processing. Since the signals select particular neuronal groups, the groups are in competition with each other in regard to their activation. For this reason Edelman dubs his theory 'neural Darwinism.'

The three tenets of the TNGS relate to the development of the anatomy of the brain; the selection from this anatomy during experience; and the emergence of behaviourally important functions through a process of signalling between the maps that result in the brain. The primary processes of development lead to the formation of the neuroanatomy characteristic of a given species. The developmental process is selectional, involving populations of neurons engaged in topobiological competition. A population of variant groups of neurons in a given brain region, comprising neural networks, constitutes what Edelman calls the *primary repertoire*. The genetic code, rather than providing specific instructions for this repertoire, imposes a set of constraints on the process of its selection.

According to Edelman, there is yet another mechanism of selection that does not generally involve an alteration of anatomical patterns: it is one based on a selective strengthening or weakening of synaptic connections during behaviour. This additional selection process produces a set of variant functional circuits called the *secondary repertoire*. The primary and secondary repertoires form maps in the brain, connected by massively parallel and reciprocal connections. Correlation and coordination of the selection events are achieved by re-entrant signaling and the strengthening of interconnections between the maps within a given segment of time.[10]

It appears, then, that mental development involves the selection of pre-existing neuronal groups by incoming signals, and the amalgamation of the groups into higher order configurations. The mechanism of selection and group constitution is to explain cognitive capacity in the brain, including the discrimination of stimuli, the formation of cognitive categories, and self-recognition.

The TNGS provides a convincing account of the selective modification of fixed behavioural patterns, including the cognitive correlates of the modified behaviours. It is less convincing when it comes to accounting for some forms of memory. For Edelman memory, whatever form it takes, is the ability to repeat a performance. Alterations in the synaptic strength of neuronal groups in a global mapping provide the biochemical basis of memory; the phenomenon is a population property created in the context of continual dynamic changes in the synaptic populations. Evidently, in such a system memory cannot issue in a stereotypic form of recall: recall must change under the influence of the continually changing context. Memory, after all, is the result of a process of continual recategorization, as perceptual categories are altered by the ongoing behaviour of the animal.[11]

It is not accidental that Edelman cites animals in connection with his account of memory: the TNGS offers a good fit in regard to some varieties of animal memory. There, what is often called 'genetic memory' constitutes the primary repertoire and, as in higher animals this is not sufficient to ensure survival, the rigidities of the behavioural routines to which it gives rise are supplemented by learned behaviours. The latter may well obtain due to re-transcriptions in the neural networks of the animal brain, i.e., through the formation of a secondary repertoire. For example, birds such as tits hunt insects randomly if various species abound in their milieu (instructed only by their genetic memory), but if one insect species is present in larger numbers than the others, they begin to hunt that species preferentially (using the neural memory of the secondary repertoire). As Beritashvili's experiments show, even fish 'recall' the location of the box where they were fed, though such memory lasts less than ten seconds. The corresponding memory in frogs and turtles comes to several minutes, in dogs to several hours, and in baboons to about six weeks.

But is memory in humans restricted to a temporary modification of performance in light of synaptic retranscription? Edelman, who recognizes that humans have developed a much richer set of psychological functions than animals, admits that these have altered the meaning of what it is to have a memory, but claims nevertheless that no new principles beyond selection and re-entry are necessary to gain new memory functions; new orderings of connections in the brain are all that is needed.[12] This claim appears exaggerated. While some forms of memory in humans could result from continual dynamic changes in synaptic populations within global mappings — for example, short-term behaviour-modifying memory — human memory is not limited to these forms: it also includes the vivid and often surprisingly accurate recall of a complex sequence of events with a vast series of associated images. These events and images could have been experienced many years ago; and they need not have any immediate behavioural correlates.

The type of memory in view of which TNGS, as other synaptic-change-based theories, ultimately breaks down is that in which events and images experienced in the distant past reappear vividly, accurately, and in detail. As noted in Chapter 6, besides their occasional occurrence in everyday life, such recall is a standard feature of NDEs (near-death experiences). Recall at the portals of death is extraordinarily clear and running at high speed; hence it is unlikely to be — as has also been suggested — a by-product of progressively dissolving synapses in decaying brain tissue. Moreover recall of an equally vivid and remarkable kind can be systematically generated in the context of regression psychotherapy.

NDE-researcher David Lorimer wrote that the only picture within which total 'life-review' experiences make sense is one of an 'interconnected web of creation, a holographic mesh in which the parts are related to the Whole and through the Whole to each other by empathetic resonance.' This must be the sort of Whole, Lorimer added, in which we and the rest of creation have our being; a consciousness-field in which we are interdependent strands.[13] This explanation, while it may be on the right tack, is far removed from the mathematical precision with which neuronal network theories are stated.

Fortunately, the choice of explanation is not limited to precise but inadequate, and adequate but vague formulations. There is an alternative to neural network theories and to metaphysical insights: it is the thesis that the events, images, and other items recalled in long-term memory are not stored *in* the brain; they are only *accessed* by the brain. In this view long-term, quasi-permanent memory is not located physically in the cerebral networks; the latter act only as the trans-ducer of signals received from an extrasomatic memory store.

The assumption of cerebral access to, rather than actual storage of, long-term and permanent memories follows from the cognitive ψ-field hypothesis. Memory is attributed here to an extrasomatic information storage medium: the ψ-field. All that goes on in the brain, just as all that goes on in the body and in every matter-energy system in space and time, is recorded in this field — the multidimensional wave interference patterns that accumulate there encode the complete history of matter in space and time. The record is a Fourier- (more exactly, a Gabor-) transform of the three-dimensional configuration-space of quanta, and of the $3n$-dimensional configuration-space of macroscale systems.

The neural networks of the brain are themselves complex configura-tions of quanta, and they leave their multidimensional wave-transforms in the substructure of the quantum vacuum. The thus created wave-fronts interfere with one another and become superposed in multiple dimensions. They are available for re-translation by systems that have the matching $3n$-dimensional configuration-space. Hence for these systems the ψ-field constitutes a selectively accessible extrasomatic memory bank. Rather than in the physical confines of the brain, it is in this extended memory bank that a lifetime's experiences are stored, and it is from here that they can be selectively retrieved.

Transpersonal memory

In most cases the ψ-field read-out of individuals selects for retrieval their own experiences. There are some remarkable cases of recall, however, where the read-out does not convey the individual's own experiences, but the experiences of another person. These are instances of transpersonal recall. Classical theories of perception are obliged to dismiss them as illusion, yet some among them, as we have seen in Chapter 6, are surprisingly well documented. The cognitive ψ-field hypothesis acknowledges their reality and offers an explanation.

We interpret transpersonal memory as the expansion of the 'band-width' of the brain's ψ-field receptivity. As already remarked, the interaction of the brain with the field presupposes Gabor-transforms that limit the infinite Fourier-transforms so as to produce a precise match between the finite spatiotemporal configuration of the individual's cerebral networks and the corresponding waveform. The bandwidth to which this transform is tuned cannot be entirely limited to the given organism, however; if it were, even personal recall could not function for long. The brain ages, like the rest of the body, and its typical configuration of neuronal structures undergoes subtle alterations. High selectivity in the tuning of the transforms would restrict read-back to the span of a few months, if not days.

If the possibility of long-term recall is to be accounted for, we must assume that the operative transforms have a non-negligible bandwidth. They must be tuned to a range of multidimensional waveforms, rather than to highly specific frequencies. In certain states, the brain is unlikely to distinguish between waveforms within a range of adjacent frequencies. When two wave interference-patterns fall within the tolerance-range of the transforms, the brain decodes both of them equally. This is the case even if one of the patterns codes the $3n$-dimensional configuration-space of another person's cerebral networks. In that event the individual recalls the other person's experiences as if they were his or her own.

In the human brain, altered states of consciousness (ASCs) enlarge the band-width of the Gabor-transforms. In such states all ψ-field signals that fall within the enlarged band-width of the transforms are processed indiscriminately. Evidence for this comes from scores of accounts of transpersonal recall in altered states. It is reinforced by recent experiments with EEG tests. These show that in altered states the brain waves of different individuals become remarkably synchronized. Experiments carried out in Italy with the 'brain holo-tester' — a device designed to measure levels of synchronization in EEG patterns between the left and right hemisphere of one person, as well as hemispheric synchronization between different persons — indicate that in deep meditation the synchronization of the left and right hemispheres increases dramatically. The tests also show that when two persons meditate together, their respective EEG patterns become

186

highly synchronized, although no sensory signal is passing between them[14] (see Figure 9).

When the two cerebral hemispheres work together, the linear, propositional and highly focused perceptions of left-hemisphere-dominated waking consciousness no longer dominate the mind. The Gestalt-oriented, nonverbal perceptions typical of the right hemisphere are not repressed but can penetrate to consciousness. On occasion they include transpersonal experiences — the retrieval of memories encoded by an analogously working brain.

The psychological and physiological features of altered states correlate with the introspective reports of persons who have mastered the art of entering such states. Yogis and other adepts at meditative techniques can reach a state of deep meditation in a matter of minutes, if not seconds. When emerging from such states they report that their consciousness was hallmarked by a great, almost transcendent tranquillity, a full separation from the worries and passions that dominate the normal wakeful state. They enter into the meditative state as if entering clear and calm water, leaving behind the turbulence of the everyday world.

The metaphor of water and turbulence is significant: it reflects the interaction of matter and vacuum in the context of human consciousness. In the pertinent metaphorical vein, we can say that, as the concerns of the everyday world are suspended, the winds that ruffle the waters of consciousness in ordinary perception die down. The brain is left with its own chaos dynamics. In this ultrasensitive state the play of the finest ripples can be registered on the calm surface of the conscious mind. The minute fluctuations that constitute the signals of the ψ-field can be registered as well.

We can now essay an explanation of several puzzling instances of transpersonal recall. These include:

— telepathic communication between individuals;
— pastlife recollections;
— natural healing; and
— simultaneous insights among individuals as well as between cultures.

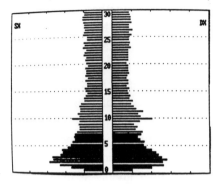 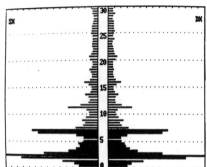

Left: Low level of left and right hemispheric synchronization in the normal waking state, with non-harmonic patterns in the EEG waves.

(Correlation value 5.9%).

Right: High level of synchronization between the left and right hemispheres in a state of deep meditation. The brain produces harmonic EEG waves, precisely repeating in the two hemispheres.
(Correlation value 99.2%).

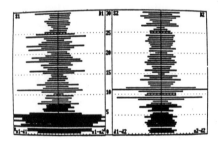 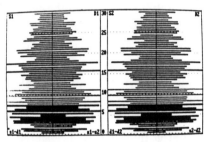

Left: Low level of synchronization between the left and right hemispheres of two simultaneously measured test subjects in the normal waking state.

Right: The quasi-identical fourfold pattern exhibited by two simultaneously measured individuals in deep meditative states, with no sensory clues passing between them.

Figure 9. Courtesy Cyber Researches, Milan, Italy.

Telepathic communication

As we have seen, the extrasensory transference of thoughts, images, emotions, intuitions and even of physical sensations, occurs most readily when sender and receiver are genetically related (truly striking instances are furnished by identical twins); when they are bound by close emotional ties (such as mothers and sons, spouses or lovers); or when they are in an altered state of consciousness (as in most controlled experiments). A close matching of the relevant brain states seems to be a precondition of effective transference. Matching states are either genetically 'hard-wired,' or they are induced by close emotional ties, empathy, or personal crises and trauma. Altered states enhance receptivity. Under such conditions the brain of the receiver gains access to some aspect of the cognitive, emotive, or intuitive content of the brain of the sender.

Pastlife recollections

In most cases also the recall of what appears to the subject as one or more past lives requires some altered state of consciousness. In regression therapy this state is induced by the therapist in guiding the patient to a deeply relaxed condition. Entering this condition the patient fails to distinguish between the recall of his or her own experiences and the experiences of other persons. Since the recall comes about due to a match between the dominant brain-state of the patient and that of the other person (or persons) whose experiences the patient recalls, the images and events that surface in the patient's consciousness have some relevance to his or her own psychological condition. Perceiving the images and events as if they were memories of lived experiences, the patient experiences what therapists call a 'karmic release.'

Pastlife experiences in young children are due to somewhat different physiological conditions. The neural networks of children are permanently in the alpha-state typical of adult ASCs: until the age of five or six years, the beta waves of normal waking consciousness are not present in the brain. Immature brains are not always able to discriminate the signals that convey the experiences of a brief lifetime from sufficiently isomorphic signals that convey the experiences of other persons. Thus children may become aware of images and impressions that are not traces of their own experiences, but traces of the experiences of people whose brain states happen to match theirs.

Consequently the images and impressions that surface at times in the consciousness of young children do not necessarily imply — as Stevenson suggests — that they have reincarnated a previously living person.[15] Rather than reincarnating the mind of someone else — or at least some traits of another individual's personality — the child's as yet fuzzily operating brain reads out from the ψ-field images and behaviours that match his or her own dispositions. The read-outs reinforce the child's dispositions and create the odd behaviours noted among others by Stevenson.

Natural healing

Two (or more) individuals in meditative states can establish direct brain-to-brain contact, as demonstrated by the phase-locking of their EEG patterns in Figure 9. On occasion such interlocking brain functions can produce telepathic phenomena, including the transference of thoughts or images. The transference can assume an active dimension; as Targ and Puthoff have shown, one of the communicating individuals can 'will' the transference of a specific thought or image. Krippner's experiments in dream telepathy confirm that willed transference can produce statistically significant results.

The read-out of another person's (willed or unwilled) experiences can create actual behaviour modification; here the past-life recollecting children investigated by Stevenson are a case in point. We can now add that also organic effects seem capable of being induced by the interlocking of two or more brain activity patterns. Such effects turn out to be subject to purposeful manipulation. The sender — a sensitive or a healer — may concentrate on a receiver (his or her patient) and 'will' an organic process.

Healers may will a non-specific healing process — they may just 'send energy' or, in the case of Byrd's experiments (cited in Chapter 6), simply 'pray for recovery.' Accomplished healers can also will specific organic processes, such as stabilizing a heart beat or enhancing blood flow to an organ. Many healers can achieve their results independently of the distance that separates them from their patients, and the results may surface staggered in time. The process calls for a space- and time-connecting field to transmit the effects, and this corresponds to the ψ-field postulate of unified interactive dynamics.

Simultaneous insights

The cognitive ψ-field hypothesis provides an analogous interpretation of the sharing of basic insights and intuitions within (and between) cultures. The interpretation comes close to Jung's original concept of archetypes and the collective unconscious. Archetypes, said Jung, arise from a vast, limitless unconscious process shared by all humanity, emerging from the accumulated experience of thousands of years of shared history. They are due to the gradual modification of genetic structure in individuals, allowing personal experience to incorporate ever more elements of the collective unconscious.

Although later in life Jung gave up trying to give a physiological explanation of archetypes and the collective unconscious (the mechanistic brain science of his time was not ready to acknowledge phenomena of synchronization between different people's brain-processes), in the commentary to *The Secret of the Golden Flower* he did write that 'the collective unconscious is simply the psychic expression of the identity of brain structure irrespective of all racial differences.'[16] Shortly before his death in 1961, Jung ventured even further. 'We might have to give up thinking in terms of space and time when we deal with the reality of archetypes,' he wrote in a letter published in the same year in German. 'It could be that the psyche is an unextended intensity, not a body moving in time. One could assume that the psyche arises gradually from the smallest extension to an infinite intensity, and thus robs bodies of their reality when the psychic intensity transcends the speed of light. Our brain might be the place of transformation, where the relatively infinite tensions or intensities of the psyche are tuned down to perceptible frequencies and extensions. But in itself,' Jung added, 'the psyche would have no dimension in space and time at all.'[17] Consequently the psyche as the collective archetypal realm, Marie-Louise von Franz commented, is eternal and

191

everywhere. When something that touches it happens at one point, it has happened at all points simultaneously.[18]

When we add the here discussed concepts of the enlargement of the band-width of the brain's Gabor-transforms in altered states, and of cerebral ultrasensitivity conferred by chaotic attractors, Jung's intuitive insight becomes clothed in the tangible substance of a theory that relates archetypes and the collective unconscious to the relationship between the living brain and the universe's basic energy field. This non-spatiotemporal field is the encoder and transmitter of all events in spacetime, including the neural network dynamics that underlie cognitive processes in human brains.

– 12 –
Creativity in the Cosmos

We have now explored the postulates of unified interactive dynamics in regard to the principal domains of scientific interest. Our explorations have taken us to the world of the quanta, the physical basis of the known universe, to the sphere of life as we know it here on Earth, and to the realm of mind and consciousness, known through neurophysiology and psychology as well as by lived experience. We can now enter the final domain of these initial explorations: that of the cosmos as a whole.

Cosmology is a physical science, yet it is one that must provide reasons for the possibility of other sciences. A cosmology that does not explain the conditions under which nature evolves beyond the sphere of physics is distinctly flawed: sound cosmological theories must show how matter configures into ever more complex and ordered systems in space and time. Cosmology, in this sense, is the mother of all natural sciences — though as a rule few cosmologists take this role to heart.

When framed in the wider context, mainstream cosmology has a problem. True, it acknowledges that matter in the universe configures into more and more complex and ordered systems, but it can only trace the evolution of such systems to random processes, oriented towards disorder.

The mainstream account goes something like this. As irreversible processes occur in the universe, the overall entropy of the system must increase. Local entropy decrease can only occur at the expense of entropy increase elsewhere within the system. Reversals of the sign of entropy change come about because the expansion of the inhomogeneous universe prevents matter from assuming an equilibrium distribution all at once. Dispersed matter searches haphazardly for equilibrium, with particles colliding and forming more complex particles and clumps of particles. The resulting configurations collide further and produce friction, slowing the entropy-oriented process even more. In this view life is a random by-product of a chance-driven and disorder-oriented process.

The above account, though it overcomes the problem of incompatibility between the second law of thermodynamics and the local build-up of complexity, is far from satisfactory. For one thing, it conflicts with our deepest intuitions and contradicts the overall tenor of our experience. More importantly, it is not able to explain the consistent orders that arise in nature; a chance-driven process, as we have indicated, can produce only divergence and not convergence. There must be more to the universe than the mechanical running down of a closed system. If cosmology is to fulfil its role as the mother of the natural sciences, it must give a better account of the emergence of order and complexity in the cosmos.

A random process in a randomly constituted universe could perhaps produce atoms, molecules and crystals, but it is unlikely to achieve the higher rungs of complexity; the fine-tuning of the universal constants required for this process, is statistically improbable. Complex systems such as those required for life, could only evolve because the constants have precisely the values they do have. And they must have had these improbably precisely set and coordinated values already at time zero, when the process got under way. How could this be explained?

Mere coincidence will not do: serendipity of this magnitude strains credibility. Could it be that serendipity was moderated by the law of large numbers — that our universe is but one among myriad universes, with its remarkable characteristics due to the fact that in a large assembly even improbable configurations become probable? Or is it that a single universe has split up into many domains during its evolution, and we live in, and observe, but one of these otherwise improbable domains, all others having been pushed beyond our horizon? And if none of this is the case, would the anthropic principle provide the answer? Are the constants the way they are because this is what could lead to a universe in which conscious beings observe them?

All these hypotheses have been advanced, but none is satisfactory.[1]

Even when mitigated by the law of large numbers, chance is not the answer. And the last resort, which is always to assume preconceived design by a cosmic intelligence, though advocated by an occasional cosmologist, is not acceptable to the scientific mentality: preconceived ends are just as objectionable to science as unrestrained serendipity.

Perhaps a hypothesis derived from the IUD postulates could shed light on this mystery. In order to explore this possibility, we should frame our analysis in the proper context: the context furnished by the known scenarios of cosmic evolution. Hence before exploring the cosmological specification of the basic ψ-field hypothesis, we shall review the main features of currently held cosmologies.

The big bang scenario

A number of cosmologies vie today for acceptance, yet for the most part they are specific variants on a standard cosmological scenario popularly known as the big bang theory. This theory was widely acclaimed when, in April of 1992, the computer analysis of about 300 million observations made over the course of the year by NASA's Cosmic Background Explorer Satellite (COBE) showed that variations in cosmic background radiation are genuine fluctuations deriving from the big bang, rather than distortions caused by radiation from astronomical bodies. The variations date back some 15 billion years to a time when the universe was about 300,000 years old. They show huge clouds of matter, the precursors of galaxies. The results agree with the standard scenario inasmuch as the variations appear to be due to minute fluctuations in the dispersion of the cosmic fireball less than one trillionth of a second after time zero.

The big bang scenario maintains that the evolution of the universe began with an explosive instability consisting of two phase-changes in rapid sequence. The first led to the rapid inflation of a Minkowski quantum vacuum, and the second transformed the inflationary universe into the more orderly expansion of the Robertson-Walker universe. Though the latter process has been under way ever since, a further phase-change took place when between fifty thousand and one million years had elapsed: in the expanding and cooling universe, matter uncoupled from radiation. When temperature dropped to 3000°K, space became transparent and leptons and hadrons established themselves as the first elements of the matter-component of the universe. Henceforth the history of this component marked the history of the universe as we now know it (see Figure 10). For the past fifteen billion years, this history has been constructive. On the astronomical level leptons and hadrons condensed into stars and stellar systems, while on the microlevel they formed atoms, molecules and crystals, and on occasion still more fanciful configurations.

Elapsed time from the beginning of the universe (or cycle of the universe)	Average temperature (°K)	Average density (g/cm$^{3)}$)	Dominant product
< 10^{-24}	> 10^{20}	> 10^{50}	—
10^{-24} – 10^{-3}	10^{15}	10^{30}	hadrons
10^{-3} – 100 sec	10^{10}	10^{10}	leptons
100 sec – 10^6 years	10^4	10^{-10}	neutral atoms
10^6 – 10^9 years	300	10^{-20}	galaxies
> 10^9 years	≈ 2.7	≈10^{-29}	stars, planets

Figure 10. The progressive build-up of the micro- and macro-structures of the universe in reference to time, temperature and radiation/matter density, from the period of inflation to the present.
(Adapted from Chaisson, Universe: an Evolutionary Approach to Astronomy, *Prentice Hall, Englewood Cliffs, 1988.)*

At the extremely high temperatures that prevailed at the very early universe there was only superheated plasma; atoms did not exist, since thermal noise had prevented electrons from associating with nuclei. But as the plasma cooled, electrons began to circulate around nuclei and a gas of atoms emerged. At that time galaxies condensed out of the plasma, and stars condensed within the galaxies. With further cooling various atoms configured into molecules. Still further cooling allowed the formation of complex molecules, transforming matter from the gaseous into the liquid, and then into the solid crystalline form. On certain planets, molecular and crystalline structures have further configured into protobionts and, provided thermal and chemical conditions proved to be favourable, could have opened the door to the emergence of the still higher-order configurations that we associate with the phenomena of life.

But in the universe as a whole, the epoch of constructive development cannot continue indefinitely: at a given time the evolution of matter must reverse into devolution. The reversal will come at different times in different places, but when it comes, it will be irreversible. In the end, all matter in the cosmos will degrade and disappear. According to current estimates, about 10^{12} (one trillion) years from now, no more stars will form. At that time existing stars will have converted their hydrogen into helium, the main fuel of the white dwarf state. Subsequently also helium will be exhausted, and galaxies will assume a reddish tint. Then, as their stars cool further, they will fade from sight altogether.

As energy is lost in galaxies through gravitational radiation, individual stars will move closer together. The chance of collision among them will increase, and the collisions that will occur will precipitate some stars towards the centre of their galaxies and expel others into extragalactic space. As a result, the galaxies themselves will diminish in size. In the same way galactic clusters will shrink, and ultimately both galaxies and galactic clusters will implode into black holes.

At the time horizon of 10^{34} years, matter in the cosmos will have been reduced to radiation, positronium (pairs of positrons and electrons), and compacted nuclei in black holes. Black holes themselves will decay in a process described by Hawking as 'evaporation.' A black hole resulting from the collapse of a galaxy will evaporate in some 10^{99} years, and a giant black hole containing the mass of a galactic supercluster will vanish in 10^{117} years. Beyond this time horizon the cosmos will contain matter-particles only in the form of positronium, neutrinos, and gamma-ray photons.

The exact timing of matter's exit in the universe will depend on whether or not protons decay. If they do, protons, and the products left over from the decay of other baryons, will vanish at the time horizon of 10^{117} years. If protons do *not* decay, this horizon will expand to 10^{122} years. At that time even non-decaying protons will evaporate in black holes formed by collapsing galaxies and galactic clusters.

In the standard scenario the fate of matter in spacetime will also seal the fate of life. The complex configurations required for the phenomena of life will vanish much before matter itself decays. The conditions responsible for this catastrophe have more to do with the evolution of the local suns of life-bearing planets than with the ultimate fate of the microparticles. Before background radiation could heat up to levels intolerable for all conceivable forms of life, or cool to equally impossible subfreezing temperatures, the suns of life-supporting planets will have reached the red giant stage. When they do, they will have expanded and engulfed all their life-bearing planets (only the most distant planets will have escaped this fate, but they will have been too cool to have supported life).

In a 'closed universe' — one that ultimately collapses back on itself — background radiation will increase gradually but inexorably. The wavelength of radiation will contract from the microwave region into the region of radio waves, and then into the infrared spectrum. When it reaches the visible spectrum all of space will be lit with an intense light. At that time life-bearing planets will be vaporized, along with all other celestial bodies.

In an 'open universe' — a universe that expands indefinitely — life will vanish because of cold rather than heat. Since galaxies will continue to move outwards, many active stars will be able to complete their natural life cycles before gravitational clumping would move them close enough together to create a serious risk of collisions. But as stars exhaust their nuclear fuel, their energy output will diminish. They will then either expand to the red giant stage, swallowing up their inner planets, or settle into lower luminosity levels on the way to becoming white dwarfs or neutron stars. At lower energy levels they will no longer be capable of sustaining whatever life may have evolved on some of their planets.

While the standard scenario has three equiprobable variants — a closed universe, collapsing back on itself; an open universe, expanding infinitely outwards; and a flat universe precisely balanced between implosion and expansion — as far as the ultimate fate of matter (and hence of life) is concerned, there is hardly any difference. In either case, the baryon number, which was long believed to have been fixed in the first fractions of a second following the big bang, will be surrendered. Protons and neutrons will either become supercompacted in the unitary embrace of the big crunch, or decay in the separate crunches of the last black holes.

Multicyclic scenarios

From the standpoint of matter, and of matter-based life, the standard scenario of cosmic evolution is quite dismal. However, other cosmologies have appeared in recent years, including some that hold distinct promise of brightening up the destiny of matter and life in the universe.

Physicists seek alternative scenarios because, apart from the catastrophic end it implies, the big bang scenario, though widely acclaimed, still faces some unsolved problems. On the theoretical plane, the big bang calls for the existence of a singularity at the origins of the universe. A singularity, however, is a region of spacetime in which the laws of physics break down. Such conditions are forbidden in Einstein's theory of gravitation: the gravitational laws do not hold when time is zero and the universe is of infinitely small size. Yet not only the big bang, also the big crunch requires exceptional conditions; both are singularities in relativistic spacetime.

On the empirical level, several observational anomalies remain, despite the previously noted confirmation by COBE of the explosive instability-based origins of the universe. It appears that the inhomogeneities in the background radiation observed by COBE are surprisingly small; and if these are the remnants of fluctuations that occurred in the density of the radiation that followed the big bang, then there is a question whether the fluctuations could have created sufficient graininess in the distribution of matter to have allowed gravitation to subsequently 'clump together' the presently observed galactic structures.

199

The gravitational clumping implied by observations of galactic structures suggests either that large-scale gravitation is stronger than presently estimated (perhaps of the order of $1/r$ rather than $1/r^2$, where r is the radius of a galactic mass), or that there is far more matter in the universe than is available for observation. In the latter event the total optically invisible 'cold dark matter' (CDM) component may be between 90 and 99 percent of the universe's total matter content. Physicists have produced entire strings of CDM models, including heavy neutrinos, Higgsinos, gravitinos, axions, photinos, and WIMPs (weakly interacting massive particles), but none is free of difficulties.

A still more fundamental difficulty is the existence of giant structures deep in cosmic space. As four highly focused (so-called 'pencil-beam') surveys show, there are extremely large-scale structures out at distances over a billion parsecs, with a succession of features at about 150-million parsec intervals. Each of these is similar to the nearest structure known as the 'Great Wall,' itself stretching across the sky for over 153.37 parsecs (500 million light years). Such giant structures are incompatible with galaxy formation mechanisms in the big bang scenario: they imply a far greater age for the universe, in some estimations more than 63 billion years.[2]

It is by no means clear, then, whether all structures currently in existence originated in an explosive instability 15 billion years ago. Astronomical observations, no matter how complete and precise, can never reach back to a timehorizon of less than 300 million years after the period of inflation: prior to that time the universe was too dense to have allowed any radiation (and hence light) to escape. Thus while it is no longer reasonable to question the occurrence of a big bang some 15 billion years in the past, it is still open to question whether this was a unique event in the history of the universe, or just one in a series of prior (and perhaps also subsequent) 'bangs.'

Of the multiple alternative scenarios, one variety postulates that the universe never started from a condition of singularity and will never reach it. If quantum theory applies to the origins of the universe, the initial 'quantum universe' must have had a non-zero radius. Making use of somewhat speculative assumptions, cosmologists show that if such a quantum universe turns out to be closed, it will not come to a final end in the big crunch but reach a state of maximum compaction from which another 'Bang' could liberate it. A closed quantum universe would go from an explosive instability through a full cycle of expansion, back to an imploding instability — and then on to the next instability. The closure of this universe would apply only to its individual cycles; in itself, the universe would have neither a beginning nor an end.

Another scenario suggests that successive cycles occur in an open, rather than in a closed, universe. This scenario takes the interaction of the quantum vacuum and matter as the basic factor. Prigogine, Geheniau, Gunzig and Nardone give a mathematical demonstration that in this interaction a possibly infinite series of cosmic cycles can be generated.[3] They show that it is a feedback effect of gravitation that procures the energy required for virtual particles to establish themselves in spacetime. Gravitation plays an unsuspected role in spacetime: not only does it drive the condensation of galactic structure, it is also at the root of the prior synthesis of matter.

The Prigogine-Geheniau-Gunzig-Nardone cosmology suggests that a gravitational mode carrying negative energy is linked with the universe's large-scale spacetime curvature. (Negative energy is the energy required to lift a body away from the direction of its gravitational pull.) The large-scale geometry of spacetime creates a reservoir of negative energy from which gravitating matter extracts positive energy, and in the unstable vacuum the extracted energy is transferred to virtual particles. Thus energetic conditions are created for the synthesis of matter particles.

As a result there is a constant and balanced interaction between matter in the large-scale structures of the universe and the quantum vacuum. In each cycle particles of matter are created in the vacuum through the energy generated by the particles that were synthesized in the previous cycle. The positive energy going into the synthesis of matter constantly and precisely compensates the negative energy generated by the curvature of spacetime owing to the gravitational attraction of pre-existing matter.

New cycles arise because expanding galaxies 'dilute' the vacuum, and as dilution reaches a critical value it creates a vacuum instability.

At that point the vacuum transits into the inflationary condition, and that phase in turn transits to the more sedate expansionary mode of the currently observed universe. The phase-transitions are governed by the creation and evaporation of 'mini' black holes of the order of 50 times Planck mass m (where m equals 2.17671×10^{-5} grams), according to the process described by Hawking. The evaporation time of these 'mini' black holes turns out to be 10^{-37} second: exactly the time required for the inflationary-phase by independently formulated theories.

Consequently the genesis of each cycle involves three stages separated by two phase-transitions. The first stage is the creation of an unstable Minkowski vacuum by the negative-energy feedback from the curvature of spacetime due to the universe's large-scale structures. The instability creates the phase transition to the inflation typical of the De Sitter universe: the second stage. During the inflationary stage the 'mini' black holes created in the first phase-transition evaporate, producing a supercooling effect which, as the second phase-transition, drives the De Sitter universe into the third stage: the spatially homogeneous, isotropic and geometrically expanding Robertson-Walker universe.

The Prigogine-Geheniau *et al.* cosmology is self-consistent. Its phase transitions depend directly on the values of three constants: the speed of light c, Planck's quantum constant h, and the gravitational constant G.

This 'self-consistent non-big-bang cosmology' outlines a perpetual mill for the creation of particles. The more matter-particles have been generated, the more negative energy is produced, transferred as positive energy to the synthesis of still more particles. Because the vacuum is unstable in the presence of gravitational interaction, matter and vacuum form a self-generating feedback loop. The critical matter-triggered instability causes the vacuum to transit to the inflationary mode, and that mode marks the beginning of another era of matter synthesis. Thus the universe we observe was not created out of an unexamined pre-existing vacuum, but arose as a new cycle within an already existing cosmic background.

The self-referential scenario

Having reviewed the principal varieties of cosmic evolutionary scenario, we can return to the problem posed in the beginning of this chapter. How is it that the values of the universal constants were precisely tuned to the evolution of life at a time when life in the cosmos could not yet have evolved?

The hypothesis we derive from the postulates of unified interactive dynamics suggests that the interaction of quantum vacuum and matter in-forms the universal constants, just as it in-forms the configuration of quantal matter itself. In other words, the ψ-effect is manifest not only in the evolution of matter-energy systems, but also in the evolution of the physical parameters that are the precondition of this evolution.

In order to scrutinize this hypothesis, let us restate the main thrust of the issues to which it is to respond. The facts to account for are these:

— The expansion rate of the very early universe was precise in all directions at a rate of better than one part in $10^{40.}$ (Had it been less precise, cosmic background radiation would not be as uniform as it is.)

— The force of gravitation is precisely of such magnitude that stars can form and exist long enough to generate sufficient energy for life to evolve on suitable planets.

— The mass of the neutrinos, if not actually zero, is small enough to have prevented the universe from collapsing soon after the big bang due to excessive gravitational pull.

— The value of the strong nuclear force is precisely such that hydrogen can transmute into helium and then into carbon and all the other elements indispensable to life. (If the value of that force were but two percent higher, all hydrogen in spacetime would have burned up before transmuting into heavier elements.)

— The weak nuclear force has the exact value to allow atoms to be expelled in supernovae (and thus be available in next generation stars for building into the more complex elements that form the basis of life).

— The weak nuclear force also has precisely the value with respect to gravity that makes hydrogen rather than helium the dominant element in the cosmos. (Had helium been the dominant element, stars would not have existed long enough for life to have evolved on their planets and, for lack of hydrogen — the principal element of water — life as we know it could not have evolved.)

We see, then, that the fine-tuning of the universal constants concerns the values associated with the basic forces and fields of interaction, as well as with the mass and with the distribution of the matter in cosmic space. These values, masses and distributions are precisely those that permit the evolution of increasingly complex matter-energy systems. Why this should be so cannot be understood by the standard big bang scenario: a universe limited to a single cycle (from big bang either to dispersion in infinite space, or to super-compaction in the big crunch) cannot tune its constants at its own beginning. But a series of self-referential cosmic cycles can: such a universe exhibits a learning curve.

In order to spell out the main features of the multi-cyclic learning scenario, we take the basic assumptions of the Prigogine-Geheniau *et al.* 'self-consistent non big bang cosmology.' This tells us that the evolution of the cosmos is the result of an interaction between the quantum vacuum and the particles of matter that are synthesized in it. We add to this scenario the postulate according to which the quantum vacuum is a fifth universal field, interacting with matter. The field acts as a holographic medium, registering and conserving the scalar wave-transform of the $3n$-dimensional configuration spaces assumed by matter in spacetime.

We now insert this ψ-field factor into the Prigogine-Geheniau *et al.* scenario. Since the scalar wavefronts created by matter propagate throughout the vacuum and are conserved in superposition, we may assume that in any given spacetime region some elements of the 'wave-function of the universe' will fall within the spacetime cone of the scalar wave patterns. Thus some patterns are likely to be given in whatever region the vacuum inflates and creates a new cosmic cycle. The patterns in the given region are minute fluctuations in the vacuum, and these fluctuations bring about progressive coherence and consistency within the successive cycles. The process can be reconstructed as follows.

Alan Guth and other cosmologists have shown that the inflation through which the presently observed universe came into being was highly, but not completely, uniform. To account for the gravitational clumping of matter into galactic clusters — and then into galaxies and stellar systems — we must assume that the initial radiation field contained minute variations that were enlarged during the inflationary period. Theory holds that these variations gave rise to scale-invariant fluctuations in the gravitational field; and the resulting fluctuations, through the Sachs-Wolfe effect, produced measurable temperate differences in the cosmic background radiation. Indeed, the differential microwave radiometer (DMR) of COBE found scale-invariant fluctuations (that is, fluctuations of which the amplitude is independent of physical size) in the temperature of the cosmic background. DMR's instrumentation could detect background radiation on angular scales greater than seven degrees; those it actually detected were of the order of ten degrees or more.

But where did these scale-invariant fluctuations come from? Although there is as yet no universally accepted answer, the most widely held view, outlined by among others Guth, Alexei Starobinsky and Stephen Hawking, is that they were produced by primordial fluctuations of the quantum vacuum. (The alternative theory traces them to the phase-transitions that followed the big bang, as the universe passed from higher to lower energy states.) In the dominant view the initial quantum fluctuations were expanded by a factor of at least 60 during inflation; they then introduced the inhomogeneities in the radiation field that gave rise to the gravitational clumping of matter in spacetime.

Currently theorists are obliged to view the primordial fluctuations as independent variables: on the big bang scenario, the universe has no history prior to inflation. However, on a multicyclic scenario the universe does have a pre-history, and the primordial quantum fluctuations informing inflation can be linked to that history — they become dependent variables within a self-consistent iterating process. In the view represented here the primordial vacuum fluctuations contain the scalar wave-transform of all matter-energy configurations that have evolved hitherto in the given region of spacetime. If so the fluctuations that introduce the inhomogeneities into the inflationary radiation field are 'in-formed' by the prior state of the universe, as that state is registered in the inflated region.

This process makes the successive cycles of the universe elements in an interlinked (non-Markovian) chain. The evolution of matter-energy in each cycle determines the primordial fluctuations that in turn determine the 'graininess' of the inflation that produces the next cycle's large-scale structures. Consequently the information carried over from prior cycles becomes a factor determining the creation of large-scale structures in the next cycle.

Of course, the trans-cyclic transfer of information does not cease with the co-determination of the dimensions of the large-scale structures. As these structures evolve and create physico-chemical templates suitable for the evolution of more complex matter-energy systems, the configurations that come about continually interact with the scalar wavefronts created in the vacuum by the hitherto evolved matter-energy systems. As we have noted, these 'secondary wavefronts' bias otherwise random evolutionary processes towards consistency with the already emerged configurations.

The trans-cyclic transfer of information creates an iterating self-referential learning scenario. An interactive, multicyclic universe correlates its physical parameters progressively to favour the evolution of complex matter-energy configurations. In each successive cycle there will be an enhanced probability of achieving:

— an initial radiation field with just the right degree of inhomogeneity to produce large-scale structures that in time become capable of producing and sustaining highly complex matter systems;

— the synthesis of just the right amount of baryons to populate spacetime;
— neutrinos with a mass (whether zero or positive) precisely such that the matter synthesized in a cycle will not collapse back after its synthesis; and
— just those values of the forces of gravitation, electromagnetism, and strong and weak nuclear interactions that permit the configuration of the baryons into increasingly ordered spatiotemporal systems.

The above scenario allows self-referentiality in the universe to extend beyond the time-horizon of a given cycle, to the cycle (and cycles) that preceded it. This creates a significant probability that large-scale structures are created in spacetime, including solar systems with planets capable of supporting life; and that on some planets the complex configurations associated with life make their appearance.

To illustrate the dynamics of the here outlined self-referential learning scenario, we come back to the metaphor of the sea, familiar from Chapter 8.

Here we envisage a sea in which a perturbation (perhaps a bubble rising to the surface) creates concentric waves that propagate from the centre towards the periphery. The receding wavefronts exercise a pressure throughout the sea, so that eventually there is another bubble creating another set of propagating wavefronts. As these, too, move outward they create their own feedback pressure leading to a third bubble — and so on. This corresponds to the multicyclic self-consistent scenario proposed by Prigogine *et al.*

We now add the ψ-field factor to the above picture: we allow that the sea conserves the traces of the wavefronts that were generated in it. As each wavefront created by a bubble passes outward, the surface does not die back to smoothness but remains subtly modulated. As a result the wavefronts created by the next bubble become modulated by the sea's enduring topography. As the successive wavefronts interact with the traces of the prior wavefronts, they add further wave patterns to it. The more wavefronts pass over the sea's surface, the more it becomes modulated, and the more it modulates the successive wave-fronts that pass over it. As the process repeats, the existing and the pre-existing patterns become mutually coherent and consistent. (For the metaphysical implications of this scenario, see Appendix for note on *The new metaphysics.*)

We may summarize the self-referential scenario as follows. The universe is spatially finite but temporally infinite. It evolves without end over a trans-cyclic topological manifold that progressively constrains random processes into forms of order. The manifold tunes the universal constants to the configurations of matter-energy that evolve successively in cosmic spacetime.

Because at present the universal constants are finely tuned, we may assume that the current cycle has not been the first. For the self-referential scenario, the evolution that the standard scenario views as the complete lifetime of the universe is but one of a potentially infinite sequence of evolutionary cycles. The universe is a temporally infinite, self-renewing, and strongly interacting system, progressively adapting itself to the evolution of complexity, and hence to the development of life — and perhaps also of mind and consciousness.

PART FIVE

Summing Up

– 13 –
The Emerging Paradigm

A new view of reality has emerged in the course of our explorations of the conceptual framework advanced here for grasping nature's unified interactive dynamics. This view deserves explication. Let us reflect, then, on the kind of paradigm that has emerged in regard to our understanding of matter, life, and mind.

The paradigm for matter

Everyday experience tells us that, in the final count, only two kinds of things exist in the world: matter and space. Matter occupies space and moves about in it — it is the primary reality. Space is a backdrop or container, of dubious reality in itself without the furniture of material bodies. This concept of reality has been revised in Einstein's relativistic universe, and again in Bohr's and Heisenberg's quantum universe. It needs to be rethought once again. The view that has emerged for us in regard to the physical foundations of the universe produces a further mutation of everyday notions about the basic furnishings of reality.

According to the panorama opening before our eyes, we cannot insist that matter is primary, while space is secondary, even if in our everyday experience material bodies are 'solid' whereas space is only the arena in which material bodies pursue their careers.

The concept of solid bodies pursuing careers in empty space is a cornerstone of the Newtonian worldview, and even though its validity has been rejected in twentieth century physics, its remnants continue to persist in the worldview of scientists. In subtle ways, the Newtonian paradigm invades even the interpretation of quantum phenomena. Although physicists recognize that space has a structure of its own, the fear of embracing the concept of a continuous medium such as the ether, together with the vexing problem of mathematical infinities, prevents them from viewing the reality of space on a par with the reality of the bodies that occupy it.

The classical view surfaces in the interpretations physicists attach to quantum experiments. Current interpretations, uncommonsensical as they are, constitute an inference from a basic assessment of the nature of reality one according to which photons are projected *across* space and *on to* screens and mirrors. The experimental apparatus consists of solid (or semi-solid) bodies, and photons bump into them in various comprehensible, and at times incomprehensible, ways. The primary reality remains the photon and the experimental equipment; whatever lies below or between them is in some ways secondary.

The reality-paradigm that emerges in our explorations provides a different picture. Space — more exactly, spacetime — has eminent reality: it is filled both with the quantal vectorial waves contemporary physics puts in place of the classical mass-points of matter, and with the scalar wave-propagations that interlink the vectorial waves within the vacuum. In this perspective we can no longer think of photons and electrons as matter-like entities projected across space and on to screens and mirrors; we should think of all microphysical events as occurring *within* the vacuum. Photons and electrons are spin-captured vectorial wave deformations of the vacuum, and screens and other bodies are standing vectorial waves — relatively static deformations that only give the impression of being solid material bodies. Indeed, in the emerging paradigm the real face of quanta is the wave-aspect; the corpuscular aspect is but the 'phenomenon' created in the context of experiment and observation.

Now, if quanta are waves, realism requires that they should be waves 'in' or 'of' something. This requirement is met: as soliton-like waves, quanta are both *in* the quantum vacuum and are integral elements *of* it. Thus if we are to be consistent, we must henceforth think of photons, electrons, as well as of screens and other laboratory equipment as actualized waves in, and of, a sub-quantum virtual energy field. When we measure quanta, we must know that we are measuring wave-patterns in a sub-quantum field. When we conduct quantum experiments, we shall realize that one complex wave experiments with other, less complex waves. If we realize this, and also that the secondary scalar-waves created by the motion of quanta are quasi-instantaneously distributed throughout our quanta-dense region of spacetime, we shall no longer be surprised at the indeterminacy and nonlocality of the phenomena we observe.

Of course, thinking in terms of a continuous field in which observed events are flow-deformations does violence to common sense. But this should not deter us: quantum physics has been violating common sense for seventy years, and the present 'violation' is in some ways less shocking than those that have gone before it. After all, if we accept the emerging paradigm for matter, we shall find a coherent explanation of the puzzling quantum paradoxes, including the simultaneous wave and corpuscular property of particles, and their lack of determinate states and simple location.

The paradigm for life

In exploring the microdomains of matter, we had to revise our everyday notion of reality and envisage a world where space is as real as the bodies that comport themselves in it. Now, when we enter the more familiar sphere of life, the shock to common sense is less acute. Yet the emerging paradigm does suggest a change in our dominant concept of the nature of life as well.

Living nature, in light of the emerging view, is not the harsh world of classical Darwinism, a world in which each struggles against all, with every organism, indeed every gene, competing for advantage against every other. In the classical worldview cooperation, even where it existed, was but a refined form of selfishness. In the new paradigm, on the other hand, organisms are not skin-enclosed and selfish entities, and competition is never unfettered. Life evolves, as Goodwin noted, in a sacred dance between the organism and the field

213

that surrounds it. This makes living beings into elements in a vast network of interrelations that embraces both other organisms, and the rest of the planetary environment.

In the socio-bio-ecosphere of this planet, the network of relations extends in both directions, from the smallest part to the system as a whole, and from the whole system to its smallest part. The former variety of interaction is uncontroversial, but the latter is surprising: it is not clear how a vast system could affect its minute parts. Yet this kind of influence is becoming recognized in field after field. First Michael Polanyi remarked on what he called 'reverse causation,' then James Campbell introduced the term 'downward causation' to describe it. Karl Popper and John Eccles employed the notion in their theory of brain/mind interaction, and Roger Sperry gave a clear-cut interpretation of it when, in his studies of brain and consciousness, he asserted that 'higher-level phenomena physically move, control the timing and otherwise directly and actively determine the main spacetime trajectories, distributions and destiny of the lower-level components.'[1]

In our corner of the universe, it is the socio-bio-ecosphere that is the highest-level system from which 'downward causation' proceeds to the organisms, populations and ecologies that inhabit our world. The resulting in-formation of organisms, populations and ecologies with the structure and dynamics of this overall system ensures consistency in evolutionary advance. It also ensures consistency in generative and regenerative processes. Particular components of the complex wavepattern of the whole system correspond to the specific morphology of organic systems. The relevant components enter as subtle 'prompts' into the developmental processes of organisms and systems of organisms. The prompts enable organisms to generate their species-specific morphology in processes of ontogenesis; to re-generate their morphology in processes of healing; and to bring forth the massively coordinated mutants that are needed in a changing milieu to achieve a leap from one species to another.

The paradigm for mind

The soliton-like embeddedness of quanta *in* the ψ-field, and the sacred dance of organisms *with* that field, indicate space- and time-spanning interconnections in the physical world and in living nature. They have their counterpart in the interactions that occur among the brains of human beings, as well as between individual humans and the world around them.

Interactions between our brain and other brains, as well as between our brain and our wider environment, imply an unsuspected degree of openness of our mind to the world. This is in vivid contrast with sceptical philosophies. For centuries, philosophers have been struggling with what has become known as the 'ego-centric predicament' — the idea that, in the final analysis, all we can know is our own mind. Of course, if we press the sceptic's argument to its utmost limits, its conclusion holds true: whatever we know is, after all, *in* our mind, and whether it refers to anything beyond it cannot be proven beyond doubt. Nevertheless, natural scientists tend to assume that at least some of the phenomena that appear in our consciousness are maps of one kind or another of the external world. This stance — known as critical realism — is by no means unreasonable. It does not assert that our consciousness maps the outside world in any direct and unequivocal fashion, only that there is some determinable relationship between what appears in our mind and what exists outside our cranium.

As we have seen in Chapter 11, in sensory perception the results of the brain's analysis of nerve signals are not direct mappings of the signals themselves. In vision, pupil and lens perform a Fourier-transform on the optical array reaching the eye, while in hearing the ear extracts signals from the analysis of the phase-coherence between external and internal oscillators. While more directly holographic transforms are at work in the analysis of the subtle scalar waves that reach the brain from the quantum vacuum, here, too, we must assume that the time- and space-transcending contents that emerge into consciousness are transformations, rather than one-to-one mappings, of the world that surrounds the brain. In every case, the brain transforms the wave propagations that reach it from the world beyond the organism into an order that, though specifically different from the presented configuration, 'contains' in some sense the latter.[2]

As a cognitive stance in science, critical realism is reasonable: there are good reasons to assume that, in a transformational sense, the brain 're-presents' the external world. The emerging paradigm for the mind specifies that this re-presentation is not limited to 'presentations' within the visible spectrum of the electromagnetic field and the audible spectrum in the atmosphere, but extends to scalar virtual-energy waves in the quantum vacuum — i.e., to the wave-transforms stored in the ψ-field.

The emerging paradigm for the mind implies that, provided that we do not repress the corresponding feelings and intuitions, 'ψ-field perception' enables us to have direct rapports and intense empathies with our fellow humans as well as with nature. The information our brain can access from the sub-quantum domain is multidimensional; hence it can include traces of all the levels of order and organization in which we are embedded. Going downwards in this multilevel structure, the accessed information can include the wave-transform of the organs and cells that constitute our body, while going upwards it can embrace the social and the ecological milieu in which we live.

Although we could — and, we shall argue, should — develop intense rapports with our fellows and with nature, few of us develop such rapports in practice. This, regrettably, is not surprising: in modern societies repression and alienation are common. Nevertheless, there is evidence that some people do have a high level of empathy with their fellows or with their environment. Poets such as John Donne and William Blake have sung of our oneness with the universe; patriots throughout the ages have dedicated their lives to country and community; and scientists including William James, E.L. Grant Watson, Abraham Maslow and Gregory Bateson have sought a detailed understanding of the close relations people can evolve with the natural orders. Traditional people always gave evidence of possessing a feeling of oneness with nature; they were well integrated in their natural environment. In the East, the Tao declared that our highest

216

good is to follow nature, while in the West Native American Chief Seattle confirmed: 'This we know. All things are connected like the blood which unites one family. All things are connected. Whatever befalls the Earth befalls the sons of the Earth.'

Our brain (and hence our mind) is potentially a window on the universe. This is a recurrent intuition. Already in the thirteenth century, Persian mystic Aziz Nasafi wrote that the spiritual world, standing like a light behind the bodily world, shines as through a window through every creature that comes into being. According to the type and size of the window, more or less light enters the world.[3] In the context of the emerging paradigm, the brain is a window far wider than the classical empiricists maintained: for them brain and mind were limited to the few wavelengths of ambient radiation to which the eye and ear can react. Physicist Raynor Johnson suggested a more apt metaphor: while in ordinary states of awareness we view the world through five slits in the tower, there are states of consciousness in which we open the roof to the sky.

For the emerging paradigm our brain is not only a window *on* the universe; it is part of the organism and hence also an input *into* the universe. Transmitted through subtle wave-propagations in the ψ-field, traffic between the brain and the rest of the universe flows in both directions. Whatever thoughts, images, feelings and intuitions enter our consciousness have their counterparts in the electrochemical activity of our neural networks, and these networks constantly read their Gabor-transforms into the field. This means that our most fleeting thoughts and vaguest intuitions are encoded in the cosmic vacuum and remain conserved in it.

Given the two-way traffic between human brains and the world, each person's thoughts and perceptions are of direct consequence to his environment, including other persons. This is because in altered states the brain does not distinguish finely shaded individual variations in ψ-field patterns — within a certain range of variation, the brain-state of one individual can be read out by another. In consequence our experiences can be accessed by others with sufficiently matching states of brain and mind. This makes for a new depth of responsibility in human beings: what we think and feel can influence our fellow beings, not only those who surround us here and now, but also those who live in distant places and in future generations.

There is a kind of immortality to human experience. If one person's memories can be recalled after he or she has died, that person's experiences can be re-lived again. It is true that people live on through the memories we have of them. These memories are more than our own recollections of other people; they are the experiences of those other people, re-lived by us as if they were our own. This does not mean personal immortality in the conventional sense. There is a factor of immortality, but it pertains not to individual minds but to the larger whole in which individual minds participate.

Intimations that the human mind is a part of a larger whole are legion: it is the fundamental stuff of religion, metaphysics and mysticism. It was present in Plato's concept of the affinity of the Soul with the world of Ideas, and in the conclusions reached by Descartes and Berkeley regarding the possibility of escape from the ego-centric predicament. It was also stated by the pragmatist William James who, following detailed investigations of the religious experience, remarked that such experience 'unequivocally testifies' that we can know 'union with something larger than ourselves.'[4] British scientist E.L. Grant Watson noted that detailed observations of the many and sundry patterns of animal, bird and plant behaviour can be illuminated by two outstanding ideas: 'First, that there is a universal consciousness pervading all things. Secondly, that the sense-organs are so contrived as to limit and direct within small compass this larger consciousness.'[5]

However, it was Gustav Fechner, the redoubtable founder of modern experimental psychology, who gave perhaps the most remarkable account of the pertinent insight. 'When one of us dies,' he wrote, 'it is as if an eye of the world were closed, for all perceptive contributions from that particular quarter cease. But the memories and conceptual relations that have spun themselves round the perceptions of that person remain in the larger Earth-life as distinct as ever, and form new relations and grow and develop throughout all the future, in the same way in which our own distinct objects of thought, once stored in memory, form new relations and develop throughout our whole finite life.'[6]

It is not as if we had a mind that is separable from the brain. Much more is it that we have a brain that is inseparable from the universe.

A mirror in the East

A cosmos that evolves from chaos — building stepwise from disorder to order, building towards complexity, structure and meaning, in harmony yet diversity, building creatively towards life, mind and consciousness, with ever closer connections — is this world strange and surprising ... or is it strangely familiar?

The image is not new: it is as old as human culture and consciousness. When we add to it that the cosmos builds through the interaction of an unseen deep that is the womb of all that exists, and a surface that is the manifest reality that surrounds us ... and that it builds cyclically, lifting towards fresh pinnacles of structure and order, returning to the womb of the deep only to re-emerge from it again and again, we get an image that has existed for millennia.

This is a basic theme of the great mystical tradition Aldous Huxley called 'perennial philosophy.' Its archetypal symbols include the Great Mother, where planet Earth is the creative source, and the Cosmic Tree and the Tree of Life, where the organic interconnectedness of roots and leaves symbolizes the connections between the source and its emanations. The philosophical and spiritual traditions of India, China, and Greece agree that there is one source, one central, self-sustaining node of being and consciousness, whence all things arise. The manifest world is an emanation or projection from this source — a source that, as we have seen, the Greeks called 'the One.' The pre-Colombian cultures, in turn, spoke of a Great Journey through which all things achieve their role and identity in nature; and the Hindus called this process *Leela* ('play'). They saw it as the concretization and distillation of primordial energy, descending from its primordial unity.

Hindu philosophy provides a remarkable account of the process whereby the deep One diversifies into the manifest Many. In this

219

account, the physical world is a reflection of energy vibrations from more subtle worlds which, in turn, are reflections of still more subtle energy fields. Existence is the creation of a hierarchy of things and beings out of a primal oneness which is pure energy: *Adi Shabd*. It first takes the form of *Sat Purush* (true being), and comes to rest in *Sat Lok* (true location). In its further emanation this outpouring energy creates *Par Brahm*, a region of spirit that is permeated by a highly refined primal form of matter: *Prakriti*. Then the primal energy tunnels into Par Brahm's lower region known as *Daswan Dwar*. The first tunnel leads to *Maha Sunna*, a great void of unplumbed depth and intense darkness. From there it courses along a channel known as the Tenth Door into *Mansarovar*, a vast reservoir. Finally, it leaves the realm of pure spirit for the domain of universal mind: *Brahm* or *Kal*. Here, together with *Maya*, the receptive or female counterpart, the cosmic energy projects into the lower planes: it takes on the coverings of individual bodies and minds. Time becomes manifest, things become subject to the laws of cause and effect, and the world turns into a duality where the positive controlling power is balanced by the negative, receptive pole. The One has journeyed from the cosmic Source, and has transfigured into the Many.

In the manifest world of today there are five principal states: earth, which is the solid state of matter *(Prithvi);* water, the liquid state *(Jal);* fire, the state of heat *(Agni);* air, the gaseous state *(Vayu);* and Akash (or *Akasha),* the primal state that has transformed into all the rest. The soul, having traversed the causal, the astral and the physical realms, is now clothed in a physical body so that it may exist and communicate at all levels of existence. Yet the soul is not intractably separated from the Source. Akash is present in every human being: it is 'closer than breathing, nearer than hands and feet.' Mystics tells us that we can be drawn into, and again become one with, the primal reality which they describe as an ocean of light, love, bliss, or consciousness.

A similar cosmological concept is present in the Sanskrit *mulaprakriti,* the original, undifferentiated source from which all things emerge through involution followed by evolution. It is also there in

Chinese cosmology as T'ai-chi, the primordial unity containing the seeds of yin and yang, universal opposites that in their incessant interaction give rise to the diversity of the observed world. The Tao gives an explicit, though purposively defocused, account of it. In Lao-Tzu's oft-quoted words: 'There was something vague before heaven and earth arose. How calm! How void! It stands alone, unchanging; it acts everywhere, untiring. It may be considered the mother of everything under heaven. I do not know its name, but call it by the word *Tao*.'[7]

The Upanishads contain perhaps the most remarkable description of this 'mother of all things.' In sixty-four verses divided into three chapters, the *Mundaka Upanishad*, one of eleven basic texts, presents the fundamental concept in the form of a tale. Saunaka, a successful worldly man, seeks out Angiras, a legendary figure to whom the knowledge of Brahman has been imparted. He asks the famous question: 'Revered Sir, what is that knowledge whereby everything in the world becomes known?' Angiras answers: 'The knowers of Brahman declare that there are two kinds of knowledge to be acquired — the higher as well as the lower. Of these the lower consists of the Rig-Veda, the Yajur-Veda, the Sama-Veda, the Atharva-Veda; phonetics, ritual, grammar, etymology, metrics, and astronomy. And the higher is that by which the imperishable is attained.'

Angiras' reply segments human knowledge into a higher and a lower form: into a knowledge of 'the deep' and 'the surface.' The knowledge of the deep is revealed to the seeker whose mind is tranquil, whose senses are controlled, and who approaches the great mystery in a proper manner. This is the knowledge of Brahman: the science of that 'which is invisible, ungraspable, without origin or attributes ...; which is eternal and many-splendoured, all-pervading and exceedingly subtle ...' (1:13)

The universe, according to Angiras, is a natural and spontaneous emanation from the Brahman, the unchanging, imperishable basis of all existence. '... Brahman expands; from him matter is born, from matter life, mind, truth and immortality ...' (1:8) 'As the spider sends forth and gathers [in its web], as herbs sprout upon the face of the earth, as hair grows upon the head and body of man, so from the immutable springs forth the universe.' (1:7) 'This is the truth. As from a blazing fire thousands of fiery sparks leap out, just so, my beloved, a multitude of beings issue forth from the imperishable and, verily fall back into it again.' (2:1)

In Raja-yoga, one of the many paths ('yogas') that lead to a knowledge of the unchanging ground of the universe, we find a detailed account of the emergence of the world from its immutable source, and its ultimate return to it. In the famed account of Swami Vivekananda, Akash is the underlying substance of all that exists, and Prana is the arch-energy that acts on and forms everything. In the beginning there was only Akash and at the end there will be only Akash again. Akash becomes the sun, the earth, the moon, the stars and the comets; it also becomes the animal and the human body, the plants, and everything that exists. At the end of one phase everything will melt back into Akash, to reemerge from it in the next.

Prana, in turn, is the infinite and omnipresent power that acts on Akash. It is motion, gravitation and magnetism; it is present in human action, in the nerve currents of the body, even in the force of thought. At the end all forces will resolve back into Prana, just as all things will die back into Akash. The latter is not passive: as the 'Akashic record' it conserves the traces of all that takes place in the manifest universe.[8]

The paradigm of surface and deep, of the manifest realm that is an emanation from the unplumbed depths of an original unity, shapes the oriental mind to this day. Gopi Krishna, founder of the Kundalini Movement, speaks of the cosmos as a boundless ocean dotted with icebergs. The ocean is impervious to our senses, but the gigantic ice-formations, transformed appearances of the underlying water, are perceptible. When we observe the world through our senses we see only the icebergs. But when we view reality internally, in *samadhi,* the icebergs vanish and water is perceived on all sides.

The cosmic ocean pervades space and time. It is the basis of all things: the energies of the visible world originate from the primordial energy that is inherent in its creative potentials.[9]

Much the same insight resurfaces in the West in the context of New Age and esoteric movements. The well-known sensitive Barbara Ann Brennan speaks of a universal energy field that is the Akashic record

222

of all that has ever happened and has ever been known. We can access this field by tuning in to its universal hologram through an extended awareness she calls 'Higher Sense Perception.' In this state we retrieve information that is stored not in our own mind and brain, but in the universal energy field.[10] The universal energy field itself is receiving increasing attention. White and Krippner, for example, noted that there is a previously undefined form of energy or matter that permeates animate and inanimate objects, as indeed all space, and connects all things together through what they call harmonic inductance.[11]

As attention focuses on unsuspected interactions and interconnections in nature and human experience, the traditionally mystical mirror is becoming clarified. It begins to shift from the spirituality of the Eastern tradition towards the uncompromising light of western scientific inquiry.

The emerging paradigm for matter, life, and mind, far from being strange and unexpected, turns out to be strangely familiar: even expected. With its inverted realm of the quantum, its in-formed world of the living, and its interconnected sphere of mind and consciousness, the concept of a creative cosmos has been foreshadowed for millennia. This is not simply coincidence. If an insight is sound, it crops up again and again in human consciousness. The most astonishing discoveries, if harboring an element of truth, inspire an 'A-ha!' experience.

The emerging paradigm is no exception. It brings to the surface of our consciousness, in a more detailed scientific form, what we, and our fathers and forefathers before us, have known all along.

– 14 –
Perspectives for Science and Humanity

Prospects for a unified science

Innovations rock the scientific enterprise from time to time, contrasting the sedate and continuous tenor of research typical of calm periods with revolutionary explorations reminiscent of the evolution of living systems in nature. Significant progress has always involved discontinuities, from Galileo, Newton, Copernicus, and Kepler, to Einstein, Bohr, Jung, Guth, Hawking, Eccles, and Pribram. Unified interactive dynamics (UID) enters this stream of nonlinear innovation with its promise to extend scientific inquiry both in depth and in range of generality.

We can best grasp the paradigm underlying UID in reference to Einstein's pronouncement that in science we seek the simplest possible scheme by which to bind together the observed facts. In the framework of the UID paradigm, binding together the observed facts is not just describing how they appear, or explaining how they function. Rather, it is to show how 'the facts' came to be. Explanation in reference to a unified dynamics specifies Einstein's dictum. It now reads: *We are seeking for the simplest possible scheme by which to understand how the observed facts are generated.*

How the facts of nature are generated cannot be understood in the simplest possible scheme by taking the interactions of quanta as 'primitive' (that is, unexplained) givens. The interactions in question are already highly complex — they have been generated by prior interactions. The simplest possible scheme by which to bind together the observed facts has to be grounded at a deeper level: at the level of the field that interconnects the quanta. This level, as we said, must be assumed to be highly structured and information-rich. It is the level of the quantum vacuum: where the interactive dynamics that generates the observed facts is rooted.

The scheme that takes the dynamics of evolution as the key factor shifts the starting point of inquiry from the quantum to the sub-quantum level. Quanta are on a higher storey rising above — and indeed rising *from* — the virtual energy field that is the vacuum. The vacuum itself is an intrinsic part of reality: its dynamics interact with particles and atoms, and the myriad configurations assumed by atomic matter in spacetime.

A vacuum-based interactive dynamics has significant promise:

1. *It provides a coherent explanation of many of the puzzles that presently confront our understandinq of the observed facts.* We obtain a new and fruitful perspective for viewing the problems of duality, nonlocality, and indeterminacy in regard to quanta, going beyond the interdictions of Bohr's phenomenalistic philo-sophy. We gain a fresh context for assessing the diversified yet self-consistent evolution of order and complexity in the bio-logical world, referring it to the creative dance between the quantum vacuum and the organic and ecological systems that arise in it. Also the farther reaches of conscious experience gain new cogency: phenomena such as permanent memory and trans-personal experience are brought within the compass of research-able facts.

2. *A sub-quantum-grounded interactive dynamics further lowers the floor of scientific inquiry.* The floor of scientific inquiry has been lowered throughout the history of modern science. First the indivisible atom of Democritus was rediscovered by Dalton and Lavoisier as the basic constituent of gaseous matter. Then the floor was lowered to the atom of Rutherford, fission-able into a nucleus surrounded by orbital electrons. A deeper basement has been reached this century at the level of Planck's

constant, with the discovery of quarks, strings and the 200-odd elementary particles that came to light in high-energy collisions. In the meanwhile the field in which these progressively more minute and abstract entities are embedded transformed from the passive Euclidean space of classical mechanics to the turbulent potential-energy-filled quantum vacuum of the new cosmology. It is logical to extend the penetration of scientific inquiry past the particulate micro-entities that populate the vacuum, to the virtual-energy field that embeds and interconnects them.

3. *A unified interactive dynamics extends the effective range of scientific research.* In the seventeenth century Galilean physics described mechanistic processes on the surface of the Earth, and subsequently Newtonian mechanics extended the range of these descriptions to all bodies moving within inertial frames. At the beginning of the twentieth century Einstein extended the validity of physical laws to accelerated frames up to the speed of light, and two decades later Bohr extended the laws of physics to the subatomic world. It now appears that relativity physics holds good only to about 10^{-8}m and that quantum physics, though it claims validity all the way to the Planck-length of 10^{-35}m, encounters anomalies (such as those associated with the energy density of the vacuum) at the level of 10^{-20}m. The postulates of UID promise to overcome many of the anomalies by referring them to sub-quantal interactions.

4. *UID also introduces improved generality into scientific theory.* As Newton generalized the laws of Galileo, and Einstein generalized Newton's laws, so UID generalizes evolutionary processes beyond the classical domain of physics, to biology and ultimately to neurophysiology and psychology. In its context evolution in the living world is not categorically distinct from evolution in the cosmos. In both domains there is a subtle but essential transfer of information between systems and environments — a self-referentiality that in-forms otherwise indeterminate processes,

turning random trials and errors into self-consistent explorations of the available dimensions of order and complexity.

In time, the interactive dynamics postulated in this study could be elaborated into a coherent and consistent, mathematically formulated science of the observed world in its principal domains. The future unified science would describe the behaviour and evolution of part-icles as well as of atoms, molecules, cells, organisms, and systems of organisms in spacetime in reference to the interaction of systems of vectorial matter-energy with subtle scalar waves propagating in the virtual gas of the vacuum. The descriptions would be quantified in terms of the phase space of the generalized positions and momenta of quanta, and of atomic, molecular and supra-molecular configurations of quanta, within the universal field. Since the number of coordinates in this phase space is vast, the full set of equations that quantify the description may never be written. But the achievable equations will have the general form

$$\mathfrak{D} \, \mathfrak{F}(i,j)$$

where a universal integral-differential operator $\mathfrak{D}$ defines the cosmic phase space density $\mathfrak{F}(i,j)$, with the i,j being the generalized positions and momenta of quanta in the quantum vacuum.

Though its promise is real and its development within the realm of possibility, the unified science envisaged here is not likely to be devel-oped through a series of incremental steps. Smooth and continuous development could be blocked by the reluctance of the mainstream science establishment to abandon some of its cherished — if ever more problematic — concepts and theories. The history and sociology of science testifies that, even though science is an open enterprise, when new data come to light that do not fit established concepts, scientists do not simply discard those concepts in favour of new and more adapted ones. As Heisenberg observed, 'any good physicist would be willing to acquire new concepts but even the best physicists are sometimes quite unwilling to leave some of the old and apparently safe concepts.'[1]

Yet, when puzzles and anomalies accumulate beyond a critical point, scientists do abandon old concepts: they have turned unsafe. In the development of science, when critical thresholds are reached there is no return to previous paradigms: progress can only be made by exploring alternative concepts and hypotheses, and testing them for applicability and consistency, as well as heuristic and predictive power.

Today, science is about to reach a critical threshold. Gone is the assurance that the fundamental features of the natural universe have been already discovered; the complacency typical of the late nineteenth century has almost vanished in the late twentieth. Anomalies are discovered in field after field, and interest in them is growing. A deepening sense of unease at the centres of the science establishment is compensated by a growing openness and sense of excitement at its innovative edge. More and more societies and associations are created for the exploration of the anomalies encountered in scientific research, and these networks are growing in prestige and legitimacy.*

Contemporary science may soon approximate a supersaturated solution — a suitable catalyst may be all that is needed to bring about a radical change in its state. Should unified interactive dynamics be elaborated so that it commands the degree of simplicity, elegance, research fertility, and confirmability that are the hallmarks of acceptable hypotheses, it could lift the current cosmological revolution to a new stage of penetration and insight. Today's puzzle-ridden disciplinary theories would then be replaced by a new and fertile unified science: the self-consistent paradigm for informed thinking about matter, life, and mind.

---

* For example, the Society for Scientific Exploration at Stanford University, publishing the quarterly *Journal of Scientific Exploration*; the Center for Frontier Sciences at Temple University, publishing the semiannual *Frontier Perspectives;* and the Scientific and Medical Network in the UK, with members in Europe, the Americas, the Middle East and the Far East and Africa, publishing the quarterly *Network Newsletter.*

Towards a new consciousness

If the dynamics of the universe from the beginning shaped the course of the heavens, lighted the sun, and formed the earth, if this same dynamism brought forth the continents and the seas and atmosphere, if it awakened life in the primordial cell and then brought into being the unnumbered variety of living beings, and finally brought us into being and guided us safely through the turbulent centuries, there is reason to believe that this same guiding process is precisely what has awakened in us our present understanding of ourselves and our relation to this stupendous process. Sensitized to such guidance from the very structure and functioning of the universe, we can have confidence in the future that awaits the human venture.

Thomas Berry, *The Dream of the Earth*

Achieving the perennial dream of a unified understanding of ourselves and the universe is not only of interest to science; it could be a critical factor in ensuring human well-being and development. A sound unified science could be an effective guide leading humanity towards the recovery of more viable ways of thinking and acting. In its cultural dimension it could inspire a naturalistic-holistic consciousness, capable of uniting people and societies with the creative cosmos that is the source of their being and resource of their existence.

Cultural historian Thomas Berry has identified the problem of our times in reference to the loss of a 'good story.' In the traditional story of the world, Western society had an agreed-upon account that shaped emotional attitudes, provided life purposes and energized action. It enabled people to answer the questions of their children, and societies to identify crime and punish transgressors. It did not necessarily make people good, nor did it take away the pains and stupidities of existence, but it provided a context in which life could function in a meaningful manner. Today the meaning and utility of that story are open to question.[2]

The traditional story, Berry tells us, originated in a revelatory

229

experience some three thousand years ago. At that time the original harmony of the universe was thought to have been broken by a primordial human fault, necessitating the forming of a human community that would participate in the divine work of redemption. But, as already noted in Chapter 1, in the turbulence of the fourteenth century, when medieval Europe experienced the plague as well as the Hundred Years' War, the powerful light of the traditional story became tarnished. Faith in divine providence was weakened, and the story split into two branches. One was the branch of religion; the other that of science. Those who continued to place full faith in religion became increasingly oriented towards the demanding tasks of redemption out of a tragic world, while those who looked to independent inquiry, though initially steeped in Christian doctrine, aspired towards more mastery over human destiny through a secular understanding of the workings of nature.

According to Berry we are in trouble because the Christian redemption-oriented branch of the story no longer offers reliable guidance, while its science branch, with its subsequent Baconian emphasis on the exploitation of nature for human ends, has degraded our habitat. Whether or not we accept this account of the crux of our problems, it is clear that, if the human community is to ensure a future on this Earth, we must go beyond the fragmented mechanistic worldview of classical science, towards the unified concept that is the basic objective of the cosmological revolution. Only a unified world concept can convey the insights necessary to grasp the problems and the opportunities that confront us in our planetary setting; only such a concept allows us to identify the remedies and apply them effectively.

The foundations we have laid here for a unified science of matter, mind and universe could contribute to the elaboration of a meaningful 'story' — one that would enable us better to know ourselves and our place in the cosmic scheme of things. A consciousness that draws on these foundations for its inspiration would help us to establish a closer rapport with each other and with nature, and the advantages of such a basis for a new consciousness are only too evident. The cosmos that creates itself through a unified interactive dynamics is a seamless totality in which the elements are organic parts of the whole. More than that, this cosmos is a totality in which all elements are constantly in touch with the whole, and hence with each other. Here all things are what they are because they are constantly in contact with the enduring record of the universe. The 'subjective communion' among the co-existing elements of the world, emphasised by Berry as the hallmark of a meaningful and functional story, is an integral feature of the new unified science which recognizes an interactively self-creating cosmos.

In this cosmos it is in the nature of things that the creative communion among the elements of the universe becomes more intense and explicit as the quarks and atoms, and the molecules and cells and organisms that emerge in the course of time pursue their evolutionary trajectory. On our planet, the potential for intense and explicit communion culminated in the cognitive and communicational faculties of human beings. But in modern societies much of this potential is allowed to lie fallow; the deeper faculties of human/human and human/world communication are not sufficiently recognized and hence not fully employed.

A creative recourse to ψ-field based self-referential dynamics could help us to rectify this situation. What we have glimpsed of this dynamics allows us to contemplate the real possibility of deriving practical guidance from the ongoing dance of our brain and body with the subtle record of our co-evolving universe.

Recovering a sound appreciation of our place and role in the scheme of things does not call for consulting the information embedded in the genetic coding of our body — as Berry suggests — nor does it oblige us to appeal to mysterious cosmic forces. We can access within our own mind the subtle signals that in-form us with the orders of the natural world. These signals have always inspired great poets and artists, front-line scientists and philosophers. Access to them does not require special gifts and inborn talent; it could be available to everyone who possesses sufficient will and motivation. All persons could learn to 'read' some elements of the in-formation that acts on their brain whether they know it or not. It is in the interest of everyone to become conscious of this ever-present yet oft-ignored information: it is the imprint of the cosmos on our organism. Deeper awareness of it could lift this subtle imprint to the level where it could influence action and guide behaviour. It could go a long way towards re-integrating human beings and communities with the bio- and socio-sphere, the vital context of Earthly existence.

Berry's insight, cited in the opening quotation, has unsuspectedly deep relevance. We are coming closer to a recognition of the evolutionary dynamics of the universe, and that we are has much to do with our need for reliable guidance in the critical times in which we find ourselves. There are no purely random events; a deeper analysis always reveals interconnections. It is up to us to undertake the required analyses and come to the needed insights. The prospects are good; the interactive dynamics at work in the cosmos is also at work in our body and mind, and tapping into it can help us create the awareness by which to guide our steps towards a more meaningful and secure future.

The perennial dream of mystics and prophets, scientists and philosophers, and thoughtful persons in all walks of life, in all cultures and all times, may achieve a new realization in our day. The consequences could be surprisingly practical: a unified science to know our way in the world, and a new consciousness to enlighten us on that path.

Appendix: Technical notes

Complexity

There are ways of measuring complexity in real world phenomena that are independent of the subjective complexity experienced by observers. The classical measure has been information content: how many yes/no choices must be made to construct a system from its elements. Using this method it has been possible to establish the information content of the DNA of several organisms, though these were mainly comparatively simple ones such as *drosophila*. Seth Lloyd and Heinz Pagels suggested a more sophisticated measure of complexity. Their 'thermodynamic depth' is a measure so formulated that it is zero for totally ordered states (such as a regular array of atoms in a crystal), likewise zero for totally random states (such as molecules in a gas), and high for intermediate states. The thermodynamic depth of a system is thus the difference between its entropy — which is the observer's lack of exact knowledge about the system — and the amount of information needed to specify all the paths by which the system might have reached its measured state. Consequently thermodynamic depth is proportional to the amount of information the process has discarded.[1]

A still more sophisticated measure of complexity has been developed recently: it relates complexity in a system to the process of its computation. The Kolgomorov-Chaitin-Solomonoff (KCS) definition states that the complexity of x is the length of the shortest program for computing x. More precisely, the measure claims that the complexity of x is the length of the shortest *self-delimiting* program for computing x — where a self-delimiting program is one which contains, at its beginning, a message disclosing its own length. (This program has been subsequently shown to be impossible to compute: the very concept of a general algorithm for finding the shortest program for computing a given entity involves a logical contradiction.)[2]

Although no fully satisfactory measure of complexity has yet been devised, there is a growing consensus that complexity measures are best calibrated when they produce zero values at fully deterministic states as well as at full randomness, and positive values in-between. The latter appear to move towards a maximum as the systems switch between regular and chaotic behaviours: at such phase transitions the information-processing capabilities of the systems are particularly high. Their complexity can be quantitatively determined following recent work by Crutchfield and Young.[3] The measures they propose are soundly embedded in computation theory and statistical mechanics. They show that, at least in principle, complexity in real world systems can be measured with arbitrarily high precision.

Fields

The field concept is not new to science; the need to link events at different points in space arose already out of Newton's theory of gravitation. 'Action at a distance' has always been an unacceptable notion: if one event at one point in space attracted another event at another point, there had to be some way of transmitting the effect from the first to the second. In the eighteenth century physicists began to interpret gravitational action as action in a gravitational field: this field was assumed to be built by all the existing mass-points in space and to act on each mass-point at its specific spatial location. It was this notion that in 1849 Michael Faraday used to replace direct action among electric charges and currents with electric and magnetic fields produced by all charges and currents existing at a given time. In 1864 James Clerk Maxwell stated the electromagnetic theory of light in terms of the field in which electromagnetic waves propagate at finite velocity. And in 1934 Einstein pointed to Maxwell's concept of field as the most profound and fruitful transformation in our concept of reality since Newton.[4] It was soon thereafter that quantum physicists began to explain particle interaction in terms of quantum field theories.

Though the Copenhagen school of quantum theory would contest it, also the fields postulated in subatomic physics require the ascription of some form of reality. Indeed, none of the known elementary particles would make sense except as a manifestation of underlying energy or probability fields. Electrons, for example, are mathematically defined as point particles (particles without spatial dimension), but such particles act in space — in quantum field theory the interaction of electrons is described by an exchange of photons within the electromagnetic field — and they can do so only if they are in some sense *in* space. Hence, logically, electrons should be viewed as point-events in spatially extended fields.

The reality of space is underscored by the fact that the photons exchanged in electromagnetic field interactions are virtual particles without independent existence apart from their interactions. The same goes for the exchange particles created in the interaction of quarks. As electrons interact by the exchange of photons, so quarks interact by the exchange of gluons. In the case of the gluon force (also called 'colour force'), the effects do not diminish with distance. On the contrary, quantum chromodynamics predicts that the force — and hence the number of gluons — increases proportionately to the distance between the interacting quarks. This would be a complete anomaly unless the

234

space between the quarks was 'filled' in some sense by an extended dynamic field.

Other phenomena that would lack every semblance of reality unless ascribed to underlying fields include the cloud-like charges of electrons (composed of quarks and antiquarks as well as of gluons exchanged between the quarks), and the transformation of quarks as a result of interactions (in weak interactions the quark changes 'flavour' but not 'colour,' while in strong interactions, when a quark absorbs or emits a gluon, the quark changes 'colour' but not 'flavour').

Chaos

Computer simulations of the dynamics of complex systems demonstrate that in chaotic states such systems develop levels of sensivity that extend even to the vacuum level.[5] This is because complex systems governed in part or whole by chaotic attractors are characterized by an ultrasensitive dependence on initial conditions.

Attractors model the geometrical shape of the dynamic forces that constrain the evolution of a system. They create limit cycles that may converge to a single point (the effect of point-attractors); exhibit some form of periodicity (periodic attractors); or exhibit trajectories that do not repeat and do not exhibit a regular pattern (chaotic or 'strange' attractors). In a system where chaotic attractors dominate, two indistinguishably close initial points may lead to widely differing end points. Initial-point differences may be on the microscale; end-point differences will nevertheless occur on the macroscale.

In an enduring system — that is, in one without fixed initial and end states — the initial-condition dependence produced by chaotic attractors amounts to parameter-fluctuation dependence. Unmeasurably fine variations in the value of an internal or external parameter produce measurable effects (this is the explosive nucleation of a minor fluctuation that became popularly known as the 'butterfly-effect'). As a result, in ultrasensitive chaotic states not just quanta, but also macroscale systems built of quanta, may be affected by feedback from the vacuum field.

Chaotic states are not as infrequent in nature as it is sometimes assumed. Realworld systems, unlike simplified mathematical models, are often governed by several attractors, and possibly by a large number of them (see Figure 7, page 144). Systems following a lawful evolutionary trajectory are dominated by point or periodic attractors: these define a regular and unique evolution-ary trajectory. Given an adequate knowledge of the state of such systems at any one point in time, one can predict (or retrodict) its state at any other time. Systems governed exclusively by point and periodic attractors are ideal-izations, however: in the real world some level of chaos is always present. This means that, *pace* Laplace, full predictability is never entirely possible: deeper analysis discloses irregularities in the trajectory of almost every system. Chaos is present — and hence chaotic attractors are called for — even in planetary motion, the classical paradigm of predictability. Minute fluctuations hallmark the planetary orbits; they are particularly prevalent in the orbit of Pluto.

The new metaphysics

The basic premises of the emerging paradigm constitute a 'metaphysics' in the sense intended by Aristotle: that is, a set of first principles. The exposition of such first principles comes logically after the exposition of the physical principles — metaphysics succeeds physics (hence its name: *meta* means 'coming after' in Greek). Since this study has been devoted to the physical principles of the dynamics through which cosmos emerges from chaos, we should now sketch the indicated — and more or less tacitly presupposed — first principles.

The metaphysics that underlies the emerging paradigm is new in specific detail, yet it bears a distinct family resemblance to evolutionary process-metaphysics in general and Whitehead's 'philosophy of organism' in particular.[6] Its principles disclose a dynamic, organically interconnected and self-referential universe.

As in Whitehead's metaphysics, above the level of quanta all things in the universe are complex entities: they are systems of matter-energy (Whitehead called them 'societies of actual entities,' or simply 'organisms'). The systems are what they are because of a two-fold interaction ('prehension' in Whitehead's term) connecting them with the rest of the universe. On the one hand, matter-energy systems 'prehend' other matter-energy systems in their region of spacetime insofar as they are relevant to their physical constitution; on the other hand the systems prehend enduring patterns that 'ingress' in them and thereby achieve concrete individuation.

In this evolutionary metaphysics, even as in Whitehead's philosophy of organisms, the reality of the universe embraces two fundamental kinds of existents, subsisting on two physically distinct levels. Existents on one of the levels are spatiotemporal 'actual entities': perceived, perceivable, or instrumentally inferrable quanta, and quantal configurations of matter-energy. Those on the other level are 'eternal objects': waveform patterns generated by actual entities but sustained independently of them. Like Plato, Whitehead regarded eternal objects as ultimate givens in reality, without derivation from empirical matters of fact. The metaphysics outlined here is in a more privileged position. It accounts for the ingressing patterns as vacuum-based wavefronts in-forming the trajectories and $3n$-dimensional configuration spaces of the existing matter-energy systems. They are produced by the presently and the previously existing systems. This means that the ingressing patterns themselves evolve; whereas in Whitehead, as in Plato, they make up a finite set, given once and for all.

236

The two levels of the universe are distinct but not discrete: they are categorically conjunctive. They are levels of one and the same cosmic reality, that is, the universe in a complete envisagement. The basic level is that of the quantum vacuum, a cosmic medium of fluctuating waves of virtual energy. The derivate level is the observed or observable spatiotemporal world: the physical universe insofar as its vacuum component is neglected.

The basic and the derivate levels of the universe are both diachronically and synchronically connected. Diachronically, the basic level is prior: it is the generative ground of quanta, the basic unit of matter-energy in spacetime. Synchronically, the quanta synthesized in the vacuum remain interlinked with their generative ground through forward and reverse Fourier-transforms. Quanta and more complex matter-energy systems translate their trajectories and configuration-spaces *into* the energy field of the vacuum as interfering wavefronts, and translate isomorphic wavefronts *out of* that field. The forward translation occurs as quanta, primary soliton-like waves in the vacuum, create secondary waves: Fourier-transforms of their spatiotemporal trajectories and configurations. The reverse translation obtains in turn as the secondary wavefronts subtly but effectively 'in-form' the dynamically indeterminate phases of the evolution of matter-energy systems.

The interaction of the two levels creates a bootstrap effect. At the logically implied (but empirically unverifiable) initiation of the process, there is 'nothing but' the quantum vacuum: a spatially and temporally unbounded sea of virtual energy. A given spatial region at a given temporal epoch (where both space and time acquire meaning only in reference to the subsequent events) suffers a critical instability, and some fraction of the energies that were liberated do not die back into the virtual energy field. They remain suspended as soliton-like nodal points: singularities of energy concentration superimposed on the encompassing virtual energy flux. The nodal points that endure in some measurable sense acquire relations both with one another and with the quantum vacuum. They create the derivate level of the universe: the level of quantal matter-energy populated spacetime.

The universe evolves through the interaction of the two levels. Matter-energy systems in spacetime leave their waveform imprint in the virtual energy flux of the vacuum, and the thereby generated wavefronts interact with the spatiotemporal evolution of matter-energy systems. The latter construct themselves through a two-fold 'prehension': of other matter-energy systems (with causal propagations transmitted by the four universal fields of inter-action), and of isomorphic elements of the already created wavefronts (trans-mitted by the ψ-field, the fifth universal field in nature). The process evolves matter-energy systems in spacetime in reference to their enduring traces in the vacuum.

The universe's self-referential dynamics is fully deterministic; it permits alternative evolutionary trajectories. Such permissiveness occurs at points of bifurcation, where the hold of dynamical forces on matter-energy systems is relaxed. The relevant states are states of chaos. Contrary to earlier interpretations, they are not entirely the prey of chance. Stochastic distribution of probabilities continue to apply, subtly but crucially in-formed by the re-translation (the 'ingression') of ψ-field wave-patterns.

Causal influences in the interactive universe are both multiple and hierarchically bi-directional. Each quantum or matter-energy system is affected by all other quanta and matter-energy systems within the spacetime cone of secondary wavefront propagations in the vacuum. By virtue of the supraluminal velocity of secondary wavefront propagations in a matter-populated region of spacetime, this cone embraces the quasi-totality of a cosmic region such as a planet. The quasi-instantly transmitted causal effects are statistical biases in otherwise random probability distributions regarding alternative evolutionary trajectories. There is thus, in addition to the hard-determinism achieved by the known dynamical forces, also a soft-determinism through patterns that Plato and Platonists ascribed to ideal realities and our metaphysics traces to the subquantum virtual energy field of the physical universe. There is no absolute chance of unrestrained randomness.

Causal influences proceed in both hierarchical directions, from parts to wholes, and from wholes to parts. Classical hard-determinism is mainly of the upwards variety, as parts in a system jointly determine the structure and behaviour of the whole system formed by them. Psi-field relayed soft-determinism, on the contrary, is mainly of the downward kind. Here the Fourier-transform of the whole system in-forms the chaotic (dynamically nondeterministic) states of its parts, introducing a subtle bias into their choice of evolutionary trajectories. Such reverse causality proceeds from the largest system within a matter-dense region of spacetime, through its various subsystems, towards its basic quantal components.

The interactive evolutionary process is cosmically extended, although it is regionally concentrated. The cosmos-wide process is not infinite: it is both spatially and temporally constrained. In space, its bounds are marked by the expansion of the super-galactic structures that result from the primal vacuum instability. In time, the process is bounded by the limited availability of the free energies required for the evolution of matter-energy systems. Inevitably, local concentrations of free energies — negative entropy sources and stores — become exhausted, whether the large-scale structures of the universe continue to expand in space, or contract back to a singularity.

As entropy overtakes the evolutionary process, its spacetime component reverses. Complex configurations of matter-energy break down, yielding to simpler ones which break down in turn until atomic nuclei, stripped of electron shells, become supercompacted in black holes. In the final 'evaporation' of black holes, the degenerate quantal remnants die back into the virtual energy field of the vacuum.

However, the spectral component of the process, unlike its spacetime component, does not reverse: the secondary wavefronts created by evolving matter-energy systems remain uncoded in the virtual-energy vacuum field. The reversal of matter-energy evolution merely produces progressively less complex additions to the ψ-field, superposing on the complex patterns generated in prior evolutionary phases. When degenerate matter has fully died back into the vacuum, no further secondary wavefronts are created: thereafter the ψ-field is quiescent.

A single-cycle universe would come to eternal rest. But there are no good reasons to assume that further vacuum instabilities would never create fresh quantal solitary waves in a freshly constituted spacetime; and some good (though abstract mathematical) reasons to assume that they may do: as we have seen, the parameters of a multicyclic open universe are intrinsically self-consistent. In such a universe the evolutionary process repeats time after time. It does not repeat in exactly the same way, however. The spectral record of the prior cycles remains encoded in the vacuum, and this record in-forms the evolution of the matter-energies synthesized in the next cycle. Thus each cycle is 'in-formed' by evolution in all previous cycles. As the process is progressively biased towards functional responses to chaos-created alternatives, evolution in each cycle becomes increasingly efficient. In successive cycles in equal times, matter-energy systems reach higher apexes of order and complexity.

Matter-energy evolution in a multicyclic universe, though cyclically reversing, becomes transcyclically irreversible. For that reason, though it escapes the temporal limits of individual cosmic cycles, the process may not attain to eternity. Ultimately, the universe will reach (though it may merely asymptotically approach) an 'omega cycle' where the complex, self-consistent orders attained by matter-energy systems in spacetime, together with the similarly complex spectral records in the vacuum, achieve a level of sophistication where complete devolution into vacuum die-back may be averted. The cyclical manifold would be then moderated by some form of continuous subsistence. But the elucidation of this post-evolutionary era of 'eternal existence,' the same as the nature of the conditions that reigned prior to the first 'alpha cycle,' go beyond the reach of any scheme of rational thought based on the empirically knowable dimensions of human experience.

References

Chapter 1

1. Werner Heisenberg, *The Physicist's Conception of Nature,* Hutchinson, London 1955.
2. The Philosophy of Niels Bohr, *Bulletin of Atomic Physicists,* Vol.XIX, 7.
3. Arthur S. Eddington, *The Nature of the Physical World,* Macmillan, New York 1929, p.341.
4. Eddington, *op.cit.,* p.276.
5. James Jeans, Interview in *Living Philosophers,* Simon and Schuster, New York 1931.
6. Werner Heisenberg, *Philosophic Problems of Nuclear Science,* Fawcett, New York 1952, p.62.
7. Werner Heisenberg, 'Development of concepts in the history of quantum theory,' *American Journal of Physics,* Vol.43, 5, 1975.
8. Ilya Prigogine, personal communication, 4 September 1990.
9. Errol E. Harris, in *New Conceptions of the Universe,* George Mason University Symposium, Washington DC, 1988.

Chapter 2

1. Murray Gell-Mann, 'A schematic model of baryons and mesons,' *Physics Letters,* Vol.8.3, 1964;
   —, *Elementary Particles.* Oppenheimer Memorial Lecture, Institute for Advanced Studies, Princeton, October 1974.
2. Steven Weinberg, 'The Search for Unity: Notes for a History of Quantum Field Theory,' *Daedalus,* Discoveries and Interpretations: Studies in Contemporary Scholarship (II), Fall 1977.
3. For an overview see Barry Parker, *The Search for a Supertheory: From Atoms to Superstrings,* Plenum Press, New York 1987.
4. Geoffrey S. Chew, *The analytic S-matrix,* Benjamin, New York 1966; Henry P. Stapp, 'Space and time in S-matrix theory.' *Physiological Review,* Vol.135B, 1985.
5. Stephen Hawking, *A Brief History of Time,* Bantam Books 1989.

Chapter 3

1. David Bohm, *Wholeness and the Implicate Order,* Routledge & Kegan Paul, London 1980.

2. David Bohm and B.J. Hiley, 'Non-relativistic particle systems.' *Physics Reports* 828 (1986).
3. Henry P. Stapp, *Matter, Mind, and Quantum Mechanics,* Springer Verlag, New York 1993.
4. Werner Heisenberg, in *Daedalus,* 87, 1958, pp.99-100.
5. Werner Heisenberg, *Physics and Philosophy,* Harper & Row, New York 1985, p.54.
6. Henry P. Stapp, *Matter, Mind, and Quantum Mechanics, op.cit.*
7. Henry P. Stapp, 'Quantum Theory and the Place of Mind in Nature,' in *Niels Bohr and Contemporary Philosophy,* J. Faye and H.J. Folse, (eds.) (forthcoming).
8. Henry P. Stapp, personal communication, 7 April 1993.
9. Ervin Laszlo, *Evolution: the Grand Synthesis,* Shambhala Publications, Boston and London 1987;
   —, (ed.), *The New Evolutionary Paradigm,* Gordon & Breach, New York 1992.
10. Ilya Prigogine, *Thermodynamics of Irreversible Processes,* Wiley-Interscience, New York 1967 (3rd ed.).
11. Ilya Prigogine and Isabelle Stengers, *Order out of Chaos: Man's new dialogue with nature,* Bantam Books, New York 1984, p.16.
12. Ilya Prigogine and Isabelle Stengers, *op.cit.,* pp.169-70.
13. Brian Goodwin, 'Development and evolution,' *Journal of Theoretical Biology,* Vol.97, 1982;
    —, 'Organisms and minds as organic forms,' *Leonardo,* 22, 1, (1989) pp.27-31.
14. V.M. Inyushin, *Elementy teorii biologicheskogo polia,* Kazakh State University, Alma Ata 1978.
15. Rupert Sheldrake, *A New Science of Life,* Blond & Briggs, London 1981;
    —, *The Presence of the Past,* Times Books, New York 1988.
16. Terence McKenna, Rupert Sheldrake and Ralph Abraham, *Trialogues at the Edge of the West.* Draft MS, rev.1.0, 22 December 1990.

Chapter 4

1. The Born-Einstein Letters, Macmillan, London 1971.
2. John Archibald Wheeler, 'Bits, quanta, meaning,' in *Problems of Theoretical Physics,* A. Giovannini, F. Mancini, and M. Marinaro (eds.). University of Salerno Press, Salerno 1984.
3. Wheeler, *op.cit.*
4. Albert Einstein, Boris Podolski, and Nathan Rosen, 'Can quantum mechanical description of physical reality be considered complete?' *Physical Review,* Vol.47 (1935).

5. John S. Bell, 'On the Einstein-Podolsky-Rosen Paradox,' *Physics*, Vol.1, 1964.

6. John D. Barrow and Frank J. Tipler, *The Anthropic Cosmological Principle*, Oxford University Press, London & New York 1986.

7. G.J. Chaitin, *A Computer Gallery of Mathematical Physics.* IBM Research Report, Yorktown Heights, New York, March 23, 1985.

Chapter 5

1. Richard Dawkins, *The Extended Phenotype*, Freeman, Oxford 1982; and —, *The Blind Watchmaker*, Longman, London 1986.

2. Michael Denton, *Evolution: Theory in Crisis*, Burnett Books, London 1986.

3. Konrad Lorenz, *The Waning of Humaneness*, Little, Brown, Boston 1987.

4. Hermann Weyl, *Philosophy of Mathematics and Natural Science*, revised edition. Princeton University Press, Princeton, NJ, 1949.

5. Jean Dorst, interview with Jean Staune in *Figaro Magazine*, 26 October 1991.

6. Etienne Wolff, in *Figaro Magazine, op.cit.*

7. Niles Eldredge and Stephen J. Gould, 'Punctuated equilibria: an alternative to phylogenetic gradualism,' *Models in Paleobiology*, edited by Schopf, Freeman, Cooper, San Francisco 1972;
   Gould and Eldredge, 'Punctuated equilibria: the tempo and mode of evolution reconsidered,' *Paleobiology*, Vol.3 (1977).

8. Niles Eldredge, *Time Frames: The Rethinking of Darwinian Evolution and the Theory of Punctuated Equilibria*, Simon & Schuster, New York 1985.

9. Stephen J. Gould, 'Irrelevance, submission and partnership: the changing role of paleontology in Darwin's three centennials, and a modest proposal for macroevolution,' D. Bendall, (ed.), *Evolution from Molecules to Men*, Cambridge University Press, Cambridge 1983.

10. M. Schutzenberger, in *Figaro Magazine, op.cit.*

11. Giuseppe Sermonti, in *Figaro Magazine, op.cit.*

12. Barry Hall, *Proceedings of the National Academy of Sciences USA*, 88, pp.5882-86.

13. Roberto Fondi, *La Révolution Organiciste*, Le Labyrinthe, Paris 1986; —, in *Figaro Magazine. op.cit.*

14. François Jacob, 'Molecular tinkering in evolution,' in D.S. Bendall, (ed.), *Evolution from Molecules to Men. op.cit.*

15. Weyl, Dorst, and Fondi, in *Figaro Magazine*, 26 October 1991.
    Alister Hardy, *The Spiritual Nature of Man*, Oxford University Press, 1981; Gordon Rattray Taylor, *The Great Evolution Mystery*, Secker & Warburg, London 1983.

16. Edmund Sinnott, *Matter, Mind and Man,* Harper & Row, New York 1957;
    —, *The Problem of Organic Form,* Yale University Press, 1963.

Chapter 6

1. John Eccles and Daniel N. Robinson, *The Wonder of Being Human,* Shambhala Publications, London 1985.
2. Karl Lashley, 'The problem of cerebral organization in vision,' *Biological Symposia,* Vol.VII, *Visual Mechanisms,* Jacques Cattell Press, Lancaster 1942.
3. J. Z. Young, under 'Memory,' *Oxford Companion to the Mind,* Richard Gregory (ed.). Oxford University Press, UK, 1987.
4. Raymond Moody, Jr., *Life After Life,* Mockingbird Books, Covington 1975; and
    —, Foreword, in David Lorimer, *Whole In One: The Near-Death Experience and the Ethic of Interconnectedness,* Arkana, London 1990.
5. Reported by Raymond A. Moody, Jr. in *The Light Beyond,* Bantam Books, New York 1988.
6. Lorimer, *Whole In One, op.cit.,* Chap.1.
7. Ian Stevenson, *Children Who Remember Previous Lives,* University Press of Virginia, Charlottesville 1987.
8. Ian Stevenson, *Unlearned Lanquage: New Studies in Xenoglossy,* University Press of Virginia, Charlottesville 1984.
9. Thorwald Detlefsen, *Schicksal als Chance* [Fate As Opportunity], Bertelsmann Verlag, Munich 1979;
    Morris Netherton and Nancy Shiffrin, *Past Lives Therapy,* William Morrow, New York 1978.
10. Stevenson, *Children Who Remember Previous Lives, op.cit.,* Chap.11.
11. Roger Woolger, *Other Lives, Other Selves,* Doubleday, New York 1987.
12. Leonard Shlain, *Art and Physics: Parallel Visions in Space, Time, and Light,* William Morrow, New York 1991.
13. Carl G. Jung, *Synchronicity: An Acausal Connecting Principle,* CW, Vol.VIII, Princeton University Press, Princeton, NJ, 1973;
    F. David Peat, *Synchronicity: The Bridge Between Matter and Mind,* Bantam Books, New York 1987;
    Allan Combs and Mark Holland, *Synchronicity: Science, Myth, and the Trickster,* Paragon House, New York 1990.
14. A.P. Elkin, *The Australian Aborigines,* Angus & Robertson, Sydney 1942.
15. Russell Targ and Harold Puthoff, 'Information transmission under conditions of sensory shielding,' *Nature,* 251 (1974);
    Russell Targ and K. Harary, *The Mind Race,* Villard Books, New York 1984.

16. Michael A. Persinger and Stanley Krippner, 'Dream ESP experiments and geomagnetic activity,' *The Journal of the American Society for Psychical Research,* 83 (1989);
     M. Ullman and S. Krippner, *Dream Studies and Telepathy: An Experimental Approach,* Parapsychology Foundation, New York 1970.

17. Quoted in Larry Dossey, *Recovering the the Soul: A Scientific and Spiritual Search,* Bantam Books, New York 1989.

18. Elaine and Arthur Aron, *The Maharishi Effect: A Revolution through Meditation,* Stillpoint Publishing, Walpole, NH, 1986;
     David W. Orme-Johnson, 'Higher states of consciousness: EEG coherence, creativity and experiences of the siddhis,' *Electroencephalography and Clinical Neurophysiology* 4 (1977).

Chapter 7

1. Dennis Gabor, 'A New Microscopic Principle,' *Nature,* 161 (1946).

2. Fred Hoyle, *The Intelligent Universe,* Michael Joseph, London 1983.

3. A.A. Michelson, 'The Relative Motion of the Earth and the Luminiferous Ether,' *American Journal of Science,* 22 (1881), pp.120-29.

4. Albert Einstein, *Proc. of Schweiz. Naturforschungs Gesellschaft,* 105 (1924).

5. Ignazio Licata, 'Dinamica Reticolare dello Spazio-Tempo' [Reticular dynamics of spacetime], Inediti no.27, Soc. Ed. Andromeda, Bologna 1989;
    Manfred Requardt, 'From "Matter-Energy" to "Irreducible Information Processing" — Arguments for a Paradigm Shift in Fundamental Physics,' *Evolution of Information Processing Systems,* K. Haefner (ed.), Springer Verlag, New York and Berlin 1992.

6. Thomas E. Bearden, *Toward a New Electromagnetics,* Tesla Book Co., 1983.

7. John A. Wheeler, 'Quantum Cosmology,' *World Science,* L.Z. Fang, R. Ruffini (eds.), Singapore 1987.

Chapter 8

1. Cf. Ignazio Licata, *Solitonic Particles Theory in Quantized Space-Time* (preprint), 1988.

2. J. Scott Russell, *Report on Waves,* British Association for the Advancement of Science, 1845.

3. H.C. Yuan and B.M. Lake, 'Nonlinear deep waves,' in *The Significance of Nonlinearity in the Natural Sciences,* B. Kursunoglu, A. Perlmutter, and L.F. Scott, (eds.), Plenum New York 1977.

Chapter 9

1. Eugene Wigner, *The Scientist Speculates,* I.J.Good (ed.), Heinemann, London 1961.
2. R.G. Jahn and B.J. Dunne, 'On the quantum mechanics of consciousness, with application to anomalous phenomena.' *Foundations of Physics,* Vol.16, 8. 1986.
3. H. Everett, *Rev. Mod. Physics,* 29. 1957.
4. Paul Dirac, in *Proc. Einstein Centennial Symposium,* Jerusalem 1979.
5. A. Aspect, P. Grangier, and G. Roger, in *Phys. Rev. Lett.* 49.9 (1982).
6. O. Costa de Beauregard, *Le Temps Déployé,* Editions du Rocher, Monte Carlo 1988.

Chapter 10

1. D.W. Duke and W.S. Pritchard (eds.), *Measuring Chaos in the Human Brain,* World Scientific, London 1991;
   B.H. Jansen and M.E. Brandt (eds.), *Nonlinear Dynamical Analysis of the EEG,* World Scientific, London 1993.
2. François Jacob, *The Logic of Life: A History of Heredity,* Pantheon, New York 1970.
3. M.W. Ho, 'On not holding nature still: evolution by process, not by consequence,' in *Evolutionary Processes and Metaphors,* M.W. Ho and S.W. Fox (eds.), Wiley, London 1988, pp.117-44.
4. B.G. Hall, 'Evolution on a petri dish.' *Evolutionary Biology,* 15 (1982).
5. Peter T. Saunders, 'Evolution without natural selection,' in *Journal of Theoretical Biology,* 1993 (in press).
6. M.W. Ho, 'The role of action in evolution,' in *Cultural Dynamics,* 4, 1991, pp.336-54.
7. Niles Eldredge, *Unfinished Synthesis. Biological Hierarchies and Modern Evolutionary Thought,* Oxford University Press, Oxford 1985.
8. M.W. Ho and P.T. Saunders, (eds.), *Beyond Neo-Darwinism: Introduction to the New Evolutionary Paradigm,* Academic Press, London 1984.

Chapter 11

1. Manfred Euler, 'Reconstructing Complexity: Information Dynamics in Acoustic Perception.' *Information Dynamics,* H. Atmanspacher and H. Scheingraber (eds.), Plenum, New York 1991.
2. J.J. Gibson, *The Ecological Approach to Visual Perception,* MIT Press, Cambridge, MA, 1980.
3. Karen and Russell DeValois, 'Spatial vision,' *Annual Review of Psychology,* 31 (1980);
   —,and E.W. Yund, 'Responses of Striate Cortex Cells to Grating and Checkerboard Patterns,' *Journal of Physiology,* 291 (1979).

4. Karl Pribram, *Brain and Perception: Holonomy and Structure in Figural Processing,* The MacEachran Lectures. Lawrence Erlbaum, Hillsdale, NJ, 1991.

5. Karl Pribram and D. McGuinness, Commentary on Jeffrey Gray's 'The neuropsychology of anxiety: An enquiry into the functions of the septohippocampal system,' *The Behavioral and Brain Sciences,* 5 (1982).

6. J.J. Gibson, *The Ecological Approach to Visual Perception, op.cit.*

7. Pribram, *Brain and Perception, op.cit.,* Lecture 9.

8. Ibid.

9. Karl Lashley, 'The problem of cerebral organization in vision,' *op.cit.*

10. Gerald M. Edelman and V.B. Mountcastle, *The Mindful Brain: Cortical Organization and the Group-selective Theory of Higher Brain Function,* MIT Press, Cambridge, MA, 1978;
    Gerald M. Edelman, *Neural Darwinism: The Theory of Neuronal Group Selection,* Basic Books, New York 1987; and
    —, *Bright Air, Brilliant Fire: On the Matter of Mind,* New York, Basic Books, 1992.

11. Edelman, *Bright Air, Brilliant Fire, op.cit.,* p.102.

12. Ibid, pp.107-8.

13. David Lorimer, *Whole in One, op.cit.,* p.22.

14. Reported in *Cyber,* Milan, 40 (November 1992).

15. Ian Stevenson, *Cases of the Reincarnation Type,* Four volumes. University Press of Virginia, Charlottesville 1975-1983; and
    —, *Children Who Remember Previous Lives, op.cit.*

16. Carl G. Jung, Commentary on *The Secret of the Golden Flower,* in R. Wilhelm, *The Secret of the Golden Flower,* Harcourt, Brace & World, New York 1962.

17. Carl G. Jung, 'Ein Brief zur Frage der Synchronizität,' *Zeitschrift für Parapsychologie und Grenzgebiete der Psychologie,* No. 1, 1961.

18. Marie-Louise von Franz, *Psyche and Matter,* Shambhala, Boston and London, 1992, p.161.

Chapter 12

1. See John D. Barrow and Frank J. Tipler, *The Anthropic Cosmological Principle, op.cit.;*
   George Greenstein, *The Symbiotic Universe,* William Morrow, New York 1987.

2. H. Kurki-Suonio, 'Galactic beads on a cosmic string,' *Science News,* 137, (1990) p.287;
   Eric Lerner, reported T. Van Flandern, in 'Major meeting on new cosmologies,' *Journal of Scientific Exploration,* 7,1 (1993), p.20.

3. E. Gunzig, J. Geheniau and I. Prigogine, 'Entropy and Cosmology,' *Nature,* 330, 6149 (December 1987);
I. Prigogine, J. Geheniau, E. Gunzig, and P. Nardone, 'Thermodynamics of Cosmological Matter Creation,' *Proceedings of the National Academy of Sciences, USA,* Vol.85 (1988).

Chapter 13

1. Roger W. Sperry, 'In defense of mentalism and emergent interaction,' *Journal of Mind and Brain,* see also *Problems Outstanding in the Evolution of Brain Function* (James Arthur Lecture on the Evolution of the Human Brain,) American Museum of Natural History, New York 1964; and
—, 'A modified concept of consciousness,' *Psychological Review,* Vol.76, 1969.
2. Karl Pribram, *Brain and Perception, op.cit.,* Prolegomenon.
3. Quoted by Erwin Schrödinger, 'The Oneness of Mind,' in *Quantum Questions,* Ken Wilber (ed.), Shambhala Publications, Boston & London 1984.
4. William James, *The Varieties of Religious Experience,* Longmans, Green & Co., London, New York and Bombay 1904.
5. E.L. Grant Watson, *The Mystery of Physical Life,* 2nd edn Floris Books, Edinburgh 1992, p.141.
6. Quoted by William James, *The Pluralistic Universe,* Longmans, Green & Co., London, New York and Bombay 1909.
7. J.J.L. Duyvendar, *Tao Te Ching,* John Murray, London 1954.
9. Swami Vivekanada, *Raja-Yoga,* Advaita Ashrama, Mayavati, Almora, University Press of India 1937.
9. Gopi Krishna, 'Kundalini for the new age,' *The Odyssey of Science, Culture and Consciousness,* Kishore Gandhi (ed.), Abhinav Publications, New Delhi 1990.
10. Barbara Ann Brennan, *Hands of Light: A Guide to Healing Through the Human Energy Field,* Chap.17, Pleiades Books, New York 1987.
11. John White and Stanley Krippner, *Future Science,* Anchor Books, New York 1977.

Chapter 14

1. Werner Heisenberg, 'Theory, Criticism, and Philosophy,' *From a Life of Physics,* Evening Lectures at the International Centre for Theoretical Physics, Trieste, June, 1968. Supplement of the IAEA Bulletin, International Atomic Energy Agency (undated), Vienna, p.40.
2. Thomas Berry, *The Dream of the Earth,* Sierra Club Books, San Francisco 1988, p.123.

Appendix

1. *Scientific American,* August 1988.
2. Ben Goertzel, *The Evolving Mind,* World Futures General Evolution Studies, Gordon & Breach, New York (in prep.)
3. J.P. Crutchfield and K. Young, *Phys. Rev. Lett.,* 63, 105 (1989); J.P. Crutchfield, 'Computation at the Onset of Chaos,' in W.H. Zurek, (ed.), *Complexity, Entropy, and the Physics of Information,* Addison-Wesley, Reading, MA, 1990.
4. Albert Einstein, *The World As I See It,* Covici-Friede, New York 1934.
5. Robert Shaw, 'Strange attractors, chaotic behaviour, and information flow,' *Zeitschrift für Naturforschung,* 36A, 1980.
6. Alfred North Whitehead, *Process and Reality: An Essay in Cosmology,* Macmillan, New York 1929; —, *Science and the Modern World,* Macmillan, New York 1925; and —, *Adventures of Ideas,* Macmillan, New York 1933.

Index